RIVAL HYPOTHESES

RIVAL HYPOTHESES

Alternative Interpretations of
Data Based Conclusions

Schuyler W. Huck

University of Tennessee, Knoxville

Howard M. Sandler

George Peabody College for Teachers

Harper & Row, Publishers

New York, Hagerstown, Philadelphia, San Francisco, London

Sponsoring Editor: George A. Middendorf
Project Editor: Joyce Marshall
Designer: Robert Sugar
Senior Production Manager: Kewal K. Sharma
Compositor: VAF House of Typography, Ltd.
Printer: The Maple Press Company
Binder: The Maple Press Company
Art Studio: Danmark & Michaels, Inc.

Rival Hypotheses: Alternative Interpretations of Data Based Conclusions

Library of Congress Cataloging in Publication Data

Huck, Schuyler W
  Rival hypotheses.

  Includes bibliographical references and index.
  1. Social sciences—Statistical methods—Problems, exercises, etc. 2. Social
sciences—Methodology—Problems, exercises, etc. I. Sandler, Howard M., 1945-
  joint author. II. Title.
H61.H87   300'.1'82   78-11228
ISBN 0-06-042975-5

This book is dedicated to our wives, Kathryn and Diane.

Contents

Problems and Solutions

		Problem	Solution

Topics and Exercises

Foreword

One of our favorite stories concerns the flea and the experimental psychologist. We can't cite the original author, since the name was left behind as the story was told and retold across many generations. Furthermore, the details of the story have undoubtedly changed somewhat in the telling, and possibly you have heard it when the main character was a fly or a spider rather that a flea. In any event, we would like to pass the story along to you as it was told to us.

> After carefully conditioning a flea to jump out of a box on an appropriate auditory signal, the "experimenter" removed the first pair of legs to see what effect this had. Observing that the flea was still able to perform his task, the second pair of legs was removed. Once again noting no difference in performance, the researcher removed the final pair of legs and found that the jumping behavior no longer occurred. Thus, the investigator wrote in his notebook, "When all the legs of a flea have been removed, it will no longer be able to hear."[1]

In the above story (which is fictional, thank goodness), the researcher's logic in interpreting his data went something like this: the conditioning of the flea's jumping behavior to an auditory stimulus obviously required that the flea be able to hear; as soon as the flea's legs were removed, it ceased to jump on cue; therefore, removal of the legs affected the flea's ability to hear. Clearly, there is another explanation for why the flea didn't jump besides the one offered by the researcher. In other words, there is a *rival hypothesis* to account for the observed results. As its title indicates, this book is about rival hypotheses.

Our Purpose

The professional working in the behavioral sciences frequently comes across summaries of research data and interpretations of those data. Most contemporary journals and formal convention sessions are replete with such interpretations. In many instances, the conclusions drawn are fully justified in light of the way the data were collected and analyzed. At times, however, the author or presenter of the research report bases the conclusions on "evidence" that has come from a study characterized by an inadequate research design, improper procedures followed during the data collection phase of the study, or faulty statistical treatment of the data. One or more of these defects may mean that rival hypotheses exist that will lessen the confidence that can be placed in the researcher's explanation of what the data mean.

In a different arena, we are all bombarded through the popular media with conclusions based upon research investigations. Just think of all the television

---

[1] G. C. Helmstadter, *Research Concepts in Human Behavior: Education, Psychology, Sociology,* © 1970, p. 94. Reprinted by permission of Prentice-Hall, Inc., Englewood Cliffs, New Jersey. Original story author unknown.

commericals that you have seen in which one brand of a product has been "proven" to be superior to the competition's brand. Or consider the more informal summaries of less biased research on popular topics (for example, political elections, sports, highway safety) that appear in weekly magazines, on the radio, in local newspapers, and during television newscasts. No doubt, the conclusions drawn in these advertisements and noncommercial reports often constitute legitimate interpretations of the data. But on occasion, the interpretive claims must be given less credence, due to the existence of an alternative explanation of why the results turned out the way they did.

People's ability to detect the existence of rival hypotheses obviously varies. Some individuals are very adept at seeing alternative explanations for the results of both formal and informal research investigations. Others, unfortunately, are less able to screen successfully the data interpretations they encounter at home and at work. Like other human characteristics, the ability or skill that we're talking about unquestionably varies by degree, and hence we might think of people as falling at various points along a continuum. If this continuum could be represented by a horizontal line, we might position people on it such that the extreme left end is reserved for people who never can detect rival hypotheses and the extreme right end is reserved for people who never miss detecting rival hypotheses. A person would be placed nearer to the right or the left according to how much ability that person showed.

This book has been written exclusively for those individuals who wish to move from their present position on this hypothetical continuum toward the right end. In other words, the single overriding objective of this book is to assist our readers in sharpening their ability to detect rival hypotheses. As we implied earlier, we are directing our efforts primarily at the "consumer" of interpretive claims made by others. However, we also hope that our audience includes people who conduct their own research, interpret their data, and then pass along the conclusions to others. If they can improve their skill at detecting rival hypotheses, we suspect that the quality of their research will improve, that their manuscripts will be accepted more readily for publication, and that they will generally feel better about providing more valid interpretations to others.

Besides helping our readers increase their ability to identify rival hypotheses, we want very much to assist people in discriminating between *possible* rival hypotheses and *plausible* rival hypotheses. With a one-group pretest–post-test design, the phenomenon of "history" is always a possible rival hypothesis. By definition, the pretest and post-test are separated in time by some sort of treatment activity that the subjects engage in, and thus it is always possible that a pre-post change in the observed measurements is attributable to some event other than the treatment. But whether history is *plausible* as a rival hypothesis to the significant increase or decrease in the data is contingent upon such factors as the length of time between the two testings, the extent to which the researcher has the subjects under control during this time interval, and the occurrence of subject-initiated nontreatment activities between the pretest and post-test periods. Given the nature of two different studies that both utilize a one-group pretest–post-test design, our goal is for the reader to be able to say something like this: "History is a possible rival hypothesis in both studies, but it is a plausible rival hypothesis in only the second study."

Before going any further, we probably should say something about our definition of the term "rival hypothesis," for this definition obviously influenced our decision about what type of material to use as an aid in trying to accomplish our goal. There are some people who might argue that a rival hypothesis is the same thing as a threat to internal validity, that the notion of internal validity is restricted to experimental research, and that therefore a rival hypothesis can only exist when the researcher is attempting to establish a cause-and-effect relationship between two variables. We have taken a broader interpretation of what a rival hypothesis is.

As we use the term, rival hypothesis implies some alternative interpretation, different from the interpretation made by the researcher, for why the data turned out as they did. Hence, we will sometimes be focusing on alternative interpretations of data that have come from experiments designed to test cause-and-effect hypotheses. But at other times, we will focus our attention on quite different types of research. For example, we will discuss a chart that appeared in the sports page of a local newspaper, listing in order the best pitchers in baseball. Clearly, the concepts of independent and dependent variables, of causal relationships, and of internal validity are not appropriate to a discussion of this baseball chart. But as you will see, there is a problem with the way the chart was set up. And there is an explanation, other than the implied reason of superior ability, for why certain pitchers are at the top of the list.

The Book's Format

To accomplish our stated objective, we have put together 100 exercises, each consisting of a problem and a solution. The problems, located in the first half of the book, present short summaries of research studies and the conclusions drawn from the data. Many of the research studies were found in more formal sources such as professional journals, convention presentations, and college textbooks. Others have come from informal sources such as newspaper articles, magazine ads, television commercials, and some personal communication. Despite the fact that the material we have written about was located in a wide variety of places, all 100 problems are similar in that they contain a direct or subtle claim that the original writer or speaker wanted the readers or listeners or viewers to believe. And in each case, we believe that there is some sort of logical problem (with the design, methodology, or analysis) that makes it possible to account for the results through one or more rival hypotheses. Your task is to detect the plausible alternative explanation.

In the second half of the book, we present a corresponding solution for each of the problems. In each solution, we point out what we consider to be the most logical rival hypothesis that might invalidate the original claim. If there are two (or more) equally plausible competing explanations, we attempt to explain each in detail. On occasion, the solution will contain a brief discussion of how the research investigation could have been conducted so as to render implausible the rival hypotheses that have been cited.

In our opinion, there is more than a passing similarity between our 100 exercises and the "Ellery Queen Minute Mysteries" that are aired over the radio in various metropolitan areas of the United States. For several years, while living in Chicago, we anxiously awaited the next occasion when Wally Phillips (of radio station WGN) would attempt to stump his audience with another minute mystery. The mysteries were great! And they might have facilitated logical thinking, as we hope our book will, except that the solutions to Ellery Queen's mysteries were often based upon tiny, obscure facts of which most individuals are not aware. In contrast, the solutions to our 100 "mysteries" should be easily identified by people who have refined their skills in detecting rival hypotheses.

As a supplementary item, we have provided a list of the places where our source material was found. If the topic of a problem turns out to be of particular interest, we suggest that you turn to Appendix A, the Bibliography, to find out where we got our material, and then hunt down the complete original research report. In fact, we strongly recommend that you do this, because our problem summaries are often condensed versions of the actual research project, with many interesting and valid portions necessarily left out. In this book, we have typically tried to describe just those portions of the investigations that relate to the rival hypotheses being discussed.

A Few Words of Warning

In order to gain the most benefit from reading this book, you must follow three suggestions that we will now pass along. In addition, there is one critical piece of information that we have not yet told you. Let's begin with the suggestions.

When we were in the process of writing this book, each of us would send the first draft of a problem/solution exercise to the other as soon as it was typed. Upon receiving these in the mail, we would sometimes turn to the solution immediately after reading the problem—without spending much time thinking about what might be wrong with the research study that had been summarized. We simply couldn't wait to see what our coauthor thought was the matter with a study that seemed on first reading to be just fine.

We predict that you, too, will have a strong urge to peek at the solution before you have given your brain a fair chance to detect the rival hypothesis. So, our first suggestion is that you overcome this urge and force yourself to do some thinking between your reading of the two parts of any exercise. In other words, don't approach the book as you do most of the other things you read. We hope that you will open and shut this book about 200 times, and we will be very disappointed with anyone who reads it cover-to-cover in a day or two.

In the process of field testing our 100 exercises, we forced our reading audience to think about each problem before looking at our solution. We did this by distribution the problem part of an exercise on a particular day, requiring our readers to submit their own thoughts about any plausible rival hypotheses two days later in writing, and then distributing the solution that we had written. Had we given them both parts of the exercise on the first day, we strongly suspect that they would have looked at the solution too soon and thereby provided us with inferior feedback—and deprived themselves of an opportunity to sharpen their detective skills.

Our second suggestion is for those readers who have memorized Campbell and Stanley's list of possible threats to internal validity. Since the phrase "rival hypothesis" is treated as synonymous with "threat to internal validity" in their classic chapter (and in many books published after 1963), some of you may be inclined to go down this list of seven rival hypotheses as soon as you finish reading each problem. At the outset, let us warn you that such a strategy is insufficient.

Of course, many of the research studies you will encounter in this book contain conclusions that cannot be so readily accepted because of one or more of Campbell and Stanley's seven threats: mortality, history, testing, maturation, selection, regression, and instrumentation. But many of the other problems will be characterized by possible problems that deal with different sorts of concepts. (We have listed several of these in Appendix B.) As we said earlier, we have not restricted our focus to traditional experiments in which cause-and-effect relationships were investigated. Hence, when you come to problems like the one that deals with the scoring averages of the top five rookies in the National Basketball Association, you will have to let your mind wander far beyond the normal threats to internal validity in order to see the flaw in the logic that we have detected. But even when the research study under consideration *is* an experiment, our concern is often with something other than mortality, history, and the like. For example, in one study based upon a respectable "true" experimental design, we feel that the human observers could have been biased in what they saw and recorded by an awareness of which subjects received the different treatments.

While our second suggestion is to think beyond the seven-item list of threats to internal validity, the final suggestion is to focus your thoughts on things other than problems of external validity. Don't get us wrong; external validity is a very important issue (or should be, if it isn't) to those who conduct research and those who consume research reports. Nevertheless, our goal in this book is to sharpen the reader's ability to detect plausible rival hypotheses—that is, alternative interpretations of why data turned out as they did. Your skill in being able to assess whether or not the results can be generalized (to other subjects, settings, or treatments) is a concern we will leave for a future book or other authors. In this book, therefore, none of our solutions will ever deal with a question of generalizability.

So much for our three suggestions. Our last warning deals with a critical piece of information that we have thus far withheld. On the adivce of one of the people who reviewed an early version of our manuscript for the publisher, we have summarized a few research studies for which there are no plausible rival hypotheses at all. When you find. these, you will turn to the appropriate solution and find a statement to this effect: "As far as we can tell, the researcher's interpretation of the data is appropriate." And since the number .05 seems to be so important to people who do research, we decided to make five of our 100 exercises of this variety. We have included these to prevent your developing the idea that something, somehow, has to be wrong with each problem you read—and also to indicate that it *is* possible to conduct research in such a way that no rival hypotheses exist to compete with the researcher's data interpretations.

The Book's Spirit

In 95 of our 100 exercises, you will find us suggesting that the original data interpretations are contaminated by one or more plausible rival hypotheses. As you read these critiques, we want you to know and remember that the motivation behind our criticism was always instructional, that in no case did we ever intend to impugn the professional competence of the original researchers, and that the conclusions drawn by those researchers may well be 100 percent valid. Let us elaborate a bit on the last of these three thoughts.

In most instances, we based our problem (our summary of the research investigation) on a published journal article. Since published reports tend to be condensed versions of longer manuscripts that the authors had initially submitted to editorial boards, it is quite conceivable that many of the rival hypotheses we suggest would quickly go down the drain if we had more complete information about the way the research studies were actually conducted. In our opinion, people reading the shorter versions that are published in journals *should* raise the same sorts of questions that we have and consequently accept the stated conclusions with a grain of salt. But at the same time, we strongly recommend that readers realize that the rival hypotheses so identified may be an artifact of the editorial process.

In reference to the competence of the original researchers, some of the interpretations we criticize were made by professional colleagues whom we see regulary at regional and national conventions. Some are more than colleagues; they are friends. We trust that they (and you) will recognize that our critiques were motivated by an attempt to help people improve their research logic, not by a desire to tear down what others had accomplished. If anyone doubts the sincerity of this claim, look closely and you will see that a study of ours has served as the basis for one of the exercises. And it's not one of those five that are free of rival hypotheses!

A Note to the Instructor

Despite our recurring dreams about this book being voluntarily purchased and read by the masses simply because of its inherently useful and charming characteristics, we suspect that out main audenece will be made up of students in college courses for which the book is a required text. For certain types of courses, this book might be selected as the core item around which the course activities will be structured; for others, it may be used simply as a supplementary text. In any event, we have done something extra in an effort to help the instructors who adopt this book for their courses.

The 100 rival hypotheses comprising this text are not arranged randomly. Instead, a concerted effort has been made to devise an ordering schema that keeps similar exercises apart from one another. The variables we kept in mind while devising this arrangement included the nature of the rival hypotheses being discussed, the substantive topic of the research investigations, the length of the problems, and the difficulty we felt the reader would have in identifying the rival hypotheses. In addition, we spread out the 20 or so exercises that came from informal sources (magazines, newspapers, and so on) and the five items that don't have any plausible rival hypotheses at all.

Some instructors may wish to have their students study our rival hypotheses in the same order that we have presented them. Others may want to assign certain problem/solution sets in a sequence that corresponds with their course syllabus and other texts. For example, it seems reasonable to assume that some instructors who are also using Campbell and Stanley's *Experimental and Quasi-Experimental Designs for Research* will want their students to begin with the rival hypotheses dealing with history, maturation, and other rival hypotheses typically associated with one-group pretest–post-test designs. For instructors in this latter category, we have included a supplementary item designed to make it easier to rearrange our 100 exercises into other orders to fit differing content structures.

In Appendix B you will find a chart in which the 100 problems have been classified by the type of rival hypothesis—history, regression, subject effect, and so on). There are 20 categories in this chart, with exercises listed under more than one category whenever the research conclusions are complicated by multiple problems. And to make certain that our classification system is well understood, a set of short definitions of the category headings is presented immediately following the formal chart.

A Final Comment

Many of our colleagues who have written books have given us the distinct impression that the process of writing was near drudgery for them. In contrast, this book has been a truly enjoyable experience for both of us. Throughout the past two years, each of us has anxiously awaited the arrival of each exercise produced by the other. We have had many lengthy conversations in which we exchanged ideas and points of view about which rival hypotheses were or were not plausible. But beyond the fun we have had putting our 100 exercises together, it has also been a very worthwhile activity. Without question, our ability to detect alternative explanations for alleged claims has increased because of this project. We are certainly not at the extreme right end of that continuum we described earlier, but we are not quite as far away as we were when we began. We sincerely hope that you will feel the same way when you are finished with this book.

So now, without further ado, it is time for you to pick up your magnifying glass, put on your thinking hat, and be off on your detective work. And as you go, we can think of nothing more appropriate to say than this little quotation that sums up the central theme of our book:

> Even having guarded against errors which might result from imprecision, variation, or bias and having arrived at a reasonable set of conclusions, we must still enquire, "What else might this mean?" The reason for doing so is painfully simple: "The value of a hypothesis is inversely related to the number of acceptable alternatives."[2]

[2]S. Shindell, *Statistics, Science, and Sense* (Pittsburgh: University of Pittsburgh Press, 1964), pp. 41–42.

Acknowledgments

We are grateful to several people for the support and assistance they gave us while this book was being prepared. Without their help, this project would have never been completed—or if it had, it would have turned out far inferior to the way it stands now.

First of all, we wish to acknowledge our students at the University of Tennessee and Peabody College who read our material and helped identify methodological or logical errors which the two of us initially overlooked. As we indicate in the Foreword, we are quite certain that we have missed certain defects; but the number of such misses is unquestionably smaller because of the assistance given to us by these students. In particular, we wish to recognize the contributions of Rebecca Smith Cooley, Jackie Cherones, and Joe McLaughlin.

There were, of course, several other people at our respective institutions who assisted us in this endeavor. On several occasions, we consulted with our colleagues concerning the plausibility of rival hypotheses related to research investigations in substantive fields different from our own. At times, these colleagues shared with us their own studies which contained unintentional mistakes. Special thanks go to Harris Gabel, Benjamin H. Layne, Kathryn B. Sherrod, Barbara Wallston, and Robert L. Williams. But beyond our students and our colleagues, we are greatly indebted to our secretaries, Cathy Pettiford and Lois Hill Davis. Although asked just to type our handwritten drafts, these two individuals filled in gaping holes that we had left, took out redundancies that we had included, improved much of our grammar and use of English, and generally made our writing far more intelligible.

Besides the contributions from people at our respective institutions, we also received significant help from individuals located elsewhere. The anonymous reviewers who reacted to our initial draft provided helpful advice and the encouragement to continue forth with the project. We are also grateful to the staff at Harper & Row for their support and technical assistance throughout the production of the book.

While the inadvertent omissions and other errors are clearly the fault of the two of us, much of what is worthwhile and good can be attributed directly to the individuals mentioned above who lent us their ideas and constructive criticism. We are greatly indebted to you all.

RIVAL HYPOTHESES

PROBLEMS

1. The Common Denominator

Over 100 years ago, the philosopher John Stuart Mill dealt with the issue of cause and effect. He attempted to set forth "canons of logic" by which cause-and-effect relationships could be determined. One of these canons was the "method of agreement." Briefly, Mill reasoned that if two or more occurrences of a phenomenon have only one circumstance in common, then that circumstance is the cause of the observed phenomenon. In our day-to-day lives, we come across numerous instances of the method of agreement being used to explain common events.

Recently, an election took place in a large metropolitan city located in the southeastern United States. One of the local newspapers was interested in why certain candidates won while others lost. After conducting a superficial investigation, the newspaper printed the following story:

> What was the common denominator that decided the races for Knox County court house offices? It wasn't incumbency since school superintendent Mildred Doyle lost. It wasn't party since three Republicans and one Democrat won.
>
> The answer is age. In all four races (sheriff, property assessor, law director and school superintendent) the younger candidate won.*

The article was entitled, "Age Was Big Factor in Knox Elections." The title and text of the article give the impression that age had a causal influence on the election outcome. After reading the article, elderly people might think twice before running for elected offices. Should they think twice, or is there some plausible rival hypothesis other than the common denominator proposed by the local newspaper?

(Turn to page 155 for solution.)

2. Sensory Deprivation

We know a few people who have the ability to concentrate on a task regardless of the auditory and visual distractions intruding upon them. If you're like us, however, even minor distractions often cause you to lose your train of thought. A dog barking in a neighbor's yard, the shadow of a person walking by your desk, an ambulance siren, even the ticking of a clock—these small sights and sounds can sometimes make us wish that we could simply flip a switch and completely shut off all auditory and visual input. But even if such a switch did exist, we probably wouldn't use it very often. For we've read about the way a complete absence of environmental stimuli can have temporary or lasting negative effects on a person's mental equilibrium.

A few years ago, a little study was conducted that seemed to show that sensory deprivation may actually have a beneficial influence on the ability to perform simple tasks. In this investigation, 60 men enlisted in the Navy were randomly selected from a group of volunteers who had been told that if selected, they would be serving in one of two "relaxation" conditions. From this group, 40 subjects were randomly assigned to an experimental group and 20 to a control group. Those in the experimental condition were put into separate cubicles that were sound-reducing and light-tight; hence, these individuals received almost no visual or auditory stimulation while participating in the investigation. The subjects in the control condition, on the other hand, could adjust the lights inside their cubicles, watch television, listen to the radio, read books, write, and even talk with one another by means of an intercom system.

The experiment lasted for seven consecutive days. Twenty-four hours before the start and at three points during the seven-day interval (after 25, 73, and 145 hours), all subjects were given a "vigilance" test. The test involved the transmission of a series of 60 short tones (beeps) through a loudspeaker into each subject's cubicle. In each 90-minute testing period, these tones were randomly spaced, with a half-minute to two-and-a-half-minute interval between tones. The task of each subject during the vigilance test was to pull a lever (located near the bed in each cubicle) immediately after hearing each tone. To equalize the testing conditions during the four vigilance tests, the lights and all entertainment equipment in the control group cubicles were shut off.

Of the 40 subjects in the experimental group, 21 remained in their sensory deprived cubicles for the full seven-day period of the investigation. However, equipment failure for five additional subjects in this group reduced the number that could be studied to 16. In the control group, 19 of the 20 subjects completed the week-long confinement in their cubicles, but partial loss of data reduced to 15 the number of valid control subjects. To equalize the two sample sizes, data for one randomly selected experimental subject were discarded.

4

The subjects' responses to the 60 tones comprising each of the four vigilance tests were scored in the following manner. If a subject pulled the response lever within two seconds of a beep, one point of credit was given; if the level was pulled after a two-second interval or not pulled at all, no credit was earned. Since there were 60 beeps at each testing period, up to 60 points could be earned. The data from the two groups of 15 men were subjected to a statistical comparison, and the results indicated no difference between the groups at the pretest period (12 hours prior to confinement), but significant differences in each of the three tests during treatment. And at each of these testings (after 25, 73, and 145 hours), it was the experimental group that made fewer errors.

The researchers who conducted this study concluded that their results strongly corroborated previous findings that individuals who experience sensory deprivation outperform nondeprived subjects on vigilance tasks. Do you feel that the results of the seven-day confinement study justify such a conclusion? Or is there a rival hypothesis to account for the results?

(Turn to page 155 for solution.)

3. A Painful Look at Hunger

Current theories of hunger place the main responsibility on a small part of the brain called the hypothalamus. The hypothalamus monitors the chemical content of the blood and triggers eating responses at appropriate times. It has even been shown that certain surgical lesions in the hypothalamus of rats can lead to nonstop eating—the rats literally eat themselves to death. Earlier theories of hunger, however, were not so sophisticated. They were based mainly on the assumption that the stomach had a causal influence on the brain—that is, since hunger pangs were often reported by those who were hungry, it seemed logical to look at the influence of stomach contractions on hunger.

One of the earliest studies in this area was done by two researchers (Cannon and Washburn, 1912) who had human participants[1] swallow a small balloon that was then inflated. The air pressure in the "gastric balloon" was affected by stomach contractions that were transmitted to a recording device. The participants were also asked to indicate each time a hunger pang was felt. The researchers took the strong positive correlation between stomach contractions and hunger pangs to mean that the contractions caused the pangs. Where did they go wrong?

(Turn to page 156 for solution.)

---

[1] "Subjects" seems more appropriate than "participants" in this context.

6

4. Beer: Brand Differences in Image

Whenever we go to certain people's houses for dinner or an evening of bridge, we get the distinct impression that the magazines on the coffee table never have been and never will be read by the host and hostess. We are confident that you, too, know at least one person who puts intellectual-type magazines out on display, hoping to impress you and other guests who attend the formal get-together or simply drop by unexpectedly. The next time you are at the home of one of these people, you might like to drop off, surreptitiously, a copy of the research study described below. If the individuals read about this investigation, it probably won't cure them of their magazine put-on; instead, it will give them a tip on how they might extend their phony "impression-ism" into the kitchen!

This research endeavor had to do with beer, and the researcher was interested in whether the images of different brands of beer vary. By "image," the researcher meant the personality characteristics we might think of as being associated with or typical of the individuals who buy and consume any given brand of beer. Of course, surveys conducted by the marketing research departments of the various beer companies could probably provide us with fairly accurate descriptions of the people who actually buy each brand; in this particular study, however, the focus was on the *perceived notions* (which potentially might be in error) that people have of the types of consumers who purchase the different brands.

To investigate the hypothesis that different brands do have different images, an experiment was conducted at the University of South Carolina. The subjects in this investigation were 157 students enrolled in a business course, and their experimental task was both interesting and simple. On the first day of class, each student was given a sheet of paper containing a short list of grocery items preceded by these directions:

> Read the shopping list below. Then try to project yourself into the situation as far as possible until you can more or less describe the student who purchased the groceries for a small informal party. Then write a brief description of his personality and character. Whenever possible try to indicate what influenced your judgment. This is a test to see how well you can size up an individual's personality on the basis of very little information.*

Six familiar items typically associated with student parties (for example, five pounds of hamburger, three packages of Sunbeam hamburger buns, and three large packages of potato chips) were identical on all the shopping lists.

*Reprinted from the *Journal of Applied Psychology*, 1976, *56*, pp. 512–513. Courtesy of A. G. Woodside.

However, the lists differed with respect to the seventh item. One-third of the subjects received lists in which the seventh item was "2 cases Pabst Blue Ribbon beer," a brand of beer that might be thought to have a good image because of its consistent increases in yearly sales plus a high market share. Another third of the subjects received lists in which the seventh item was two cases of a different brand of beer (unnamed in the technical report), a brand that conceivably would have a bad image because of its decreasing sales and a lessening share of the market. The final third of the subjects received lists that did not contain any beer item at all, just the six items on the other lists. The three versions of the shopping list were randomly mixed (by means of a table of random numbers) and distributed among the 157 subjects who were unaware, of course, that three versions were being used.

After the written descriptions of the hypothetical party planner had been collected, two judges evaluated each description and classified each sentence as being positive, negative, or neutral in affect. (If a sentence had both positive and negative components, judges were instructed to score it as neutral.) The two judges evaluated the 157 papers independently of one another, yet there was a 94 percent agreement between them on the scoring of the 539 sentences produced by the subject pool. To avoid any rater bias, the two judges scored each paper without knowing which of the three versions of the shopping list had been given to the author.

Upon subjecting the judges' evaluations to a formal statistics analysis, the researcher discovered that the descriptions from the Pabst group, when compared with each of the other two groups, contained a significantly greater proportion of positive statements and a significantly smaller number of negative statements. A separate statistical analysis focused on the 157 subjects and their net scores, defined as the numerical result obtained by subtracting each subject's number of negative sentences from the number of positive sentences. By means of these net scores, each subject could be classified as being positive, negative, or neutral in the description of the party planner. The results were that a significantly greater (smaller) percentage of the Pabst subjects were classified as positive (negative) than was the case in either of the other two groups. The non-Pabst beer group produced the smallest percentage of positive descriptions, even smaller than the no-beer control group.

The researcher interpreted his significant findings as support for the hypothesis that different beer brands carry different images. Clearly, this study's conclusions imply that a cause-and-effect relationship had been found to exist, with the causal variable being the brand of beer contained in the shopping list and the effect variable being the positive, neutral, or negative nature of the written description of the shopper's personality. In your opinion, were the differences obtained truly attributable to the seventh item on the shopping list? Or can you identify one or more plausible rival hypotheses that complicate and potentially invalidate the conclusions associated with this study?

(Turn to page 156 for solution.)

5. Seasonal Variation in Personality

The Minnesota Multiphasic Personality Inventory (MMPI) is one of the oldest and best self-report personality instruments in existence today. It was first published in 1943, and since then literally thousands of research investigations have been conducted using the MMPI. In the opinion of at least one author, the MMPI "is one of the most widely used of all the available personality inventories and has certainly been more widely reported in the literature than any other inventory" (J. Horrocks, 1964, p.554). A different authority in the field of testing, Jum Nunnally, states unequivocally that the MMPI "represents the apex of research and detailed test construction in the area of adjustment inventories" (Nunnally, 1970, p. 360).

The MMPI is made up of 566 statements concerning different areas of life experience, such as "I often feel a tight knot in my stomach." To each of these statements, examinees indicate whether the statement is an accurate description of themselves by selecting one of three response options: true, false, or cannot say. Based upon the total set of responses, the inventory yields eight clinical scales, each of which is intended to measure the relative presence or absence of a separate form of mental illness. For example, three of these scales are entitled "Psychopathic Deviate," "Hysteria," and "Hypochrondiasis."

Although the names of the clinical scales correspond to labels attached to patients living in mental hospitals, the MMPI is typically administered to people on the outside, like you. The purpose is to determine the components of one's personality structure and the possible existence or likely development of psychological problems. Recently, two researchers wondered whether there might exist seasonal variations in the way people respond to the MMPI. It may be, they hypothesized, that people feel better about themselves at certain points of the year than at other times. And if this were so, then a valid interpretation of the MMPI results would necessitate knowing when the examinee responded to the inventory items.

To investigate their hunch, the researchers initially administered the MMPI to 40 college students in December, six weeks before the end of the fall semester. Then, these same examinees were given the MMPI a second time in April, again six weeks before the end of the academic term. A statistical comparison was made, for each clinical scale, of the average score from the December testing and the average score from the April testing. On three of the eight scales (the ones identified earlier), there was a significant difference between the two means. And in each case, the group of college students appeared to be more normal (that is, less troubled) in the spring than they were in the early winter.

Based upon their statistical findings, the researchers argued that the data "suggested a relationship between seasons in question and performance on the

MMPI." Even though you, personally, may feel more depressed in the winter than in the spring (especially if you're not a winter sports enthusiast), do you accept the conclusion of this research investigation? Or are there any alternative explanations to account for the more normal scores among the 40 college students in the spring?

(Turn to page 157 for solution.)

6. Mind Your Ms and Qs

Like most Americans, we drink many more soft drinks than can possibly be good for us. For a while it seemed as if worldwide increases in the price of sugar would put most of these drinks well out of the reach of the average college professor; however, sugar prices unfortunately dropped. Thus, we are in the unhealthy position of finding too many such beverages in our shopping carts.

The following story appeared about an advertisement in a weekly news magazine as well as in the local newspapers—you may have seen it yourself. It seems that the Pepsi-Cola Company decided that Coke's three-to-one lead in Dallas was no longer acceptable, so they commissioned a taste-preference study. The participants were chosen from Coke drinkers in the Dallas area and asked to express a preference for a glass of Coke or a glass of Pepsi. The glasses were not labeled "Coke" and "Pepsi" because of the obvious bias that might be associated with a cola's brand name. Rather, in an attempt to administer the two treatments (the two beverages) in a blind fashion, the Coke glass was simply marked with a "Q" and the Pepsi glass with an "M". Results indicated that more than half chose Pepsi over Coke. Besides a possible difference in taste, can you think of any other possible explanation for the observed preference of Pepsi over Coke?

(Turn to page 158 for solution.)

7. Immediate Feedback

In some university courses, students take tests but never really find out how they did until the academic term is over and their final course grades are posted or sent through the mail. More often than not, however, students receive feedback on their test performances within a few days of the class session in which they were tested. Usually, the nature of this feedback is a letter grade on the test, plus an indication of how the student's total score compares to the total test scores earned by the others. In many instances, the student receives no feedback on the correct answer to each specific test question.

Recently, a research study was undertaken to see if learning could be facilitated by giving students immediate feedback on individual test items. The subjects were 253 undergraduates enrolled in a psychology course. The tests in this course consisted of four multiple-choice quizzes given during the academic term, plus a comprehensive final examination administered at the end of the course. The final exam, like the four quizzes, was made up of multiple-choice questions.

Each of the 35 items on each quiz was projected on a screen for 45 seconds. During this time, the student had to select the best answer from among the available choices. After the thirty-fifth question of each quiz had been presented, the answer sheets were collected; then the students were shown 18 of the quiz questions again while the instructor announced what the right answer was and why it was correct. At the time of the final examination, 38 "feedback" questions and 38 "nonfeedback" questions were repeated verbatim from the earlier quizzes.

For the purposes of this experiment, two final exam scores were computed from each student's answer sheet. One of these scores indicated how well the student did on the 38 feedback items; the other score indicated performance on the 38 nonfeedback items. A statistical comparison of these two sets of scores revealed that students obtained higher scores on the group of questions for which feedback had been provided.

The obvious implication of this study is that immediate feedback on specific test questions facilitates learning. A cause-and-effect relationship is more than just hinted at, with feedback being the presumed cause and learning (as measured by final exam performance) being the effect. As college instructors who give lots of quizzes and who believe in the principle of immediate feedback, we are tempted to hold a bias in favor of the results obtained in this investigation. Nevertheless, we feel that there may be one or more rival hypotheses that prevent a clear interpretation of the study results. Can you think of any variables, other than the immediate feedback concerning correct answers, that may have caused the group of students to perform differently on the two parts of the final examination?

One rival hypothesis that we thought about was item difficulty. We felt, at first, that the students might have performed better on the feedback items simply because those items were easier than the nonfeedback items. However, a close reading of the researchers' technical report shows that an attempt was made to control this variable. This was done by selecting items for the final exam in such a way that feedback and nonfeedback items were matched on the basis of how hard they had been on the quizzes. Therefore, the notion of item difficulty differences is *not* the rival hypothesis we have in mind.

(Turn to page 158 for solution.)

8. Wilt Thou Take This Plant...

As any backyard gardener knows, newly planted vegetables or flowers need lots of sunshine and water to grow properly. Some nutritious plant food often helps, as does an occasional dusting for insects or disease. To help the plants grow quickly, the gardener must keep certain things away—such as rabbits, the lawnmower, and small children who think the rose or tomato is a red ball. Recently, gardeners have also been told to keep loud noises away from their growing plants.

In a large metropolitan city, the Sunday newspaper has a column in the spring and summer entitled "Your Lawn and Garden." One Sunday, the column dealt with fertilizer, planting seeds from magnolia trees, watering dogwoods, and noise. With respect to the last topic, the article went as follows:

> A year or so ago we had much to say here pro and con about how plants appreciate a kind word now and then and that such treatment helps them to thrive. A researcher at Drexel University in Philadelphia says that while science still doesn't know if plants appreciate kindness, it has learned that they don't like to be yelled at. It has nothing to do with tender feelings. Apparently, loud noise increases the amount of water normally given off by the leaves, causing the plants to wilt and grow at a slower rate.
>
> The researcher, Dr. Arthur Lord, a physics professor, and some of his students discovered this in two experiments with coleus plants. In the first experiment a student grew two coleus plants under the same greenhouse conditions, except that one plant was exposed to about 100 decibels of noise, approximately the same as a person would hear while standing on a busy subway platform. After 1½ weeks of continuous exposure the sound-treated plant wilted.*

Let us assume that the phrase "same greenhouse conditions" means exactly the same everything—same amount of water, same amount of natural and artificial light, same type of soil, same amount of insect and disease repellant, and so on. Let us also assume that a coin was flipped to determine which of the two coleus plants would receive the noise treatment. Even if both of these assumptions are true, there is still a plausible rival hypothesis—other than noise—to explain the outcome. What is it?

(Turn to page 159 for solution.)

14

9. Imaginary Friends

Occasionally in the past our children reported to us on their imaginary playmates (who were often held responsible for whatever mischief occurred in our homes). We always listened attentively and wondered about the expense of psychotherapy for young children. Having failed to come to a reasonable conclusion on the latter point, we were naturally attracted to an article entitled "Imaginary Companions and Creative Adolescents." Thinking that there may yet be hope for our preteenage children, we dove into the article.

What we found was a study in which 800 adolescents from schools with "outstanding records" in "creative student achievement" were classified into eight groups of 100 according to sex, creativity (more versus less), and field of interest (boys—scientific versus artistic, girls—art versus writing). All students were asked if they had ever had an imaginary companion. Comparisons were then made between the more creative and less creative groups (based on teacher evaluation as well as on two tests of creative thinking) on the frequency of reported imaginary companions. Significant differences were found for boys between the two artistic groups, and for girls between the two writing groups.

Since for most of the boys (but not the girls), "artistic" meant writing, the authors concluded tentatively that the presence of an imaginary companion was related to creativity in the area of writing. This conclusion is made all the more appealing when we consider that many authors make a fortune by sharing with the rest of us a particularly vivid imaginary character. Should we start lining up lucrative contracts for our children?

(Turn to page 160 for solution.)

10. Pre- and Postreward Delay

As you probably know, psychological learning theories are sometimes in conflict with one another in their attempts to explain why people or animals behave the way they do. In an effort to settle such controversies, basic laboratory experiments are often conducted. Based on the competing theories, hypotheses are derived that predict how the experimental subjects will respond when given a particular task. Then, after data have been collected from the subjects as to their performance, such data may turn out to be consistent with the hypotheses of Theory A and inconsistent with the hypotheses of Theory B. Given such an outcome, the experimental results are interpreted as providing support for—but not proof of—Theory A and an indication that Theory B should be refined. Let us now take a look at one instance in which two theories were in competition and the way an experimental study was undertaken to help settle the dispute.

Using rats, a straight running box, electrical timers, and a sugar solution, researchers had previously demonstrated that the animals would run faster from the starting end of the running box to the drinking cup at the other end if on earlier trials they were given the sugar solution as soon as they finished their trip. But if there was a delay between the time they got to the reward cup and the time they actually received the sugar solution, the rats tended not to run so quickly on subsequent trials. Even though this observable phenomenon was clear cut and could be duplicated, not everyone offered the same explanation of why the rats would run more slowly under the delayed treatment condition. In particular, those who subscribed to contiguity theory disagreed with those who believed in reinforcement theory.

On the one hand, learning theorists in the contiguity camp would argue that the stimulus conditions of the goal box (at the end of the running box) often resemble those of the running box itself, that the rat's behavior while waiting for the reward becomes a conditioned response, and that this conditioned response (of sniffing around) then generalizes, on succeeding trials, to the stimuli of the runway. On the other hand, reinforcement theorists would simply say that the behaviors of the rat during the waiting period in the goal, since they are followed by a reward, become learned; hence, upon finding itself in the running box on subsequent trials, the rat doesn't "know" whether running behavior or nonrunning behavior will bring forth the reward.

While the contiguity and reinforcement theories would explain the slower running behavior differently, they would both predict that the prereward delay would lead to a performance decrement. Consequently, the two theories can't be differentiated on a prereward basis. Recently, however, a researcher conducted an experiment in which there was a postreward delay. In this study, some of the rats ran down to the goal box, got their reward, and then were kept in the goal box for a period of time before being removed. Since behaviors exhibited by the rat in the goal box during this delay period came after the presentation of the reward, reinforcement theory would predict no decrease in running speed on subsequent trials. In contrast, contiguity theory would predict that rats given the postreward delay would run more slowly on future trials. According to contiguity theory, the nongoal-oriented behavior of the rat (during delay) constitutes responses to essentially the same stimulus components that exist in the runway; hence, the rat's behavior during postreward delay becomes conditioned and thereafter impedes performance on successive trials.

The subjects in this study were 60 male hooded rats, each about 100 days old at the beginning of the investigation. These 60 rats were randomly divided into six subgroups of ten, each of which was then run through the experiment under one of the three delay conditions and one of the two goal-box conditions (thus forming a 3 × 2 factorial design). The three delay conditions were 30 seconds of prereward delay, meaning that the rat had to wait in the goal box for half a minute prior to receiving the sugar solution; no delay, meaning that the rat was given the sugar as soon as it got to the goal box; and 30 seconds of postreward delay, meaning that the rat was detained in the goal box for half a minute after it had consumed its reward. The two levels of the goal box factor were a goal box somewhat similar in dimensions to the 2-foot runway set up between the starting box and the goal box, and a goal box that was much larger (in terms of width, length, and height) than the runway.[1]

The procedures of this investigation were relatively straightforward. Each rat was run through the experiment a total of 80 times, but on each trial it was tested under the single combination of treatments to which it had been assigned (for example, 30 seconds of predelay in the small goal box). And to prevent any sort of order effect from becoming confounded with treatment conditions, rats from the six groups were counterbalanced across trials in the sequence in which they were tested. The reward—0.3 millimeter of 20 percent sucrose solution—was held constant across all six comparison groups and all 80 trials. To make this reward effective, all rats were deprived of food and water for 12 hours prior to each trial.

On each trial, each rat was measured (by clock timers activated by the researcher and stopped automatically when the rat passed through an electrical eye and touched the reward cup) on two dependent variables. One of these was *latency,* defined as the time it took the rat to move from the starting box to a point 6 inches down the running box. The other was *running time,* defined as the total time it took the rat to move from the starting box to the reward cup postitioned in the goal box. For each of these measures, a rat's 80 scores across the various trials of the experiment were averaged together, and then separate analyses were made of each set of scores.

Results indicated no significant difference between the rats' starting

---

[1] Goal boxes of two sizes were used since the regular, smaller goal box is normally so small as to make it difficult for the rat to move around and emit the behavior that theoretically will become a conditioned response.

speeds and running speeds under the no-delay and postreward delay conditions but showed that each of these conditions produced faster times than the prereward delay condition. On the other hand, size of the goal box was not related to performance on either response measure. These results were taken as support for reinforcement theory, for this theory had predicted no difference between the no-delay and postreward delay groups, regardless of goal box size. In contrast, contiguity theorists would have predicted that the postreward delay rats score lower on the two dependent measures than those in the no-delay condition, expecially when the goal box was large so as to permit nongoal-directed behavior.

We hope that you now have an insight into the way basic laboratory researchers sometimes set up and test hypotheses to support or not support the theories from which the hypotheses have been derived. However, apart from that possible insight into the function of laboratory experimentation, we want you to focus on the causal conclusions of this particular study. Was it really the 30-second delay prior to reward that caused 20 of the rats to move more slowly, on the average, out of the starting box and down the runway to the reward cup than did the 40 rats in the other two delay conditions? Or do you feel that a plausible rival hypothesis exists to explain the significant findings?

(Turn to page 160 for solution.)

11. Air Force Officer School and Dogmatism

According to a personality theorist named Milton Rokeach, dogmatism can be defined as "a relatively closed cognitive organization of beliefs about reality, organized around a central set of beliefs about absolute authority which, in turn, provides a framework for patterns of intolerance and qualified tolerance toward others."[1] In less formal terms, the person who is highly dogmatic tends to be closed-minded, inflexible, and often more concerned about the status of a communication source than about the substance of what's being communicated. We are confident that you know at least one person who fits this description.

Many people believe that the structure of the armed services and the inherent chain-of-command basis of communication attract highly dogmatic volunteers. Military commanders, of course, disagree; they claim that they have a need for officers who are open-minded, tolerant, and able to win the respect and loyal cooperation of the personnel they direct. Aside from this question as to the type of person attracted to a military career, a researcher recently wondered whether a 14-week stint at officer training school would affect the participants' degree of dogmatism. Would this training program cause the junior officers to become more or less dogmatic, or would it have no effect on dogmatism? And would the influence of the 14-week program be the same for those participants who began with high levels of dogmatism as it was for those who began with low levels?

The subjects in this investigation came from a pool of 764 officers who completed the three-and-a-half-month Squadron Officer School (SOS) at Maxwell Air Force Base in Alabama. As the researcher saw it, there were several facets of the SOS program that might have made for a change in dogmatism. For example, each student was given extensive feedback from peers, the opportunity to discuss the personality characteristics of other trainees, a chance to deal with unstructured situations, and experience in planning military strategy in areas divorced from his field of expertise. These and other similar activities might, according to the researcher's hypothesis, cause the students' dogmatism levels to decrease over the 14-week time interval.

During the first and last weeks of training, all students in the SOS program were given a copy of the Rokeach Dogmatism Scale, Form E. (In this study, it was titled the Rokeach Opinion Scale.) This measuring instrument is made up of 40 statements, each of which is rated on a –3 to +3 scale so as to indicate the

[1] Milton Rokeach. "The Nature and Meaning of Dogmatism." *Psychological Review*, 1954, *61*, p. 195.

extent of one's disagreement or agreement. Two of the statements go as follows: "Most people just don't know what's good for them," and "A group which tolerates too much difference of opinion among its own members cannot exist for long." From among the SOS students who completed and returned the Rokeach Scale at both the pretest and post-test periods, 250 were randomly selected. Then, based upon an examination of the pretest scores, the 250 subjects were subdivided into five groups of 50 subjects each. In terms of the dogmatism continuum, these subgroups were described as high, above average, average, below average, and low.

The data were statistically analyzed in two ways. First, the pretest mean for all 250 subjects was compared to the overall post-test mean. Results indicated no significant difference. Next, a two-way analysis of variance was used to see whether the five subgroups were changing in a similar fashion between the beginning and end of the SOS program, or possibly not changing at all. The pre- and post-test means for the five subgroups turned out as follows:

		Pretest	*Post-test*
Grouping	High	170.04	161.14
based on	Above average	151.02	145.42
pretest	Average	138.12	137.26
performance	Below average	126.12	128.78
	Low	108.24	117.32

The statistical analysis indicated a significant interaction between subgroups and pre-post trials. (Such an interaction simply means that the change from pretest to post-test is not the same for all subgroups.)

Based on the subgroup means presented in the preceding table and the significant statistical finding, the researcher stated that "Subjects high in dogmatism on the pretest tended to become less dogmatic by the last week of training while those scoring below the mean tended to become more dogmatic" (Gleason, p. 35). In a way, it looks as if the SOS training program causes the participants to become more homogeneous in terms of dogmatism. Before drawing such a conclusion, however, it might be worthwhile to stop and ask whether there are any plausible rival hypotheses to account for the statistically significant result.

(Turn to page 161 for solution.)

12. A Penny for Your Thoughts

Although we enjoy games of many kinds and even understand the rules to a few of them, we would not qualify as game theorists. Game theorists are mathematicians who specialize in economic models of human decision-making. One such model that was once quite popular in psychology is the two-person Prisoner's Dilemma (PD) game. The PD game has its origins in the story of two prisoners in custody on suspicion of committing a crime. They are each told separately that if either confesses and the other does not, the confessor will be treated leniently and the nonconfessor harshly. If both confess, then they will both be treated severely (though not as severely as in the first case). Finally, if neither confesses, their punishment will be moderate. Thus, each prisoner is in a dilemma. Individually he is best off to confess when his accomplice does not (competitive choice); but, collectively the pair is best off when neither confesses (cooperative choice).

In the study we wish for you to consider, a variation of this situation was used, with each person asked to choose between two alternatives—red (R) or black (B) —and then rewarded according to schedule (B-B: 3,3; B-R: 0,4; R-B: 4,0; R-R: 1,1). In this example, black is the cooperative choice and red the competive choice, in that the maximum payoff to the pair is B-B (6 units), while the maximum payoff to one is B-R (4 units) and to the other is R-B (4 units).

This version of the PD game, with a payoff unit of 1¢, was used with a group of first-year medical students at the University of Kentucky in 1963. The author of that study was attempting to show that personality factors (not normally considered by game theorists) were influential within this model. An adjective checklist was used to measure the students on a variety of personality dimensions: need abasement, aggression, autonomy, deference, dominance, and nurturance. Each student then played the PD game with a confederate[1] of the experimenter who always made the cooperative choice (B). The student had the option to cooperate (B-B) or to exploit (R-B) the confederate. Students were then categorized as extreme if they made 22 or more choices (out of 30) of the same color. The fifteen most competitive students were contrasted with the nine least competitive students using the Mann-Whitney U-test, and differences were found for all characteristics but nurturance and dominance. The author took this as support for the influence of personality factors in this economic model. Do you agree?

(Turn to page 162 for solution.)

---

[1] A "confederate" is not an old Southerner. Rather, it is a person who is "in cahoots" with the experimenter, behaving or talking in a predetermined manner.

13. Pretest Sensitization

When reading a summary of an experimental study, you are probably inclined to take the researcher's results and presume that the treatments would be about as effective for your students (or animals or patients) as they were for the researcher's subjects. Whenever you do this, you are operating on the premise that the research investigation has high "external validity." Simply stated, studies possessing high external validity have results that generalize—that is to say, the results hold true for subjects other than those used by the researcher. Clearly, such generalization is important for anyone who consumes the professional literature, for it would be silly to read about empirical investigations if it were known that the conclusions held true only for the specific subjects involved in the experiment.[1]

There are, of course, several reasons why a treatment may not work very well when you use it, even though a researcher has offered somewhat conclusive evidence that the treatment had a terrific effect in the formal investigation. Maybe you're giving the treatment to people (or animals) who are different in some physiological or psychological way from the subjects used by the researcher. Possibly, the treatment worked in the formal experiment because of the Hawthorne effect. Or, the discrepancy between your assessment of the treatment's worth and the researcher's assessment could be due to a novelty phenomenon; that is, the treatment may lose its effect after the novelty of it wears off.

While there exist long lists of threats to external validity[2] one of the more likely reasons why a researcher's results do not generalize is "pretest sensitization." This phenomenon, which is also referred to as test reactivity or pretest-treatment interaction, is often associated with experiments wherein the subjects are pretested prior to receiving the treatment. Quite conceivably, the pretest will sensitize the subjects to what's important about the forthcoming treatment, and consequently they may perform much better on the post-test (with significantly more improvement than a pre- and post-tested control group). But when you use the exact same treatment with the same type of individual in an applied setting, the treatment may not seem to have much of an impact at all, simply because you're not doing an experiment and are not pretesting anyone—and are therefore not providing the pretreatment sensitization needed to make the treatment work.

[1] Usually, the notion of external validity refers to setting generalization as well as to subject generalization. Sometimes it is important to assess the ability of the results to generalize across different treatments.

[2] See D. T. Campbell and Julian C. Stanley's classic text entitled *Experimental and Quasi-Experimental Designs for Research* (Chicago: Rand McNally, 1966) and G. H. Bracht and G. V. Glass' article "The External Validity of Experiments," *American Education Research Journal*, 1968, 5, pp. 437–474.

Recently, a pair of researchers from Massachusetts conducted a study to see whether pretest sensitization was associated with experimental investigations in the field of counseling. Their goal was "to assess the degree of reactivity of pretesting on selected outcome criteria in counseling" (p. 128), and they used 27 college students as their subjects. These individuals were randomly divided into two groups, both of which received counseling. However, only one of the two groups of clients was administered the pretests: the Maladjustment Scale (Mt) and the Unidimensional Depression Scale (D_{30}) from the MMPI. After an equal number of counseling interviews, all 27 subjects were post-tested with the two MMPI scales. A statistical analysis of the post-test data revealed a significant difference between the two groups on the Mt Scale, and not surprisingly it was the pretest group that showed significantly greater adjustment.

The researchers concluded that their results provided partial support for the hypothesis that pretesting reactively interacts with counseling, and they ended their formal report by asserting that:

> pretesting may sensitize the client to counseling, which results in greater, or perhaps sometimes fewer, client benefits than if no pretesting were performed (Haase and Ivey, p. 128).

We want you to focus on the measuring instrument that did, in fact, lead to a significant difference between the two comparison groups. Relative to this Mt Scale, are you willing to accept the researchers' claim that pretest sensitization brought about the significant finding? Or is there an alternative explanation for why the two groups ended up with dissimilar adjustment scores on the post-test?

(Turn to page 162 for solution.)

14. Brainstorming

Every so often, most groups of individuals—especially groups in work settings —encounter problems of one sort or another. Before selecting a course of action to deal with the problem, the group may engage in a "brainstorming" session. The purpose of such a session is to generate lots of ideas, and the hope is that the best solution to the problem will appear among the suggested ideas (and then be recognized as the best idea by the group members).

Several research investigations have demonstrated that individual brainstorming is superior to group brainstorming. That is, more and better ideas are usually generated when people work on their own instead of together. One researcher, however, has hypothesized that group brainstorming might be equally or more effective than individual brainstorming if the technique of "synectics" is used within the group sessions. With this technique, each group member in turn is required to act out the central object associated with the problem. For example, if the problem or task were to come up with some brand names for a new type of hot dog that was ready to be marketed, the group members would be asked to lie down on the floor one at a time for one minute and play the part of a hot dog. During each minute, all members of the group, including the hot dog on the floor, would suggest as many new brand names as they could.

To determine whether the technique of synectics was worthwhile, the researcher who suggested its use conducted an experiment. The purpose of this study was to compare the regular brainstorming technique with the brainstorming-plus-synectics technique. The 88 male subjects came from an introductory psychology course. The subjects were divided into four-man groups, with the regular brainstorming groups being run through the experiment during the first half of the academic term, and the synectics groups during the second half of the term. All students received course points for their experimental participation plus $2.50 an hour.

Each of the four-man groups had the same nine problems to work on, and these problems were presented in the same order to each of the brainstorming and synectic groups. These problems were to devise (1) brand names for a cigar, (2) uses for old bricks, (3) possible problems of people getting taller, (4) brand names for a bra, (5) uses for newspaper, (6) procedures for getting more tourists to come to the United States, (7) brand names for an automobile, (8) uses for old coat hangers, and (9) consequences of everyone suddenly going blind. (It certainly would have been interesting to observe the synectics group act out some of these problems!)

On each of these nine problems, each of the four-man groups was measured in terms of the total number of different ideas generated. A closed-circuit television was used to record all suggestions from all groups. The average number of ideas for the synectics groups was computed for each problem, as was an average for the regular brainstorming groups. A statistical comparision of these two brainstorming techniques was performed on the data associated with each problem. Hence, nine comparisions were made. On five of these comparisons, a significant difference was found between the two averages —and in each case a significantly greater number of ideas was associated with the brainstorming-plus-synectics groups. Even on the four problems that did not yield a statistically significant result, the synectics group mean was higher.

The researcher concluded that the synectics strategy for group problem solving was more effective than typical brainstorming. This conclusion is based, of course, on the differences between the average number of ideas generated by groups using the two approaches. Do you accept this conclusion? If not, can you identify a plausible rival hypothesis to account for the results?

Before turning you loose on this problem, let us say one thing about the type of data collected. As you will recall, each four-man group was simply measured in terms of the number of suggested solutions generated. You may be thinking that this type of data is not too scientific, that a good technique might lead to a small number of really good suggested solutions. However, the researcher pointed out in the technical report that previous research had shown the total number of ideas generated to be the most sensitive indicator of treatment effects. Therefore, let us agree that the type of data collected has nothing to do with any rival hypotheses which may be associated with this experiment. Focus your personal brainstorming energies in one or more other directions!

(Turn to page 163 for solution.)

15. Model Drinking

Alcohol has recently regained its position as the drug of choice among young adults. Such previously fashionable drugs as cocaine and marijuana have (fortunately) begun to fall from grace. Nonetheless, alcohol addiction is a serious problem and among the most expensive—in both dollars and lives—that our society currently faces. In light of these facts, the following study of drinking behavior in three volunteer male college students should be of some interest.

The purpose of the study was to see if an individual's rate of drinking could be influenced by the rate of another person; that is, do people drink faster around fast drinkers and more slowly around slow drinkers? Two psychologists set up a simulated tavern complete with a bar, bar stools, tables, and a bartender. This tavern only served beer in 12-ounce glasses that were "calibrated decoratively" at 2-ounce intervals. Three graduate student confederates[1] were trained to drink at varying rates (accurate to within a half-ounce every five minutes), and then each was assigned to one of the three participants in the study.

The study used a design in which each student served as his own control. Thus, in this study, each participant was first placed in a baseline condition (A), followed by a slow rate condition (B), another baseline (A), a fast rate condition (C), and another baseline (A). (For obvious reasons, this was called an ABACA design.) All sessions were one hour long. In the baseline sessions the confederate matched his drinking rate to that of the participant, while in the experimental sessions the confederate model drank at a rate that was either one-third greater or one-third less than the participant's baseline rate. In the experimental sessions, two other confederates were also present who drank at a rate opposite to that of the model (faster in the slow session, slower in the fast session).

Graphs were presented for each individual subject that "clearly showed that each subject's consumption was influenced by the drinking rate of the single model confederate" (Garlington and Dericco, p. 209). One practical application of these findings might be for local mental health centers to hire slow drinkers, who would be assigned to sit in a fast-drinking bar in order to bring down the rate of drinking. Alternatively, tavern owners could hire fast drinkers to increase the rate (assuming that they do not already do so!).

Would you hire such people as a result of this study? Or would you be more likely to apply for the job?

(Turn to page 164 for solution.)

---

[1] A person working for the experimenter.

16. Required Textbooks in College Courses: Are They Needed?

The cost of a college education is skyrocketing. And while we usually think of tuition, room, and board as accounting for the largest chunk of the student's expenses, the financial outlay associated with other little items typically adds up very quickly. For example, we have known students who went into their campus bookstore with a list of the texts required for their new courses and left the bookstore with a $150 dent in their checking account. Little wonder that someone finally conducted a study to see whether students could learn as much without a required text as they normally do when one is required.

The research project in question took place over a two-year period at Marquette University in Milwaukee, with the focus of the study being an introductory course in psychological statistics. During the first semester of the 1974–75 academic year, 35 sophmores majoring in psychology signed up for this statistics course. On the first day of the term, the students were given a syllabus that stated, in part, that there was no text required for the course nor any specific book even recommended, and that they would be receiving various handouts containing formulas, problems, and the necessary statistical tables. A year later, the same course was again offered to 33 psychology majors. This second group of students also received a course syllabus on the first day of the term, and it was identical to the one used the previous year—except that it listed the required text and where it could be bought.

The same instructor was used for both sections of this statistics course, and each time the course was taught "in a traditional manner which relied heavily on lectures and discussions, with occasional demonstrations" (Quereshi, p. 2). The two groups of students received the same set of handouts (containing the formulas, problems, and tables); they met for the same number of class sessions; and they were given the same number of quizzes and take-home exercises. Furthermore, the specific quiz and exercise items remained constant from one year to the next, with identical directions and credit being given for correct responses.

Since complete data (scores on the three quizzes and the take-home exercises) were not available for nine of the students in the first class nor for eight of the students in the second class, the statistical comparison of student performance without the text versus performance with the text was based on sample sizes of 26 and 25, respectively. From the data provided by these 51 subjects, no significant difference was found to exist between the two groups with respect to their take-home exercise scores. However, a significant difference *was* associated with the in-class quiz scores, with the students in the required-text group earning higher scores than students in the no-text group. With these results as ammunition, the researcher concluded that "using a textbook in conducting an undergraduate course in psychological statistics has a definite beneficial effect on performance on closed-book, subject-mastery tests or quizzes" (p. 2).

Whether or not the findings of this study generalize to the specific courses that you take or teach clearly depends upon several important considerations—for example, the nature of the text used, the type of students enrolled in the course, the degree to which the instructor's lectures correspond with the text, and so on. However, we would like you to put aside the issue of generalization for the moment. Instead, focus on the results obtained by this particular researcher at Marquette during the 1974 and 1975 fall terms. Was the significant difference between the two groups' quiz performances brought about by one and only one causal variable, the presence or absence of the required text? If not, can you point out one or more explanations that make you unwilling to accept the researcher's conclusions, as they relate to *his own* research subjects?

(Turn to page 164 for solution.)

17. Claustrophobia

At times, we all experience things that are traumatic. For example, at the tail end of our undergraduate careers we—along with all other seniors at our college—had to take a four-hour multiple-choice test that determined whether or not we graduated. If we didn't score high enough, we would not get our degrees—even though we might have done well in every course we took for four years. That, most assuredly, was a traumatic situation! At other times, most of us probably create situations for other people that are frightening for them. For example, as college professors we now administer final examinations at the end of our courses, and the trauma experienced by at least some students is clearly visible as they prepare for and take what may be the only test upon which their grade will be based.

When responsible for the traumatic feelings that other people experience, we often will attempt to change ourselves or the environment such that the other person will have absolutely no need to feel frightened. But at times, our professional responsibility may demand that we do something to or for people even though we know that it will be a semitraumatic experience for them. Surely the dentist knows that a visit to the dental chair is quite frightening for many patients. And as professors, we know that most of our students hate to take tests. Nevertheless, drilling to fill cavities and testing students to evaluate their achievement are necessary parts of, respectively, the dental and academic professions. One might ask, however, whether an event can be made less traumatic by giving it out in small doses rather than all at once. Instead of giving one final examination, we could administer several short quizzes throughout the academic term. Might this alternative strategy reduce trauma?

We do not have the answer to this question yet, at least for college students and test situations. In a different arena, however, an experimental study has been conducted to see if trauma can be reduced by having subjects experience it in small doses. The subjects in this study were 16-week-old puppies, and the traumatic experience involved being placed in a very small box, so small that the puppies could just barely turn around. All puppies were put into this box for ten minutes; however, a random half of the puppies were in the box for ten consecutive minutes while the other half of the subject pool had one minute inside the box, one minute out of the box, one minute in, until they had experienced a cumulative total of ten minutes in the box. The number of yelps made by each puppy while in the box was recorded, and a significant difference was found to exist between the average number of yelps emitted by the two groups. The puppies who were in the box for ten consecutive minutes

This problem is based on a study taken from Benton J. Underwood, *Psychological Research*, © 1957. Adapted by permission of Prentice-Hall, Inc., Englewood Cliffs, New Jersey.

yelped, on the average, almost three times as frequently as their counterparts, thereby supporting (in the researcher's view) the "small-dose" hypothesis for reducing trauma.[1]

There is, of course, a possibility that being in the small box was *not* traumatic for the puppies used in this experiment. With animals, trauma can only be inferred from their behavior; we can't ask them whether they are experiencing trauma. Nevertheless, let us assume that the box *was* a traumatic situation and that a record of yelping behavior *was* an appropriate way to assess which dogs were experiencing the most trauma. Even if we make these assumptions, there may be a plausible alternative explanation to account for why the small-dose group yelped less. In fact, we feel there are two rival hypotheses in competition with the researcher's claim that the all-at-once group yelped more because of the way they were experiencing the trauma. Can you identify either or both of these alternative explanations?

(Turn to page 165 for solution.)

[1] The mean number of yelps for the all-at-once group was 1104, or almost two yelps per second while in the box; the mean for the small-dose group was 347 yelps for their ten minutes in the box.

18. Hypnosis and Biofeedback

A ninteenth-century physician named F. A. Mesmer was among the first to investigate hypnotism in a scientific manner. Although "mesmerized" is now used almost exclusively to mean "fascinated," it was at one time synonymous with the term "hypnotized." Many claims have been made over the years for the power of hypnosis, but our favorite involves the use of hypnosis to create a temporary state of deafness in the hypnotic subject. We have never understood how the subject heard the command to come out of the hypnotic state!

Hypnotism was also involved in a recent study of *biofeedback*.[1] The researchers were primarily interested in seeing whether or not some individuals could exercise voluntary control over their peripheral skin temperature, as measured by the relative warmth of their hands. In this study six college students were selected for their *hypnotic talent* (ability to be hypnotized) and their "extensive" previous hypnotic training and experience. Four of the students had some experience in meditation; two were still actively pursuing meditation during the experimental period.

Participants were hypnotized before each experimental session and then asked to make one hand warmer than the other. Some began with the right hand and some with the left—the hand chosen alternated from one session to another. Headphones were used to carry a biofeedback tone to the participants. The tone would shift toward the right ear when the right hand was becoming relatively warmer, and the frequency of the tone would also increase as the temperature differential increased. At the end of the session the hypnotic state was lifted.

The results indicated that participants *were* able to create temperature differences between their hands. However, different approaches were used. For example, some would raise the temperature of the target hand, while others would lower the temperature of the nontarget hand. Still others would raise the temperature of both hands at different rates and thus create the desired difference. One thing the participants did share, however, was a "high degree of motivation and involvement" along with the belief that the experiment was both a "helpful and valuable experience." In addition, all participants felt that the hypnosis had helped in their attempts to exercise control over their skin temperatures.

The researchers concluded that "some individuals are capable of achieving voluntary control over the autonomic processes involved in peripheral skin temperature regulation" (Roberts *et al.*, p. 168). We agree. They also pointed out a confounding factor in the study, involving the case of

---

[1] The use of external feedback to allow one to control such physiological processess as heart rate or blood pressure.

the learning that took place. What would you have listed as plausible rival hypotheses to the claim that hypnosis was the causal variable that allowed people to control their skin temperature?

(Turn to page 166 for solution.)

19. How to Stop Smoking

Of the people who smoke cigarettes, cigars, or pipes, many want to continue their habit. On the other hand, there are lots of smokers who are tired of finding small holes in their clothes and furniture, are scared of the probable consequences for their health, and are conscious of the money that they are literally burning up. Within this group of smokers who would like to quit, a few can do so with apparent ease. But for the majority, it is exceedingly difficult to kick the habit. We're sure you know someone who has "permanently" quit smoking on several occasions, each time to find that the nasty habit somehow creeps back into their everyday routine. (Or maybe you yourself are an example of this type of person.)

Several techniques have been used to help people quit smoking, such as filters that progressively screen out more and more of the smoke, group get-togethers patterned after Alcoholics Anonymous, and the substitution of gum or candy for tobacco whenever one experiences the onset of a "nicotine fit." In addition, a multitude of books and articles have been written on the subject. Unfortunately, all such attempts to help smokers become nonsmokers have met with limited success. Consequently, we expect there to be a great deal of interest in a recent study that seems to show that an entirely different approach produces quick and lasting results.

The subject used in this investigation was a 27-year-old female who volunteered to be in the experiment. She had been smoking an average of 30 cigarettes per day for several years, and she had previously made five attempts to quit smoking. However, each of these attempts ultimately failed, and the longest interval of self-imposed abstinence was a four-month period.

The new approach to help this subject kick the habit was called "aversive smoking," and the treatment consisted of nine 30-minute sessions held on the Monday, Wednesday, and Friday of three consecutive weeks. During these treatment sessions, the subject was involved in three activities. First, she was asked to light up a cigarette and smoke at her normal rate while handling cigarette litter. Here, the subject was asked to run her hands through a five-pound bag of cigarette litter, and she was also encouraged to put her head right over the bag to smell the aroma as she smoked her cigarette.[1] The second activity required that the subject smoke at a faster-than-normal rate while a machine blew warm, stale, smoky air at her face and body. In the third activity, the subject was encouraged to drink water (as a substitute activity) whenever she felt an urge to light up a new cigarette at home, at work, or at social events.

Before, during, and after the three-week period of treatment, the subject

---

[1] To prevent the subject from becoming endangered by the bacteria normally present in cigarette litter, the bag's contents in this study were sterilized—making it clean litter.

maintained a record of how many cigarettes she smoked each day. During the baseline period (the week prior to treatment), the subject reported smoking an average of 30 cigarettes per day. During the treatment phase of the study, the subject's smoking rate decreased steadily, and there was absolutely no smoking reported for the final eight days of this three-week period. Throughout the six-month follow-up period (which included a "booster" treatment session once each month), the subject reported complete abstinence. During the final follow-up booster session, the subject indicated that she had no desire to smoke and that the sight of other people smoking was quite distasteful to her.

According to the researchers, the dramatic change in the subject's smoking behavior was most likely attributable to the litter part of the treatment. While she was handling the cigarette litter in the plastic bag, ashes quickly found their way under the subject's fingernails; this was considered to be especially disgusting to the subject, and she reported nausea and at least once actually vomited. Even though she washed her hands thoroughly following the litter-handling episodes, the subject found it quite horrible to smell the ash residue on her arms and hands throughout the day and to see small particles of the cigarette litter lodged under her fingernails.

The data associated with this study appear to document an amazingly strong cause-and-effect relationship. The effect variable is a drastic change in smoking habits, while the causal variable is a series of short sessions involving cigarette litter, smoky air, and talk of water. Are you willing to accept the researchers' conclusions about the worth of their "aversive smoking" treatment, or do you see any plausible rival hypotheses that might explain the results?

(Turn to page 166 for solution.)

20. Class Attendance Plus Study Versus Study Versus Nothing

When you were in college, we're sure you had lots of courses in which class attendance was downright essential to passing the examinations. We're also somewhat confident that you ended up in a couple of other courses in which the instructor's lectures were completely unrelated to the test questions—thus making it possible to pass the course by simply reading the text assignments. And although *you* never signed up for them, we suspect that you knew other people who occasionally took courses that students could pass without doing anything at all.

Not too long ago, a pair of researchers conducted an experiment to see whether the students who received the most complete training would be the ones to score the highest on post-training examinations. One of the three training conditions involved in-class instruction plus outside reading assignments; the second condition involved just the reading materials; and the last condition involved neither instruction nor reading. Of course, the researchers' hunch was that the first group would perform better than the second, and that the second group would perform better than the third.

The subjects in this experiment were 51 college students enrolled in an educational psychology course taught at the University of Georgia. These subjects were assigned in a random manner to six subgroups, and then two of the subgroups were randomly assigned to each of the three treatment (training) conditions. Subgroups I and IV received both in-class instruction and out-of-class reading material. The reading material was Mager's short text entitled *Preparing Instructional Objectives*,[1] and the in-class activities involved about 100 minutes of training related to the text's content. This training dealt with evaluating objectives to see if they were stated behaviorally, recognizing the components of well-stated instructional objectives, and determining whether test items were appropriate for given objectives. Subgroups II and V studied the same text outside of class, but they received none of the in-class training activities. The final two subgroups, III and VI, did not learn at all about behavioral objectives—they simply read an article on student unrest and wrote a critique of this unrelated paper.

After the three treatments had been applied, a 30-item test was administered to all 51 subjects. This test was based upon the material presented in Mager's text, and it did not contain any questions that were unique to the in-class activities associated with the first treatment condition. This 30-item post-test had 20 true-false items plus ten additional items that

[1] Robert F. Mager. *Preparing Instructional Objectives*. (Palo Alto, California: Fearon Publishers, 1962).

35

required the examinee to underline the performance criteria (if any) associated with given objectives.

For the purposes of statistical analysis, the data from the two subgroups receiving the same treatment were combined. The resulting mean scores for the three treatment conditions turned out as follows:

Mager text + instruction (Subgroups I & IV)	Mager text by itself (Subgroups II & V)	No text and no instruction (Subgroups III & VI)
$\overline{X} = 25.06$	$\overline{X} = 21.66$	$\overline{X} = 13.41$

A one-way analysis of variance was used to compare these three means statistically, and the results indicated overall significance. Then, a follow-up analysis was conducted to see if the in-class instructional activities were worthwhile. In the words of the researchers:

> Following the analysis of variance, the mean for Groups I and IV was contrasted with pooled means for Groups II & V and III & VI to see whether the addition of class instruction led to significantly better test achievement when added to the reading of the Mager text. A D′ contrast (Scheffé method, as described by McNemar, pp. 285–86) was used. Accepting alpha as .05 (K = 2.526), 2/48 df, D′ for this contrast was 7.24. As hypothesized, subjects who received the most complete training achieved highest scores on the training test.

It is possible that you are unfamiliar with some of the technical jargon of this quotation, such as alpha, D′ contrast, and K. Nonetheless, the first sentence clearly indicates that the mean for the subjects receiving the text plus instruction was compared against the average performance of all other subjects (that is, those in subgroups II, III, V, and VI). Are you willing to accept the researchers' claim, based on a significant finding in this follow-up analysis, that "the addition of the class instruction led to significantly better test achievement when added to the reading of the Mager text?"

(Turn to page 167 for solution.)

21. Charity Begins at Home

At one time or another we all receive solicitations for charitable organizations. Maybe these solicitations are sort of randomly distributed throughout the year, with only a small amount of seasonal variation. It often seems, however, that the first solicitation of spring signals an onslaught of similar requests. Since we already have aggregate nouns for geese ("gaggle") and larks ("exaltation"), perhaps it would be appropriate to use a "solicitation of charities" to cover these springtime activities. Regardless of when they send out their representatives, we strongly suspect that charitable organizations would be interested in research on the factors that influence the probability and the amount of giving by an individual.

In one such study, two researchers examined the responses of 240 adults contacted in the course of an actual door-to-door fund-raising drive, in an effort to study the "effect of verbal modeling on contributions to charity." Participants in the study were randomly assigned to one of 16 groups, each of which received a different combination of verbal information. The experimenter gave the participants information about the percentage of their neighbors who donated (more than three-fourths or less than one-fourth), the amount the neighbors donated (more than $5.00 or less than $1.00), the reason for the participant to donate (to fulfill their social responsibility or just to feel good), and the level of need of those helped by the charity (desperate as opposed to "could use your help").

The amount donated was used as the dependent variable in a 2 x 2 x 2 x 2 analysis of variance. The results of this analysis indicated a significant difference between the percentage conditions, with people giving more when told that over three-fourths of their neighbors had previously contributed. Also, a significant interaction was found between that factor and the factor dealing with the reason for giving. Additional analyses showed that combining social responsibility with the information that others gave a large amount resulted in the collection of more money. This led the researchers to conclude that giving verbal information about the behavior of others was "sufficient to elicit modeling behavior" (Catt and Benson, p. 83).

Would you apply the results of this study if you were running a local fund-raising drive?

(Turn to page 168 for solution.)

22. Professional Socialization in Nursing School

One of the major goals of faculty members and administrators in the health professions is to help students adopt realistic views of their future jobs. The rationale behind this goal is very simple, and it is based upon empirical research. Students who have accurate expectations of their work roles tend to be more satisfied and more likely to remain in the profession.

The term *professional socialization* has been used to describe the process by which students acquire appropriate perceptions of their professional roles. As you might suspect, faculty members play an important role in this socialization. In fact, it has been hypothesized that this process can be identified by seeing whether the students come to adopt more and more of their mentors' ideas and attitudes and values as they progress through their formal training program. Several researchers have attempted to document this phenomenon of professional socialization in both medical schools and nursing schools, but these efforts have been hindered by the unavailability of a well-designed, standardized measuring instrument. Fortunately, however, two individuals have recently joined efforts to develop such a scale for use with student nurses.

The new instrument, called the Nurses' Professional Orientation Scale, contained 112 items that described behaviors often displayed by nurses when on the job. (Two of the items were: "Question instructions when the reason for them is not clear," and "Accept the death of a patient with no overt emotional signs.") Each respondent was asked to rate the importance of each of these behaviors for the practicing nurse, and a five-point scale was provided with the possible choices extending from "extremely important" to "undesirable."

Scoring weights for the item responses were established by administering the scale to 94 nursing faculty members at three universities. For each item, it was possible to determine the percentage of faculty who selected each of the five response options, and these percentages (rounded to the nearest 10 percent) became the weights associated with the five options. Thus, if a student chose a response that had previously been endorsed by 90 percent of the faculty respondents, the student earned 9 points on that item; if the student chose a response that had been selected by only 80 percent of the faculty, the student would earn only 8 points, and so on. By means of this scoring system, students would earn high total scores on the Professional Orientation Scale if they rated the 112 traits in a fashion similar to the responses of the faculty members.

Once constructed, the 112-item scale was administered to 488 students enrolled in four-year baccalaureate nursing programs at Michigan State University, Wayne State University, and the University of Illinois. This subject pool was randomly split into two halves, and an item analysis was conducted (using data from the 244 students in the first half) to identify the better items. (An item was considered to be good if more seniors agreed with the faculty than juniors, more juniors than sophomores, and more sophomores than freshmen.) As a result of this item analysis, 52 items were thrown out, leaving 60 items in the final form of the instrument. Then, total scores on the shortened 60-item scale were computed for the 244 students in the second half of the subject pool.

To validate the new scale, the students in the second half of the subject pool were subdivided on the basis of year in school. Then, the average score on the 60-item scale was computed for each of these four subgroups. These average scores were 132.9 for freshmen, 154.3 for sophomores, 176.1 for juniors, and 193.5 for seniors. When these were compared statistically, it was shown that the mean for each class was significantly greater than the mean for the class below.

In the technical report of this study, the researchers stated that their results indicated:

> that the nurses' professional orientation scale measures a shift in the student's view of the profession that was positively related to the length of the training experience. The congruence between student and faculty ratings of items increased significantly with each year of training experience. (Crocker and Brodie, p. 234).

And in general, the researchers felt that their data supported the contention, expressed and held by believers of professional socialization, that there exists a definite trend for students to gravitate toward the faculty way of viewing the profession as graduation nears.

Within this study, there is a clear cause-and-effect relationship being discussed. The causal variable allegedly is "amount of training," with the effect variable being "tendency to agree with the faculty." Based on their data, the researchers are asking us to believe that nursing students come to agree more with the faculty view of the profession because of the contact the two groups have had with one another. Are you willing to accept this conclusion? Or do you feel that there are alternative explanations to account for the statistical findings?

(Turn to page 168 for solution.)

23. Counseling Practicum

During their formal training in their master's program, prospective school counselors are exposed to research articles, theory, and role models. It is not unlikely that during this period, students develop an initial set of thoughts concerning ideal counselor characteristics. Near the end of the graduate program, however, students are often placed, through a practicum course, into a field setting so the counselor-trainees can put into practice the things that have been learned and, of course, learn some new things. As a result of this field-based experience, one might ask whether there is a change in the perception of the desirable characteristics associated with a competent counselor's role and responsibilities.

In an attempt to answer this question, a pair of researchers recently conducted a study at Northwestern Illinois State College. The subjects in this investigation were 36 graduate students in guidance and counseling, all of whom had completed 30 credit hours of required courses and were enrolled in the practicum experience. This eight-week experience involved four half-days a week in a public school, with supervision provided by local school personnel and the college faculty. Besides conducting individual and group counseling sessions, the practicum students also performed a variety of typical guidance activities.

At the beginning and end of the eight-week practicum experience, each of the 36 subjects was administered the Occupational Characteristics Index (OCI). This instrument provides 12 scores, each associated with a trait that workers might have to varying degrees (for example, organizational realist, leader, innovator). On each administration of the OCI, the practicum students were asked to indicate the ideal characteristics that they believed a counselor should possess. For each of the 12 traits, prepracticum and postpracticum means were computed and compared statistically.

The results of the data analysis indicated that the 36 practicum students, on the average, changed from pretest to post-test with respect to 11 of the 12 OCI scales. At the end of the practicum experience, the students believed that five of the traits were more important than they had thought prior to their eight-week field experience; however, for six other traits there was a feeling after the practicum that these traits were less important. Hence, there appeared to be substantial evidence that the practicum students had changed their perception of what an ideal counselor was like.

The researchers clearly attributed this change to the field-based practicum experience that had taken place during the eight weeks between the pretest and post-test. For example, near the end of the formal report of this study, the investigators state that "on-the-job experience did provide a statistically significant change in their perception of the ideal counselor characteristics" (Langley and Gehrman, p. 79). Do you agree with this interpretation of the data? Can we assume for certain that it was the counseling practicum that brought about the change? Or might there be one or more plausible rival hypotheses to account for the change in perception?

(Turn to page 170 for solution.)

24. Where the Wild Goose Goes

Before the advent of journals such as *Animal Behavior*, much of the early work done by ethologists was published in "bird" journals such as *Auk*, the journal of the American Ornithologists' Union. Since birds are usually considered to be timid, easily frightened, and not particularly intelligent, it was logical that some of this early work attempted to establish which aspects of stimuli in the environment would produce escape reactions in birds.

One such study examined the reactions of young ducks and geese (raised in the laboratory) to a cut-out silhouette of a bird that resembled a hawk (short neck, long tail) when moved on a string in one direction and a goose (long neck, short tail) when moved in the other direction. The birds behaved as though they were trying to escape when the silhouette was in the first position, but not when it was in the second. Since the wings on the silhouette were symmetrical front and back, the difference in responses could not have been based on wing shape. Thus, the researcher, Nobel-prize-winning ethologist Niko Tinbergen, concluded ducks and geese respond to "shape in relation to direction of movement" and not just to shape alone.

The ducks and geese were obviously alarmed when the hawklike silhouette went flying by. What other explanation for their alarm comes to mind?

(Turn to page 171 for solution.)

25. Crashing into the Rear of a Taxi

Far too many people die each year in auto accidents. A greater number survive such accidents only after sustaining injuries that often leave them maimed for life. Although a great deal of money has been expended in an attempt to develop automotive equipment that will protect the occupants during a crash (padded dashboards, air bags, and the like), suprisingly little money has been devoted to research on the development of equipment that helps to *prevent the accident altogether.* Given the choice, we suspect that just about everyone would rather ride in cars that do not have accidents than in cars that simply keep you from getting jostled around and cut (and possibly killed) when involved in a smash-up.

In spite of the small amount of money earmarked for the design of preventative equipment, it is encouraging to know that at least a few researchers are working along these lines. Recently, Dr. John Voevodsky attempted to decrease rear-end collisions—specifically, the kind where the first of two vehicles stops quickly while the second car does not. The new piece of equipment that Dr. Voevodsky designed was an amber-colored warning light positioned on the rear of the experimental vehicles at the same height as the regular red stop lights. The warning light was connected to the brake pedal, and it pulsed at a rate that varied exponentially with the amount of deceleration. Hence, as more and more pressure was exerted on the brake pedal to stop the car, the amber light would go off and on faster and faster to warn the driver behind of the impending quick stop.

The vehicles used to test the worth of the new warning lights were taxicabs located in San Francisco. These vehicles were used rather than privately owned cars because they are driven a much longer distance each day—and driven in the type of traffic situations that typically involve rear-end accidents. Of the fleet of 503 taxis owned by the cab company, some of the vehicles were equipped with the warning light apparatus while other taxis remained unequipped and served as the control group. Neither before nor during the experimental period were the taxi drivers involved in any education program concerning the operation or function of the deceleration warning light, nor did they get to choose which taxis they would be driving. The dispatcher assigned the drivers to equipped or unequipped vehicles at his discretion, ignoring any preference of the drivers.

During the 11-month test period, data were collected for each group on the number of rear-end collisions, the number of drivers injured, and the cost of repairs associated with these collisions, all adjusted on the basis of miles driven per cab. These data indicated that the equipped cabs had a significantly smaller number of rear-end accidents and less than one-half the number of injuries to the drivers. Furthermore, the average cost of repairing the cab following a rear-end collision was $398 (per million miles driven) for the equipped cabs versus a figure of $1041 for the cabs in the control group.

The data associated with this study give the clear impression that it was safer to be riding in an equipped rather than an unequipped cab. But was it the deceleration warning light that brought about the smaller number of accidents? Your first thought is probably that the cab drivers were simply more cautious when in the equipped cars, and thus the true causes of the differential accident rates could have been the drivers rather than the new light. However, the researcher anticipated your thinking and has argued that it doesn't hold. In the formal report of the research, he states:

> This criticism does not apply because the collisions are due to the drivers of the cars that follow the taxis and not to the taxi drivers. That the taxi driver has not become more cautious because of driving a taxi equipped with a safety device is attested by the lack of change in the collisions in which the taxicab driver ran into the rear-end of a car in front of him. The drivers of equipped taxis produced 7.1 such collisions per million miles, and those not equipped produced 8.1 such collisions per million miles. When this difference is tested statistically . . . the difference is not significant. (Voevodsky, p. 272). *

Do you accept the researcher's claim that the cause of the lower rear-end accident rate among the equipped cars was the warning light? Do you trust his reasoning about why the drivers themselves do not constitute a plausible rival hypothesis? Or do you feel that there is some other alternative explanation (besides the drivers) to account for the cause-and-effect relationship presumably identified in this study?

(Turn to page 171 for solution.)

*Reprinted from the *Journal of Applied Psychology*, 1974, *59*, p. 272. Courtesy of J. Voevodsky.

26. Angina Pectoris

Angina pectoris is the medical term used to describe a severe pain that some people feel in their chests. The pain is caused by too little blood getting from the mammary arteries to the tissue around the heart, and many physicians believe that this condition, if allowed to worsen, will eventually bring about a heart attack. Consequently, several different remedies have been tried, ranging from doing nothing (and hoping that the problem will simply go away) to surgery.

The surgical techniques used to deal with angina pectoris also vary. Sometimes the arteries are scraped out; on other occasions, they are ligated bilaterally. This latter procedure involves tying the main mammary arteries to improve circulation to the cardiac region among the existing secondary routes and maybe even encourage the development of new routes. Since there are, in this case, alternative surgical techniques aimed at correcting the same problem, it is encouraging to know that research studies are sometimes conducted to assess the worth of each technique. Let us now consider one such investigation.

In this particular study, there were 50 patients suffering from angina pectoris. Each of these individuals was surgically treated by using the procedure wherein the internal mammary arteries are ligated. Between two to six months following the operation, the patients were contacted and questioned as to the status of their physiological problem. Of the 50 patients, 34 were clinically improved: 18 reported no angina whatsoever following the operation while 16 experienced fewer and less severe seizures. This rate of improvement (34 out of 50) is significant at the 0.05 level.

About a year after this first investigation was published, a very interesting follow-up article appeared in the medical literature. The physician-researchers associated with this second study were somewhat skeptical about the results of the first investigation, and in particular they had questions about the wisdom of using the 50 patients "as their own controls" and the presumption that their condition would remain unchanged unless treated. So, a new study was undertaken to reassess the value of ligating the mammary arteries.

This second study involved 17 patients who were suffering from angina pectoris. These subjects were split, in a random fashion, into two groups—an experimental group of eight and a placebo control group of nine. The individuals in the experimental group were operated on and had both mammary arteries ligated. The subjects in the placebo control group were also operated on, but they did not receive the ligation; instead, they simply received the type of skin incision similar to that required to perform the ligation.[1] The patients, of course, were all under the impression that they had received the complete surgical procedure, and the doctors who conducted the postoperative evaluation of the patients' status were kept in the dark as to their experimental or placebo group affiliation. In other (more technical) words, this experiment was conducted in a "double-blind" fashion.

When the resulting evaluations of postoperative status were compared, there was no difference between the two groups of patients. Moreover, the rate of improvement in both groups was comparable to that reported in the first research article. Based on these results, the authors of the second study wrote:

> After observing some of the dramatic results afforded by only bilateral thoracic skin incisions, one seriously questions how much of the reported clinical improvement after thoracotomy is actually dependent upon the patients' psychological reaction to surgery rather than an enhancement of coronary-artery blood flow or other physiologic alteration.

Hence, the researchers associated with the second investigation were arguing that the frequency and severity of chest pains decreased following the operation simply because the patients *expected* the operation to work. And the phrase "placebo effect" was used to describe this self-perceived improvement brought about by the psychological expectation of improvement.

The second study appears to demonstrate that the actual tying of the mammary arteries is not the causal agent that brings about relief from angina pectoris. Instead, the researchers have pointed to the patient's psychological expectation of improvement as the true cause. Do you agree with their rival hypothesis, which they feel explains the results of the first study (in which there was just one group of 50 patients), or do you think that there may be some *other* alternative explanation—besides psychological expectancy—to account for the improved postoperative condition in all three groups of the two studies?

(Turn to page 172 for solution.)

---

[1] You may be thinking that the "operations" on the placebo subjects were cruel, unfair, and unethical. However, part of a recent television documentary on the topic of unneeded surgery could be used to defend the procedures of this study. The theme of the documentary was as follows: many operations (such as tonsilectomies) are thought to be necessary and are therefore performed quite frequently but maybe they are *not* really necessary. The only way to find out for sure is to randomly split a group of patients who seem to need the operation into two groups and then operate on those in one group but not the other.

27. Psychotherapy Revisited

One of the main plausible rival hypotheses to any study of psychotherapy is that of statistical regression. Individuals tend to enter therapy at an extreme point in their lives and, thus, tend not to be at such an extreme later on. This would generally be the case even in the absence of therapy. We are not criticizing the effectiveness of psychotherapy, only pointing out the difficulty of doing research in this area. Under these conditions, the need for studies that follow up psychotherapeutic programs should be obvious.

One such study investigated the effects of four psychotherapy programs (including one control condition) on the following three diagnostic groups: nonpsychotic patients, short-term psychotic patients, and long-term psychotic patients. The researchers compared the results of a six-month follow-up with the results of the original study, as well as those from an 18-month follow-up of the same patients. The data consisted of responses to a nine-item questionnaire given to 86 of the 96 participants in the original study. Among other topics, the questionnaire addressed employment, rehospitalization, and general adjustment.

At the end of six months, significant diagnostic group differences were found in the areas of degree of illness, employment, having friends, and remaining out of the hospital. These differences continued to exist at 18 months, although other earlier differences in community adjustment had disappeared by this time. However, significant differences in employment between the three diagnostic groups that had existed at six-months ceased to exist by the time of the latest follow-up.

The researchers concluded that "the disappearance of significant employment differences by 18 months suggests that psychotherapy effects are of short-term duration" (Fairweather and Simon, p. 186). They also recommend the development of a social support system in the community for people similar to those in their study. While we might agree with their recommendation, we are not sure the data support it. Are you? (To prevent our initial paragraph from misleading you, regression in not a problem in this particular follow-up study.)

(Turn to page 172 for solution.)

28. Passing Out

Because some males are taller and stronger and less apt to cry, females are often referred to as the "weaker sex." However, enough statistical evidence has now been accumulated to challenge this long-standing stereotype. For example, infant mortality rates are lower among females, and males tend to have shorter life spans. Recently, further data have been reported on another difference between the two sexes, and once again it is the females who show up as superior.

The researcher who collected this new evidence is Dr. John McGimpsey of the dental surgery department of Belfast University, and his study focused on the frequency with which people pass out in the dental chair. The rate for men was three times higher than it was for women! And the lead sentence in the magazine report of this study asserted: "Men are the weaker sex when it comes to visiting the dentist."

Since most fainting episodes occur before noon, Dr. McGimpsey suggested that the difference between the male and female rates may be attributable to men's not eating a proper breakfast at the beginning of the day. Others might argue that the sex difference in fainting rates is caused by differential exposure to pain and suffering. Given the traditional division of labor, some mothers at home see, and have to deal with, far more cuts and bruises and broken bones than do their husbands, and as a result they may develop a higher resistance to the pain and suffering that they themselves might encounter.

Assuming that the statistics on passing out in the dental chair are valid, do you accept the breakfast or exposure explanations for the higher rate among males? Or, are there any plausible rival hypotheses to account for the difference between the two sexes?

(Turn to page 173 for solution.)

29. Nine Out of Ten Better in One-Fourth the Time

As most college students would agree, new teaching methods are quite unusual in our undergraduate or graduate institutions. Consequently, we often hear the complaint that instructional innovation begins in elementary school and only gradually moves up. Despite the probable truth of this complaint, there is a new instructional approach being used to teach foreign language in college, and it seems to work. This teaching method was developed by John Rassias at Dartmouth College, and it is called the Intensive Language Model.

Rassias' instructional model divides the academic year into three ten-week phases. During the first phase, students are on the Dartmouth campus in the classroom. From the moment the course begins, students are forced to communicate at a rapid rate in spite of improper accent, vocabulary, and grammar. They immediately engage in short conversations (on such subjects as going to a train station), and they also memorize one-minute "micrologs" written by Rassias that explain how to do something (for example, make a crepe). In small groups, the students are also drilled by junior and senior apprentice teachers who ask students an average of 65 questions an hour. Both professors and apprentice teachers alike become uninhibited actors—sometimes with costumes—as they attempt to create a classroom atmosphere that keeps students excited about the learning process. During the second ten-week period, students go abroad to live with foreign families and to study under the supervision of an American professor. The final phase ends up back at the Dartmouth campus with an optional ten-week literature survey.

In an attempt to document the worth of Rassias' teaching model, the weekly news magazine describing it presented three types of evidence: student testimonies ("It changed my life"), increasing enrollment figures, and test results. With respect to the third type of evidence, the magazine article stated that "tests given to students at 200 colleges show that first-year language students at Dartmouth are more fluent after only 20 to 30 weeks of instruction than 9 out of 10 language majors elsewhere are at graduation."

We have no doubt that Rassias' Intensive Language Model works better than the traditional foreign language courses we had in college. This instructional approach sounds truly exciting—especially if funds are available for the teaching apprentices and the ten-week period of study in a foreign country. But we are concerned about the third type of evidence presented to document the model's effectiveness. The implication of the statement on test results makes it appear as if Rassias' method of teaching *caused* students to perform far better, after only one year, than other students on different campuses who spent four years studying. Is there a plausible rival hypothesis to account for this set of test data?

(Turn to page 173 for solution.)

30. Flexible Time

One of the supposed benefits of college teaching is the flexible schedule we are allowed to keep. We often point with pride to the fact that we do not have a 9-to-5 job. This leads our nonacademic friends to believe that any time not spent in class is automatically available for basking in the sun or other such pursuits. In contrast, our families can't seem to understand why someone with such a flexible schedule has to work nights and weekends.

The notion of fitting schedules to people rather than people to schedules has recently led a number of business firms to try a more flexible approach in which, for example, workers can start as early as 7:30 A.M. or as late as 10:00 A.M. Assuming a seven-and-three-fourths-hour workday, this provides a core period from 10:00 A.M. to 3:15 P.M. during which all employees would be present. This plan would be of great benefit to many workers who are constrained by their children's school schedules or would like to commute at off-hours. Three researchers decided that a study of worker productivity under the conditions outlined above would provide valuable information to companies considering such a plan.

Productivity data were collected on 246 employees in one of five natural groupings over a four-month period. Within two of the groups there were "experimentally designated" control groups, while in two others the productivity was contrasted with levels measured prior to the beginning of the study. Since no prior data were available in the fifth group, it was only possible to analyze productivity within the experimental period. The analysis of variance showed no treatment effects for either of the first two groups; however, pre-post differences were found to be significant in the third and fourth groups. No significant trend was found in the fifth group.

The researchers failed to come to a clear-cut decision on the impact of flexible working hours but did indicate that no adverse effects were found. Do you see anything that they may have overlooked?

(Turn to page 174 for solution.)

31. Fore!

Although we consider ourselves to be relatively athletic and sports-minded individuals, we do not play golf very often. The primary reason for our infrequent appearance on the links is simply our inability to get that seemingly innocent little ball from the tee to the green in a reasonable number of shots. Almost every time we swing the club, the ball hooks to the left or slices to the right—assuming, of course, that we haven't whiffed! It sure would be nice if some sporting goods company could invent a ball that wouldn't hook or slice, or simply a ball that would travel a long distance, since most of our shots (even the few straight hits) trickle along the ground and only occasionally make it to the fairway.

For golfers who share our concern about finding a ball that gets good distance, a recent magazine advertisement by the Rawlings Golf Company has probably caught (or will soon catch) your eye. Rawlings claims to have invented a new ball—called the Toney Penna DB—that travels farther than other balls when hit. (Incidentally, the letters "DB" stand for the phrase "distance ball.") The reasons provided for the new ball's distance quality are somewhat technical. We suspect that most avid golfers are in the dark, along with us, when it comes to terms such as "high-rebound core," "a rugged Surlyn cover," "weight distribution point," "centrifugal action," and "longer spin." However, the comparative test results provided in the advertisement are not difficult to understand. In fact, they are very thought-provoking!

To substantiate their claims, Rawlings had the Nationwide Consumer Testing Institute conduct a little experiment in which the new Toney Penna DB was compared to five other specific balls. In this experiment, each of 51 golfers hit 18 balls (three of each brand) off a driving tee, using a driver and new balls. The average distance (in yards) that each brand ended up being from the tee was reported as follows:

1.	Toney Penna DB	254.57
2.	Titleist Pro Trajectory	252.50
3.	Wilson Pro Staff	249.24
4.	Titleist DT	249.16
5.	Spalding Top-Flite	247.12
6.	Dunlop Blue Max	244.22

After presenting these results, Rawlings tells the reader that "as you can see, while we can't promise *you* 250 yards off the tee, we *can* offer you a competitive edge, if only a yard or two. But an edge is an edge."

The test results provided in the advertisement (and the way Rawlings talks about these results) make it seem as if there is a cause-and-effect relationship between the type of ball used and the distance you can expect to hit the ball off the tee. Although this may in fact be the case, we submit that there are some alternative explanations for why the Toney Penna DB turned out to get the best average distance. To be more specific, we feel that there are three plausible rival hypotheses to account for the results, besides the alleged engineering success of those who invented Rawlings' new ball.

(Turn to page 174 for solution.)

32. Six Weeks on Nothing but Bread and Water

As you undoubtedly know, the magazine *Consumer Reports* publishes information on the quality of all sorts of consumer products—washing machines, cars, movie cameras, soap, and so on. Often, the recommendations provided to the consumer are based upon a simple brand-by-brand comparison of cost, advantages, and disadvantages. (For example, one particular brand of fly-fishing reel was given a poor rating because, among other things, spool removal required the use of a coin or tool and the line-guide opening was small.) In some instances, however, the performance or durability of various competitive brands of a product are compared to one another within the context of an experimental investigation. The purpose of such studies, of course, is to determine whether a cause-and-effect relationship exists between the brand used and the criterion variable of interest (some measure of performance).

In a recent issue of *Consumer Reports,* various brands of bread were discussed in terms of their relative nutritional quality. Altogether, 33 different brands were compared. Included were white, rye, wholewheat, oatmeal, and pumpernickle; some from large bakers such as Pepperidge Farm and some of the supermarkets' own brand. The comparative nutritional quality of these 33 brands was not assessed as you might think—the labels were not checked to see how much of the body's daily nutritional needs each bread provides, nor was a laboratory analysis conducted to determine what was actually in each brand. The rationale for not doing these things was presented, as was the justification for using the somewhat unusual experimental precedures employed. Strange as this might seem at first, the nutritional value of the various breads was assessed by feeding them to laboratory rats as an "only food." Unless you've read the article, you'll have to take our word for it that the arguments offered in defense of rats as subjects were convincing, so let's agree that it was all right to use this approach rather than the label comparison, laboratory analysis approach, or some other approach you might think of.

Here is a description of the experimental methodology utilized to make a comparison of the 33 brands of bread. The abbreviation "CU," which you will come across in this quotation, stands for Consumers Union, the nonprofit organization that publishes *Consumer Reports.*

> The testing was done by a CU consultant, using newly weaned male hooded rats. To accustom the animals to their new environment and get some idea of their individual growth rates, we fed them a standard laboratory ration for one week. Then the test began. CU's consultant used 36 groups of rats, six animals to a group. Thirty-three groups were put on the breads and three were set up as comparison groups—one on laboratory rat feed as a control, one on eggs, and

54

one on milk. Rats in the milk group were allowed unlimited amounts of milk; those in the other 35 groups were given unlimited amounts of the test food and water.

For 16 weeks, our consultant studied the animals' growth rates, the condition of their coats and teeth, and the way they utilized the test foods. Nervousness was noted, as were poor calcification of bones and any other abnormalities.*

The results indicated that one of the 33 brands of bread "results in growth and health better than that achieved on the rat-feed control, the eggs, and the milk," while none of the other 32 brands came close to matching the growth and health of the control groups. The phrase "results in" certainly has the sound of a cause-and-effect statement. However, we wonder if any of us would be well advised to run out to the store to buy a loaf or two of the winner—Thomas' Rite Diet Bread.

Let's assume that the 216 rats were randomly assigned to the 36 treatment conditions, and let's also assume that the measured characteristics of the rats (growth rate, condition of teeth, and so on) were subjected to a statistical test that indicated that there were, in fact, significant differences among the 33 brands. Even though we might make these assumptions, we feel as if there is something in the methodology that is not as it should have been. In other words, we think there is a plausible rival hypothesis to account for the results. What do you think?

(Turn to page 176 for solution.)

33. To Insure Promptness

One of the new "theme" restaurants opened not far from us last year. The theme in this case was old-time movie stars, and it would have been fine had the movie stars been represented by posters on the walls or the napkins and so on. Unforunately, the management chose to have the waiters and waitresses in costume as such characters as Donald Duck, Humphrey Bogart, Superman, and a dancing bear on roller skates. On our first and last visit to this establishment, our table was graced by the presence of Harpo Marx. Since "Harpo" never spoke, our first reaction was to celebrate the good fortune of not having to suffer a bad Cagney imitation; however, we had forgotten about the bicycle horn. As a consequence of a most unpleasant lunch, the tip was an inverse function of the number of times the horn squawked in our ears. Next time, we'll ask for the bear.

A group of social psychologists at Ohio State University was interested in tipping as a function of group size, as seen from a diffusion of responsibility theory developed in the "helping behavior" literature.[1] That is, a person is more likely to help when alone than when in a group, since all of the responsibility is on the person when alone. In a group, the same responsibility can be spread out among all members. Accordingly, as group size increases, each person's share of the responsibility should decrease.

The results obtained by the Ohio State researchers confirmed their expectations in that, while most tips were around 15 percent, single diners tipped more (almost 19 percent) than did those dining in groups (13.5 percent). Extrapolating, the authors recommend that waiters and waitresses greet requests for separate checks with glee rather than dismay, since this might short-circuit the diffusion of responsibility. As less-than-affluent college students, however, you might consider eating in large groups; but is it really, as the authors claim, cheaper by the bunch?

(Turn to page 176 for solution.)

[1] B. Latane and J. M. Darley. "Group Inhibition of Bystander Intervention." *Journal of Personality and Social Psychology*, 1968, *10*, pp. 215–221.

34. Do the Blind Sometimes See?

As you probably know, the subjects used by psychological researchers are often rats, not people. There are many reasons for this practice, of course, and prominent among them is the fact that things can be done to rats that could never be done, at least by any ethical researcher, to humans, like performing unnecessary operations on the subjects, injecting hormones into their bodies, administering electric shocks, and then sacrificing them at the end of the study. Although this manner of treating an animal—even a rat—sounds quite cruel, the ultimate goal is to make discoveries from such experiments about why animals behave the way they do and then hope that these discoveries can be used to understand better behavioral variations among humans.

Not too long ago, a pair of researchers at the University of Wisconsin conducted a study focusing on the possible effects of neonatal hormonal injections on the behavior of female rats during adulthood. Other researchers had previously verified that such injections at critical periods in infancy could decrease the frequency of feminine sexual behavior, increase weight and length, and also change the texture of the rat's coat. However, it was not clear whether androgen treatment would also have an effect upon other types of behavior. Specifically, these researchers were interested in the variable of resistance to shock. And they were also curious as to whether combinations of infant and adult hormone treatments might affect this variable in different ways.

The subjects in the Wisconsin study were 78 female rats of the Holtzman strain. These rats were divided into eight treatment groups, with somewhere between eight and eleven subjects assigned to each treatment condition.[1] The eight comparison groups were administered different combinations of infant and adult hormonal treatments, and when the rats were about 115 days old, the primary data of the experiment were collected.

At this point, rats were put individually into an operant-conditioning chamber. This piece of apparatus is simply a cagelike box with two ends, top, and bottom made of metal, and the front and back made of glass. When put into this chamber, the rat walked around on a grid-type floor that could, if the researchers so desired, transmit an electrical shock to the inhabitant. This chamber was set on the top of a sturdy table in a room than was dark except for one 15-watt bulb positioned directly behind the back wall of the chamber. This light was quite sufficient to allow two human observers, seated 4 feet

This problem is based on a study taken from the *Psychological Bulletin*, 1972, *78*, pp. 70–71. Courtesy of W. W. Beatty.

[1] The sample sizes varied because the researchers wanted to equalize the eight groups in terms of average body weight following the injections during infancy.

from the front wall of the chamber, to see clearly what the rat was doing when in the box.

After each rat was in the box and two observers were in place to watch what happened, the researchers began to administer a series of 13 shocks varying in intensity from very, very mild (0.05 ma.) to quite strong (0.08 ma.). Each shock lasted for half a second; there was approximately a ten-second intertrial interval (rest period) between shocks; and the 13 shocks were presented first in ascending order of intensity and then in descending order, for a total of ten trials. Thus, each rat was shocked a total of 260 times throughout the ten trials.

The two observers independently classified each rat's motor response to each of the 260 shocks into one of four mutually exclusive categories. Either the rat gave no response, or she "flinched" (defined as a contraction of any part of the body), or she produced a "flinch-shuffle" (defined as a flinch followed by foot movement), or she jumped (said to occur when all four feet left the grid). In addition to these motor behaviors, the observer also noted whether or not each shock prompted a "verbalization"—that is, some sort of audible moan or scream of pain (or request that the darn experiment stop).

The observers' record forms were first examined to determine whether they agreed on what they saw and heard. To a large extent, they did; the interrater agreement was 86 percent for the motor responses and 94 percent for the vocalizations. Then, each rat's threshold level was established. This was simply the lowest current level to which responses of a certain type (for example, a flinch) occurred on 50 percent of the ten trials. There were four such thresholds computed for each rat (for the flinch, flinch-shuffle, and jump motor responses, and for vocalizations), and these were the data used to compare the eight treatment groups. As it turned out, the various comparison groups did, in fact, show up as significantly different on the four thresholds.

The researchers concluded that the observed differences were attributable to the varying hormonal treatments, with a cause-and-effect hunch allegedly being verified. Unfortunately, there is a rival hypothesis to this interpretation of the data. Before we turn you loose to hunt for the problem associated with this investigation, we should point out two additional facts about this study's methodology. First, rats from the eight treatment groups were tested in a random order. And second, the two observers were not given information about each rat's treatment group affiliation.

(Turn to page 177 for solution.)

35. Humor, Curiosity, and Verbal Absurdities

What is humorous to some people is not humorous to others. But why does this variability exist? Several different reasons have been suggested, and surprisingly (at least to us), one of these explanations is based upon Freud's psychoanalytic theory. From this point of view, the person who frequently sees humor is "more able to think like a child, to escape the restraints of rationality and logic, and to feel secure enough to explore further into his/her environment." In the eyes of two recent researchers, this description seemed somewhat synonymous with the notion of being curious. And to test the validity of their thinking, a simple research study was conducted in 1972.

The researchers theorized that people with high levels of curiosity would be more likely to see things as humorous. However, in their study, they didn't want to deal with the messy problem of trying to assess whether or not someone thinks something is humorous. (Clearly, it's possible for a person to see humor a great deal of the time without giving evidence—a smile, chuckle, or boistrous laugh—that something funny has been perceived.) Therefore, the researchers decided to measure people's ability to detect verbal absurdities ("She picked up the melted ice cubes and dropped them into the pail"). They felt that humorous events or statements often contain some sort of absurdity in them, and consequently you have to be able to see the absurdity before you can respond (possibly just in an internal way) in a humorous manner.

The subjects in this study came from a pool of 191 fifth-grade children from Delaware. Curiosity scores on these subjects were derived from teacher ratings, peer ratings, and self-ratings (equally weighted to arrive at the final score). All ratings were based on data-gathering techniques possessing high reliability, and students ending up with high composite scores were those who (according to the ratings) reacted positively to new elements in their environment, showed interest in learning more about themselves, scanned surroundings for new experiences, and explored stimuli to find out more about them. Once the curiosity scores were in, the total subject pool was divided into upper and lower halves. The students were not given information, however, about which subgroup they were in.

All 191 students were then administered a 51-item test of verbal absurdities, made up of 27 items (like the one presented earlier) wherein an absurdity was present, plus 24 items that were "normal" (like, "She hurried to class so she would not be late for her first class"). Each subject's task was to put a check next to any of the items that contained parts that "make them look foolish." And it was the researchers' hypothesis that students with high curiosity scores (those in the upper half of the distribution) would detect more of the true absurdities than those students with low curiosity scores.

Before contrasting the verbal absurdity scores of the high- and low-curiosity comparison groups, the researchers decided that "intelligence might also be a factor in recognizing verbal absurdities" (Maw and Maw, p. 559). If intelligence were to be correlated with curiosity, then observed differences between the groups (in verbal absurdity scores) might be more attributable to intellectual differences than to curiosity differences. In other words, maybe high intelligence causes an individual to exhibit curious behavior and to perform well when asked to detect verbal absurdities. So, IQ data were collected on the 191 subjects, and it turned out that a moderately high correlation ($r = .55$) did in fact exist between curiosity scores and IQ.

Because of this correlation, and in order to control for intelligence, the researchers decided to match their subjects on the basis of IQ. Accordingly, they took each pupil having a curiosity score in the upper half of the total group of 191 and then tried to find someone else in the lower half of the total group who had a similar IQ. If such a person could be found, then the two individuals became a "matched pair" and were included in the final phase of the study. If a good match could not be found for person X in the high or low group from among the individuals in the opposite group, then person X was discarded from the study. As a result of this matching process, the upper and lower groups each ended up containing 51 subjects.

When the verbal absurdity scores for these two groups were compared, it was found that the average score for the 51 pupils in the high-curiosity group (23.06) was significantly higher than the average score in the low-curiosity group (18.77). Clearly, this difference was not brought about by intellectual differences between the two groups, for intelligence had been controlled through the matching. (The mean verbal IQs for the two groups were 103.71 and 103.80; the mean nonverbal IQs were 100.61 and 100.24.) Therefore, in looking at the discrepancy between the two verbal absurdity average scores, the researchers stated that "these results may indicate that high-curiosity children seek more when they read and thus are able to see small absurdities" (p. 558).

Do you accept the implied cause-and-effect conclusion? Were the 51 subjects who earned an average score of 23.06 on the verbal absurdities test able to outperform the other 51 subjects *because* of their higher levels of curiosity? Or might there be one or more alternative explanations, besides curiosity, to account for the significant difference that was obtained?

(Turn to page 179 for solution.)

36. Quantity? Versus Quality

As college professors we are always concerned with the quality of educational programs in our own or closely related disciplines. Thus, we were naturally attracted to an article by Cox and Catt in a recent issue of the *American Psychologist* that gave a rank ordering of doctoral programs in psychology. The rankings were based on departmental productivity in 13 journals published by the American Psychological Association (APA) during the years 1970–1975. In addition to a composite list, rankings were also reported for each journal separately. The lists were then contrasted with a list of "reputational" ratings compiled earlier in 1970 by Roose and Andersen. Lest you worry, the productivity index for each department was adjusted to reflect the number of faculty members in each.

In general the authors concluded that the reputations of the older, more established programs in many cases were no longer deserved, as indicated by disparities between the reputational ratings and the less subjective authors' productivity ratings. Although the time of measurement (pre- versus post-1970) could account for some of the disparity, Cox and Catt discount this explanation in favor of concluding that programs once "in the limelight" have "now faded." They also suggest that their index, while not perfect, is more appropriate than a questionnaire asking about "reputation." Do you agree?

(Turn to page 180 for solution.)

37. Speed and Death on the Highway

Unfortunately, many people die each year on our highways in automobile accidents. Hence, it is understandable that several researchers have attempted to identify the causal reasons for traffic fatalities. We say causal *reasons*, since it is clear that a number of factors combine either to increase or decrease the chances that you will be in an accident or survive an accident. For example, research has shown that one such factor is alcohol consumption. Holding other things constant, as a driver increases the amount of alcohol in his or her blood system, reaction time is slowed and there is an increased probability of being in an accident or even being killed.

Of course, researchers have studied other factors that may be causally related to traffic fatalities. One of these factors is speed, and recently a short article appeared in Scripps-Howard newspapers dealing with speed and deaths. In part, this report went as follows:

> Most motorists are aware that Americans are not observing the national 55-mile-per-hour speed limit as zealously as they did when it went into effect about three years ago. And it's beginning to show up in the highway death toll.
>
> In 1973, nearly 55,000 lost lives in automobile accidents. In 1974, there was a decrease of almost 20 percent, and of 2 percent more in 1975. In 1976, however, highway deaths increased slightly; from 44,690 in 1975 to 44,807 last year.
>
> With vacation season coming on, it surely behooves motorists to observe the 55-mile-per-hour limit. Otherwise, they may become a part of the new statistical trend.*

In this article, it is clear that the authors believe that a cause-and-effect relationship exists between speed and fatalities. So do we. However, we do not feel that the statistics cited (particularly the increase in fatalities from 1975 to 1976) necessarily indicate that motorists were disregarding the 55-mile-per-hour speed limit more in 1976 than in 1975 or in the year before when the national speed limit was put into effect. In other words, we feel that there is a plausible rival hypothesis to account for the observed data. Do you agree with us?

(Turn to page 181 for solution.)

38. Getting a Bank Loan

At one time or another, all of us are probably in need of a little extra money for something important in our lives. It might be a mortgage on our first house, a new car, a long overdue vacation trip, or any one of a long, long list of possible items. But whatever our specific purpose for the extra money, we all hope that the loan officer at the bank will make a decision on the basis of *relevant* data (such as our proven ability to pay back past loans, our current employment status, and so on). Most assuredly, we expect the decision to be completely unrelated to things such as our religious affiliation, our hair color, or our opinion concerning parental discipline.

A few years ago, three researchers attempted to collect data to determine whether the amount of money approved for a loan was influenced by irrelevant information about the applicant. In particular, the researchers were interested in whether the financially *unrelated* attitudes of a loan applicant might be related to the extent of assistance provided by the bank. And as you might suspect, the researchers hypothesized that the chances of getting the loan approved would be greater when the applicant and the loan officer held similar attitudes on the nonmonetary irrelevant topics.

Naturally, it would have been very difficult (if not impossible) to conduct this investigation inside an actual bank. Accordingly, a simulation study was carried out on a university campus. The subjects were 53 students enrolled in a graduate finance course in the School of Business Administration, and each of these individuals was asked to assume the role of a loan officer at a bank. There was only one decision to be made by each of the 53 subjects, since there was only one person applying for a loan in this simulation study. The "applicant" was met only through written documents; in fact, this applicant did not exist in real life at all, and the information concerning him, although somewhat typical, was hypothetical.

On the day of the experiment, each of the subjects (the "loan officers") was given a packet of materials. Inside was an actual loan application used at a local bank, and it contained the usual information concerning the applicant's age, occupation, bank account, car payments, and so forth. Also included in the packet was an eight-item attitude inventory—supposedly filled out by the applicant—dealing with such topics as birth control, welfare legislation, the place of women in today's society, and such. These materials in the packets were identical for all 53 subjects.

After examining the information in the packet, each subject was asked to make a decision regarding the loan request. Using a seven-point scale, each "loan officer" indicated how much money should be approved—with the seven choices ranging from nothing to over $5,000. Once these decisions had been made, the packets of materials were collected and the final item of the study was distributed. This was a blank copy of the same attitude inventory that had been included in the loan applicant's packet, and the subjects were asked to record their own attitudes toward the eight topics.

The seven-point attitude inventory had three response positions on either side of a neutral midpoint. The researchers, in scoring each item on the inventory, simply determined whether the loan officer (one of the 53 subjects) was on the same side of the neutral point as the hypothetical loan applicant.[1] And the overall index of attitude similarity between each subject and the loan applicant was computed as the percentage of the times when their two responses fell on the same side of the neutral midpoint. Hence, when a loan officer and the applicant agreed on six of the eight attitudinal items, the index of similarity was 75 percent.

After an index of attitude similarity was computed for each of the 53 subjects, these individuals were divided into subgroups on the basis of the similarity indices. Some of the subjects responded in the same way as the hypothetical applicant on 7 of the 8 items (footnote 1 explains why no one agreed on all 8), some agreed on 6 of the 8 items, and so forth. Then, for each of these subgroups, the average amount of money approved for the loan was computed. There was a statistically significant difference between these subgroup averages, with the groups having higher similarity indices approving more money than the groups having lower indices. In fact, the 15 subjects who were in most agreement with the hypothetical applicant approved almost $2,000 more than did the subjects who held the most drastically opposed attitudes!

On the basis of their data, the researchers concluded that the loan decisions had been determined, at least in part, by the attitudinal similarity between the loan officer and the applicant. And these were attitudinal topics, you will recall, that were totally irrelevant to the financial matter under consideration. In the words of the researchers, "an applicant who favored, for example, increased welfare legislation would have either helped or hindered his chances for a large loan depending on the position of the loan officer concerning welfare legislation" (Golightly *et al.*, p. 522).

Clearly, a cause-and-effect relationship is implied by this study. The effect variable is the amount of money approved; the causal variable is the degree of attitude similarity between the applicant and the decision maker. Do you accept this conclusion? Or is there an alternative explanation for the obtained results?

(Turn to page 182 for solution.)

---

[1] The attitudes of the loan applicant were generated by randomly selecting a number between 1 and 7 for each item on the inventory. On one of the eight items, the response randomly selected was 4, the midpoint.

39. The Four-Day Workweek

We initially found the prospect of a four-day workweek appealing but quickly changed our minds upon learning that each day would be ten hours long. What is really needed is a combination of a shorter workday, a shorter workweek, and a higher salary. Unfortunately, should such a utopian combination ever arise, we are quite sure that college professors would be excluded from participating. Nonetheless, it is time to consider the next study.

Two researchers were able to convince the executive committee of a large manufacturing company to use two of its four manufacturing divisions (located throughout the Midwest) as experimental and control groups in a study of the four-day, 40-hour (4-40) workweek. The experimental group of 106 subjects was put on the 4-40 plan while the control group of 104 worked a normal five-day, 40-hour (5-40) week. After 13 months, one of the remaining two divisions (with 111 people) was converted to the 4-40 plan and studied for an additional 12 months. Thus, data were available over a 25-month period for two of the three groups, and for a 12-month period on the third. Attrition in the three groups was negligible.

Preliminary analyses showed the three groups to be comparable at the beginning of the study on such measures as age, seniority, absenteeism, and salary. During the study, pretest and post-test self-report data were collected on job satisfaction, stress, and absenteeism, along with supervisor ratings of work performance. The major findings were of improved job satisfaction in the 4-40 group during the initial 13-month period (not sustained over the entire 25 months of the study), and improved productivity.

Thus, the researchers concluded somewhat tentatively that although there were short-term benefits of the changeover, these tended not to persist. How would you interpret these results?

(Turn to page 183 for solution.)

40. Newspaper Advertising

Each year, millions of dollars are spent on newspaper advertising. Obviously, the people who pay for the ads feel their financial outlay is worthwhile. In other words, there is a presumed cause-and-effect relationship involved here, with the newspaper advertising being the cause while subsequent increased sales constitute the effect. But do the ads really bring about, in a causal sense, more consumer purchases? Recently, two researchers conducted a little study designed to answer this simple yet important question.

The setting for this study was a small town in northern Illinois (population about 3000). The subjects were 142 female customers who regularly purchased items at a grocery store. A list of 28 items appeared in the local newspaper for four consecutive days prior to the day of the study. Each of these 28 products was advertised at a reduced price, and the purpose of the study was to determine whether this advertising made a difference in sales of these items.

Following the four days of advertising, the data of the experiment were collected. The procedural aspects of the study on this fifth day were as follows. As each subject came through the checkout counter, the clerk examined her purchases to see if any of the advertised sale items were included. If one or more of the 28 items were about to be bought, the clerk was instructed to ask whether or not the consumer had read about the sale items in the newspaper ad. Although several of the subjects came back to the store a second (or third) time on the data-collection day of the study, responses from each consumer were recorded only for her first time through the checkout counter.

Results of the study indicated that all 142 subjects purchased one or more of the 28 advertised items. Ninety-nine of the subjects stated that they had read about these items in the newspaper while 43 subjects admitted that they had not. Based on these figures, the researchers concluded that "reading the newspaper advertising seemed to increase purchase of advertised items more than not reading the paper" (Peretti and Lucas, p. 693). To probe the data further, each subject's socioeconomic status (SES) was assessed by the store clerks (who knew the customers quite well) through an instrument called the Index of Status Characteristics. Using this SES information, a group of lower-class consumers was compared with a group of middle-class consumers. Results indicated that a significant difference existed between the two groups, and in the words of the researchers, "advertising tended to affect lower-class consumers' buying more" (p. 693).

Based upon the data that were collected in this study, can we conclude that a cause-and-effect relationship has been established? Does newspaper advertising lead to increased purchasing behavior? And does the alleged effect really exist more for lower-class consumers than for those in the middle class?

(Turn to page 184 for solution.)

41. The Dentist's Drill

If you're like us, a trip to the dental office to have a cavity filled is a frightening, anxiety-provoking experience. We would rather do just about anything else—weed the garden, count paper clips, mow the lawn—no matter how boring. Unfortunately for our health, we put off going to the dentist to have our cavities taken care of far longer than we should. When we finally get there and into that awful chair, we immediately request the largest possible dose of novocaine, gas, or any other pain reliever. But even that does not solve the problem. As we sit there with a drill in our mouth digging a hole in one or more teeth, we may not be able to feel the drill but we sure as anything hear it. That noise of the drill grinding away at our teeth is by far the worst part of the whole awful trip.

But what about the dentist? Is it possible that the noise created by the drilling process has an adverse effect on the dentist, as well as on the scared-to-death patient? A recent study has been conducted to deal with this question, and the results make it seem as if the answer is yes. Here is the complete text of the research summary, which was in a nationally distributed and widely read magazine:

> Young people who become dentists to earn money and serve the public should consider another factor. Dentists work in an environment that can be detrimental to their health. A recent study of dental students at the University of Tennessee found they suffered a significant loss of hearing within three years of using high speed drills. These instruments reduce a patient's pain but gradually turn some dentists deaf or impair their hearing. The researchers in Tennessee recommend that dentists wear earmuffs or plugs on the job.*

It is interesting to us, and saddening, that the researchers' recommendation concerning earplugs or earmuffs took into consideration only the dentist. Don't they realize that the patient squirming in the chair not only hears the same noise but also interprets it as pain!

The results of this study indicate that the dental students experienced a significant hearing loss over a three-year span after beginning to use a dental drill. The research report, entitled "Dentists Beware," clearly implies that the hearing loss was caused by the noise created by the drill. The recommended solution (earplugs or earmuffs) again implies this cause-and-effect interpretation of the data. If all new dentists were to follow this recommendation and begin wearing earplugs or earmuffs, or if a noiseless drill were to be invented, could we indeed expect to find that dental students would no longer experience a hearing loss during the time they are attending dental school? In other words, is there a plausible rival hypothesis for the findings of this research investigation?

(Turn to page 185 for solution.)

42. Psychotherapy Revisited Again

Earlier in this volume (see Problem 27) we discussed both the importance of and some of the problems with a study that examined the long-term effects of therapeutic intervention. Given the popularity of psychotherapy among college students, we didn't think that you would mind a second study in the same area.

Using a variety of psychological instruments, two psychologists in Chicago tested 93 college students before they entered therapy and then at the end of therapy. Eighteen months after the second testing, they were able to locate and test 69 of their original group. Comparisons made between the post-therapy and follow-up scores showed no significant differences, thus leading the researchers to conclude that the students did not continue to improve in the post-therapy period. This was in contrast to the expectations of those psychologists, who believed that psychotherapy sets the stage for future growth on the part of the client.

Although any improvement from the pretherapy to post-therapy testing might be a consequence of regression toward the mean, this would not be a factor in a change (or lack of change) in the post-therapy period. What other rival hypotheses are there to the finding of no difference?

(Turn to page 186 for solution.)

43. Animadversion

On a number of college and university campuses, faculty members are required to collect evaluations of their instructional skills from students. Sometimes these teacher evaluations are used to help make decisions regarding promotion, tenure, and salary increments; more often than not, however, the purpose is simply to give the instructors some feedback so that their teaching skills can be improved. But regardless of the intended purposes of the teacher evaluations, there is some question as to when students should make an assessment of their instructor. To be more specific, one might ask whether it would be best to collect the students' evaluations of their teacher before or after the students are given feedback as to their performance in the course.

If students find out how well they do on a test (or for the entire course) before rating their instructor, then it is possible that the teacher evaluations will be biased. Students who receive good grades might unconsciously rate the instructor higher than would have been the case if the evaluations had been requested prior to the distribution of grades, and likewise students who receive poor grades might tend to give their instructor a poorer evaluation. The bias in both groups' evaluation of their teacher would involve mirroring *back to* the teacher (in the rating) the evaluation that they, the students, *received from* the teacher. Among students who receive poor grades, this bias probably stems from an unwillingness to accept blame for the undesirable outcome, and the term "animadversion" has been used to describe this type of error in teacher evaluations.[1]

To test this hypothesis about animadversion, two researchers recently conducted a little study. The setting was a university course in business, and the content dealt with industrial relations. Following the midterm examination, the papers were graded and returned to the students for review. Then, the students were given 3 x 5 index cards and asked to rate the professor's effectiveness in teaching the course. These rating took the form of a grade (A through F), the instructor was not present when they were made, and the students were told that the ratings would go to the department head and not influence grades in the course.

The 85 students enrolled in the business course were subdivided into five groups on the basis of the grades earned on the midterm examination. Then, within each of these five groups, the distribution of grades given to the instructor was determined. In other words, the researcher simply figured out how many of the "A" students gave the instructor an A, B, C, D, and F, how many "B" students gave the instructor each of these ratings, and so on for each

---

[1] In general, animadversion means criticism prompted by prejudice or ill will.

69

group. When subjected to a formal statistical analysis, these data indicated a significant difference among the comparison groups. And as you might suspect, the students receiving the poorer grades tended to give the instructor the poorest ratings.

Had there been no significant difference in the way the student groups rated the instructor, the researcher would have interpreted the data as indicating no bias. But as it was, the results were said to substantiate the animadversion error. Furthermore, the suggestion was made that administrators require faculty to collect teacher evaluations before any examinations are given, "thus depriving the rater of the contamination information" (Schuh and Crivelli, p. 259).

What do you think? Did the students receieving poor grades rate the instructor poorly because of their poor midterm performance? Has a legitimate cause-and-effect relationship been identified? Or is there a plausible rival hypothesis?

(Turn to page 186 for solution.)

44. The Ultimate Martini

Many manufactured products have a specific designated purpose or function. To increase sales (and financial profit), the manufacturer often advertises the product for a secondary purpose with hope of establishing a new market area. For example, Johnson & Johnson originally advertised their baby shampoo for babies. Now, Johnson & Johnson are directing their baby shampoo ads towards adults, telling Mom and Pop that they will enjoy this product just as much as their kids do. Clearly, if Johnson & Johnson's Baby Shampoo could capture a portion of the adult market, this company's profits would increase. As another example, Jello is now being advertised not solely as a gelatin dessert, but also as an ingredient for Bundt cakes.

Rum is traditionally used to make a variety of drinks (most notably rum and Coke, daiquiris and rum collinses). Recently, Bacardi and Company, Ltd.—one of the largest producers of rum—has attempted to persuade the drinking public to use rum in martinis. (A martini is usually made with either vodka or gin.) Bacardi's full-page ad in a national magazine contains a picture of three glasses filled with a clear liquid and ice. One of the glasses is labeled "Bacardi," one is labeled "vodka," and one is labeled "gin". The three glasses and their contents look identical except for the labeling. Below the picture is the following text:

> The ultimate martini test? It's one in which there aren't any olives, lemon twists, or even the slightest hint of vermouth to change the basic liquor taste. It's just ice and the liquor itself. Which is exactly how 550 drinkers in 21 cities tasted a leading gin, a leading vodka, and Bacardi rum in an independent taste test. And without knowing which was which, 41.4% of them preferred Bacardi, 34.4% vodka, 24.2% gin.
>
> Why Bacardi? Smoothness and taste, we were told. And for a dry martini, there just aren't better reasons. So put in your vermouth and your olive. And enjoy!*

This advertisement, entitled "Bacardi Rum Tops Vodka and Gin in the Ultimate Martini Test," gives the impression that the best martini has the smoothness and taste found in Bacardi rum, not vodka or gin. In other words, Bacardi rum brings about (causes) the "ultimate" martini. Martini drinkers, what do you think? Do you accept this implied cause-and-effect relationship, or is there some alternative explanation? And even if you're not a martini drinker yourself, would you, based upon this advertisment, begin to make rum martinis for your guests?

(Turn to page 187 for solution.)

---

*Taken from a magazine advertisement, "Bacardi Rum Tops Vodka and Gin in the Ultimate Martini Test." Reprinted with permission from Bacardi Imports, Inc.

71

45. Modeling Clay

Jean Piaget is a well known Swiss psychologist whose ideas have transformed the field of developmental psychology over the past few decades. Many students associate him with conservation tasks, such as how a child learns that 200 cc of water is the same in a tall skinny glass as in a short fat glass, despite the difference in level of the water. A similar task involving a clay ball and a clay cylinder (each with the same volume of clay) was one of a number of conservation tasks used in a study comparing modeling and nonmodeling instructions given to six-year-olds.

In this study, a random sample of 28 Chicano children were drawn from the first grade of a school located in a *barrio* area of Tucson, Arizona. The children were all from Spanish-speaking homes and were in their first few months of school (median age was 6.3 years). The children were randomly assigned to one of two groups, each group included seven boys and seven girls. Some children (those in the modeling group) were allowed to watch the experimenter transform an object from one shape to another while listening to another child (the model) answer the experimenter's question about the transformation. Those in the nonmodeling instructions group were not shown the transformation process but were instead presented with "before" and "after" objects. This group was told that the objects were equivalent ("There is just as much wood now as there was before because they both had the same amount in the first place" Rosenthal and Zemmerman, p. 398). Analysis of variance showed significant differences between the two groups, with the modeling group showing superiority on the conservation tasks. Furthermore, according to the authors, the nonmodeling instructions produced no reliable changes. Do you agree that the modeling approach is clearly superior?

(Turn to page 188 for solution.)

46. Procrastination

If your job is anything like ours, you have certain tasks or engage in certain activities that are actually fun and even exciting. But then on the other hand, you probably could enumerate several tasks or activities associated with your work routine that are boring or sometimes emotionally painful, and that you never look forward to. Unfortunately, the typical way that we handle these negative aspects of our job, if we're given the opportunity to do so, is to procrastinate and hope they will go away. At home, we also tend to put off dealing with distasteful chores, discipline problems, and the yearly income tax maze. Imagine how excited we were to see a formal research study on the topic of procrastination.

This particular research endeavor was not set up to discover any tips that could solve our (and possibly your) procrastination problem, but it certainly was an interesting little study. The focus of the investigation was on the way adults draw pictures of the human figure and whether or not procrastinators tend to draw different type of pictures than those who do not procrastinate. To be more specific, this research study constituted an attempt to see whether Machover's theory—that people who are evasive and fearful of making commitments tend to produce profile drawings of the human figure—could be supported by data gathered from an applied setting.[1]

The subjects of this investigation were selected from the pool of female students who applied one year to the School of Nursing at Middleton State Hospital in New York. Each year, student applications were received and evaluated during a ten-month period (November through August) prior to the start of classes in September. Of the students expressing a desire to attend Middleton's School of Nursing in the year of the study, 65 early applicants (defined as those who applied between November and February) and 61 late applicants (defined as those who applied between May and August) were administered the Human Figure Drawing Test. The researcher felt that the last applicants, by definition, "were more inclined to be evasive, to put things off, to procrastinate, and so to reflect a fear of commitment" (Wolfson, p. 570). Accordingly, he predicted that there would be more profile drawings among the 61 late applicants than among the 65 students who applied early.

The results were interpreted as supporting the researcher's hypothesis. More than twice as many of the late applicants produced profile drawings as did early applicants, with the difference showing up as significant when subjected to a formal statistical test. The final sentence of the technical report was as follows: "It appears from these findings that drawing one's own sex in profile on the human figure drawing test does indeed occur with significantly

---

[1] Karen Machover is a psychologist who has concentrated on personality theory and who developed the Draw-A-Person Test.

greater frequency in those who procrastinate, evade responsibility, and defer making commitments than among those who face problems in a more forthright fashion, act sooner, and are presumably more likely to take the proverbial bull by the horns" (p. 570).

This research study was correlational in nature, and we do not think that there was any attempt to establish a cause-and-effect relationship. The researcher was simply trying to see whether the characteristic of procrastination tends to be associated with generation of profile drawings. The answer he has given us is yes. Are you willing to accept this conclusion? Or is there some alernative explanation, besides procrastination, to account for the significantly larger number of profile drawings that were produced by the late applicants?

(Turn to page 188 for solution.)

47. Grip Strength and Sleep

We know a few people who wake up early each moring with pleasant dispositions and boundless energy for the day's activities. However, most of our acquaintances are just like us. Upon hearing the alarm clock go off, we first reach for the telephone or wonder who in the world is ringing the doorbell. Then, realizing that it's the alarm clock, we immediately reset the clock for five or ten minutes later. It seems like only a few seconds go by, then the alarm goes off and the entire cycle begins again. On some occasions, we suspect that the darn clock has been reset at least five times. And on most occasions, when we finally do get up we feel groggy, lost, absent-minded, and in dire need of a hot cup of coffee.

In general, our bodies feel weak in the morning when we first get up. Recently, a pair of researchers attempted to collect some data to show that people are not as strong on arousal from a full night's sleep as they are after having been awake for several hours. The subjects in this study were 20 male college students, and the instrument used to measure strength was a dynamometer. This instrument measures grip strength, and it is simply held in one's hand and squeezed as hard as possible. A nonreturn dial indicates the amount of pressure exerted on the dynamometer by the squeezer, and such measurements are frequently used in the field of exercise physiology as an index of overall muscle power.

The subjects in this study were given some practice with the dynamometer, and then experimental measurements were taken on each subject for six consecutive days. On the first and sixth days of data collection, a measurement of each subject's grip strength was made sometime between 12:00 noon and 2:00 P.M. On the four intervening days, measurements were taken immediately after arousal. During days two through five, each subject was allowed to determine when his alarm clock would go off. But when it did, every subject had to assume a standing position and squeeze the dynamometer. On each of the six days of data collection, each subject had to use his right hand when gripping the dynamometer. (All subjects were right-handed.) And during their efforts to show how strong they were, the subjects could move their right arm into any preferred position so long as it (or the dynamometer) did not press against the body or any other object for leverage.

A statistical analysis of the data revealed a significant difference between the morning scores and the afternoon scores. On the average, the subjects were 15 percent stronger in the afternoon. As a group, the 20 subjects were fairly consistent in their performance, and there were no significant differences between the two afternoon means (from days one and six), nor were there any significant differences among the four morning means (from days two through five).

The obvious implication of this study is that sleep causes a decrease in body strength, at least to the extent that overall muscle power can be successfully measured by a dynamometer. Do the procedures associated with this research study warrent such an inference? Or might there be one or more alternative explanations (besides sleep) to account for the lower scores that were recorded in the morning upon awakening?

(Turn to page 189 for solution.)

48. An Object Lesson

A young woman just graduating from college was in our office recently to discuss her application to graduate school. Among the things she mentioned was a claim that she had been born in 1956. As we explained to her, we have trouble accepting the fact that anyone could have been born after about 1950, and she was obviously misrepresenting the situation badly. Imagine our surprise at later being on a doctoral committee responsible for a study involving children born in 1972. Will wonders never cease?

The study was of "two-year-olds' use of objects in peer interaction," and it looked at descriptive data collected in the naturalistic setting of a day care center. Each of 8 two-year-olds was observed every day for 25 days, with records kept on object-related behavior whenever the target child was engaged in social interaction with another child. Findings were based on the total number of social interactions; that is, all interactions of the target child and the child with whom he or she was interacting were recorded for a ten-minute period. The eight children varied in terms of the number of interactions in any given period (with a range from less than five to more than 20) and also in the number of ten-minute periods in which they were being observed as the target child. Among the findings reported were that the younger children (2–2½ years) engaged in more object conflict than did older children (2½–3 years), and that the older children engaged in more social interaction than did the younger children. Assuming that these children actually exist (and they do), what questions might you have asked at the final doctoral examination?

(Turn to page 189 for solution.)

49. Teaching Experience for Counselors

Many school administrators, when in a position to hire a school counselor, prefer to employ an individual who has had previous experience in the classroom as a teacher. In fact, many states require a minimum of one year's teaching experience before they will consider granting a counseling certificate. The assumption here, of course, is that a school counselor will do a better job working with students, teachers, and parents if the counselor has seen at first hand the varied problems that both teachers and students encounter in the classroom.

However, not everyone believes that teaching should be a necessary prerequisite to counseling. Some argue that many graduate students who would make outstanding counselors turn away from this field because they consider the teaching requirement to be an unnecessary detour. Others ague that the teaching experience may actually hurt (rather then help) the counselor! According to some counselor educators, teaching experience may be *disadvantageous* because it makes it difficult for past teachers to begin treating students as clients rather than as pupils. Many counselors who have previously been teachers—so the argument goes—are never able to shift from the advisory, tutorial, and information-dispensing role they assumed in the classroom to the accepting, nonjudgmental, and therapeutic role needed in the counseling office.

Clearly, research evidence is needed to help resolve this controversial question. And this is precisely what a group of researchers attempted to produce in a recent study. The question was simple: Does teaching experience have a positive or negative effect on the subsequent behavior of the counselor? Likewise, the methodology of the study was relatively simple. The subjects were 21 student-counselors who were completing the supervised practicum at the University of North Dakota. These counselors were assigned to three groups (seven per group) according to their past teaching experience—either none, two years, or at least seven years. Each of these 21 subjects was then asked to turn in two tape-recorded interviews with high school students. The middle 15-minute segment on each tape was analyzed by two trained judges in terms of the total number of counselor remarks made during the 15-minute period and the number of evaluative (judgmental) counselor comments.

The results indicated that each of the three groups produced about the same number of total remarks during the 15-minute segment of the tape. However, the number of evaluative comments was *not* the same. Whereas about 30 percent of the remarks were judgmental in the two-year and seven-year groups, only 9 percent of the remarks coming from the counselors with no teaching experience were of this nature. A statistical comparison between these two percentages indicated that they were significantly different.

There is no question but that this investigation was attempting to establish a cause-and-effect relationship. Near the beginning of the report, the authors stated, "The purpose of the present study was to investigate the effects of teaching background on the tendency of counselors to use evaluative remarks when interviewing," and near the end they concluded, "apparently, teaching experience of relatively short duration (two years) is sufficient to establish the pattern of behavior" (Mazer *et al.* pp. 82, 83). Do you accept this conclusion? Or might there be some other explanation, besides differences in teaching experience, that could account for observed differences in the percentage of evaluative comments made during the taped interviews?

(Turn to page 190 for solution.)

50. Caffeine, Alertness, and Visual Monitoring

A few people we know are able to drink cup after cup of (nondecaffeinated) coffee between dinner and bedtime and yet experience no difficulty whatsoever going to sleep. Not us, however. Even the thought of coffee keeps us awake! Consequently, we avoid consuming any of this beverage past 4 P.M. on days when we're planning to retire at our usual time.

On the other hand, we will readily go out of our way to make or purchase a hot cup of the black stuff if we're sleepy and know that we must remain awake for ten or more hours—for example, when we get up each morning, or especially when we're driving across the country at night (a good time for travel because our children tend to be darling little angels while asleep but veritable monsters on trips when awake). Needless to say, we became very interested in a recent research study dealing with caffeine and its presumed ability to keep people like us awake and alert.

The subjects in this investigation were 100 male volunteers drawn from various universities in the Washington, D.C. area. These subjects were randomly divided into five groups of 20 subjects, with each group required to perform a simple but boring task under a different treatment condition. We'll explain what these treatment conditions were in a moment, but first allow us to describe the subjects' task. We think you will agree that its boring nature fully justified the monetary gift given to the subjects in appreciation of their participation.

Five subjects (one from each treatment condition) were put through the experiment at a time. They were taken into a semidarkened room and seated about 12 feet from a display board. Tall panels (room dividers), positioned on both sides of each subject's chair, cut off his view of the other four subjects; these panels did not, however, obstruct the subject's view of the display board. After being seated, each subject was given a spring-loaded toggle switch that could be depressed by pushing down with one's thumb. (After being pushed, the toggle switch automatically returned to its original position, ready for the next response from the subject.)

The display board had two 1-inch round red lights initially spaced 6 inches apart. At random intervals of one and one-half to three and one-half minutes, the two red lights were automatically driven apart, in a horizontal direction, at a relatively slow rate of 12½ inches per minute. Once they started to move apart, the two lights continued to move away from each other for 30 seconds. Then, the lights automatically returned to their initial positions 6 inches apart and remained in place until the next trial begin. There were 80 such trials spread out over a period of four uninterrupted hours.[1]

---

[1] The movement of the two red lights was meant to approximate what you would see if driving at night 60 yards behind another vehicle that all of a sudden began to travel 92 percent as fast as your car.

Each subject's toggle switch was connected to a separate clock. On each trial, everyone's clock began automatically at the instant the two red lights started to move, and it stopped when the toggle switch was depressed. The number of seconds the clock moved (on each trial) measured the time it took for each subject to observe the lights moving apart and respond by pushing the toggle switch. Appropriately, this dependent variable was called "response latency." And as you might suspect, the researchers predicted that response latency would increase over the four-hour duration of the experimental session.

The independent variable (the treatments) in this study involved pills given to all subjects (with water) at four points in time: just before the first trial on the monitoring task, and at the beginning of hours two, three, and four. The subjects were informed before volunteering that the research study would involve a drug, but were not told what the drug actually was—only that it was medically safe. During the experiment, the pills were administered in a double-blind fashion, meaning that neither the subjects nor the person distributing the tablets knew how much of the drug was being administered at any of the four points in time.

The drug used, as you have undoubtedly surmised, was caffeine. The five comparison groups differed in terms of their caffeine treatments as follows. The placebo group received pills containing no caffeine throughout the study. The other four groups started out with a placebo pill (right before the testing session began), but thereafter each was given one dose of caffeine, either a small or large dose at the beginning of either the second or third hours of the experimental session. Thus, one of the treatment groups got a small dose of caffeine at the beginning of hour two and placebo pills at the beginning of the other three hours; another treatment group got a small dose at the beginning of hour three and placebo pills at the beginning of the other three hours, and so on. The small dose was equivalent to one 100-mg No-Doz pill on sale at various stores, while the large dose was equivalent to two No-Doz pills. (The manufacturer's recommended dosage of No-Doz is 100 mg, and the double dose was used to make sure that caffeine's effect, if present, would be observable.)

The researcher's hypotheses, of course, were that the placebo group's performance would worsen over the four-hour monitoring session, that each of the four treatment groups would improve its performance following the administration of the caffeine tablets, and that the double dose of caffeine (as compared to a single dose) would cause the response latency to be smaller and/or to remain small for a longer period of time. Upon subjecting the data—made up of 80 response latencies for each subject in each of the five groups—to a formal statistical analysis, it was found that the first two hypotheses were confirmed. In the placebo group, the reaction time measures increased from one hour to the next, while in the other four groups these scores were about the same as in the placebo group until the caffeine was consumed—after which the reaction times quickly improved. However, a double dose was not found to be associated with better or longer-lasting performance.

In this study, the researchers were clearly trying to establish a cause-and-effect relationship. The causal variable was the ingestion of caffeine, and the effect variable was response latency. Even though you may have spent years avoiding coffee at night because you suspected that such a relationship does exist, are you willing to accept the researchers' claim that their data clearly show that "caffeine helps to repress the tendency toward response blocking that is generated by extended performance on a monotonous task" (Baker and Theologus, p. 426)? If not, what rival hypothesis can you think of to account for the treatment groups' performance improving right after they were given caffeine?

(Turn to page 191 for solution.)

51. Barricade Your Opponents

While the title of this problem may remind you of the Edgar Allan Poe story in which someone is bricked up in the cellar, it is, instead, a recommendation made by H. W. Kelsey, a well-known British author of advanced texts on contract bridge. Since, in addition to our scholarly pursuits, we are avid bridge players, it was with great interest that we read one of Kelsey's chapters on bidding.

The tactical advice given in that chapter may be stated quite simply: If in bidding you have a choice between bidding "scientifically" and making life difficult for your opponents, always choose the latter. According to Kelsey, whatever is lost in accuracy is regained by not providing the opponents with adequate information on which to base their defense to the final contract.

By escalating the bidding very rapidly to a high level, you can make life very difficult for your opponents. Bidding sequences such as "One No Trump/Three No Trump" or "One Heart/Three Hearts/Six Hearts" are much less revealing than the parallel sequences of "One Club/One Diamond/One No Trump/Three No Trump" and "One Heart/Two Diamonds/Three Hearts/Four Hearts/Five Clubs/Five Spades/Six Hearts." Bridge players often refer to the former sequences as "blasting" or "barricading."

As does any author with a theory, Kelsey presents a number of examples of bridge deals in which his recommended strategy was successful and the more scientific strategy was doomed to failure. Most intriguing, however, was his summary of a report published in the 1969 *Annals of the International Bridge Academy*. According to Kelsey, "A study of 1,556 World Championship deals revealed that the most successful contracts were those reached in the fewest bids" (pp. 100–101).

Can you think of any reasons why we should not incorporate Kelsey's recommendation into our bidding system?

(Turn to page 191 for solution.)

52. Some Shocking Nonsense

A *memory drum* is not a musical instrument that you can't forget. Rather, it is a piece of equipment used by psychological researchers in experiments on learning and forgetting. To get an idea of what a memory drum looks like, visualize a tall glass mounted on its side so the open part of the glass and the normal bottom of the glass are pointing left and right rather than up and down. A memory drum looks like such a glass except that it is made of metal and it only has one opening—a horizontal slot on the side. The researcher can put written material into the memory drum so that only a certain part of the material is visible through the window or slot at any given time, and more often than not the written material consists of single words—sometimes real words ("car") and sometimes nonsense syllables ("hij").

In one experiment, the researchers took a memory drum and filled it with 15 nonsense syllables. Then, each of the 55 college students used as subjects had to learn the list. The learning process was as follows. First, the subject sat in front of the memory drum and watched as each nonsense syllable, in turn, became visible through the drum's slot. Then, after the last syllable had appeared, the first syllables began to appear again in the same order; here, however, the subject was asked to state out loud what each item was going to be *before* it appeared in the drum's slot. Whether or not the subject correctly anticipated the next nonsense syllable, it appeared in the drum for the subject to see. Hence, there was immediate feedback following each subject's guess. Each subject stayed at the memory drum until the entire list of 15 nonsense syllables was learned, a task defined as one complete trip through the list without making any mistakes. (As you might suspect, it took most subjects several attempts before they could get all 15 items correct.)

Just to make the experiment a little more interesting (and also to test a portion of Freud's theory of repression), five of the 15 nonsense syllables were associated with the administration of a mildly painful electric shock. These five shock-syllables were"Jul," "Sab," "Hij," "Yur," and "Cil." Whenever one of these syllables appeared in the memory drum, the subject received a small jolt through wires attached to his or her ankles, even if the subject correctly anticipated the syllable. Thus, the only way for a subject to stop getting shocked was to get through the entire 15-item list one time without making a mistake. Otherwise, back to the beginning of the list and a guarantee of five more shocks.

After the data had been collected and analyzed, the researchers reported that it took the 55 subjects an average of 18.6 trips through the list to learn the "neutral" (non-shocked) items, versus an average of 16.8 trips through the list to learn the "affective" (shocked) items.[1] A statistical test was utilized to

---

[1] The research report does not indicate clearly how these two averages were computed. We suspect, however, that the full 15-item list was subdivided—for analysis purposes—into two parts:

84

compare these two means, and it turned out that 18.6 was significantly larger than 16.8. Hence, the affective material yielded better learning scores.

Did the subjects in this experiment learn the shock-associated words more quickly because of the shock? Or is there one or more plausible rival hypotheses to account for the alleged cause-and-effect relationship? To help guide you away from a wrong answer, it should be pointed out that the five affective items were not learned faster because of their placement order in the 15-item list. (Studies have shown that in learning experiments like this, the items at the beginning and at the end are learned more easily than items in the middle.) To prevent order from being a problem, the researchers divided the total subject pool into three subgroups, and each group was given a different arrangement of the 15 nonsense syllables. Within each of the three arrangements, the five affective items were distributed equally throughout the list.

Therefore, besides the issue of how the 15 nonsense syllables were arranged, can you think of any competing hypotheses that might explain the results?

(Turn to page 192 for solution.)

---

a ten-item "neutral" part and a five-item "affective" part. For each part, it would be possible to find out how many times a subject went through the list before getting all items on that part correct. This would be the subject's score, and these scores could then be averaged across the entire subject pool.

53. Affirmative Action Has Been Too Successful

The title of this problem reflects the conclusion drawn in a recent study from the *Educational Record.* The study resulted from the author's concern that the trend away from women's colleges and towards coeducation, accompanied by the increased hiring and promotion of female faculty at coeducational schools, would lead to decreased achievement among talented young women. In order to investigate this potentially worrisome phenomenon, 500 women were selected at random from each of three editions of *Who's Who of American Women* (the total number of subjects was 1500).

Most of the conclusions drawn from this study were based on data from the more than 1100 college graduates in the sample. The major findings were that in comparison with coeducational colleges, women's colleges have not only graduated about twice as many achievers per 1000 graduates, but they also employ about twice the number of female faculty per 1000 students. In addition, although a strong relationship was found between the number of achievers and the number of female faculty, no relationship was found with the number of male faculty. Finally, a strong relationship was also found between the number of achievers and the number of male students.

The author concluded that the female faculty served as important role models for talented young female students, and that coeducational colleges put pressure on these women to take on traditionally feminine roles (wife and mother) in proportion to the number of men present. This author believed that affirmative action has led to the demise of the most beneficial training grounds for women—women's colleges with a small male faculty, no male students, and lots of good role models. Do you agree?

(Turn to page 192 for solution.)

54. Food Additives and Hyperactivity

There is no question that certain types of food or drink have a causal influence on behavior. For example, if we force a runner to consume enough alcoholic beverage before a race, we will most assuredly observe a detrimental effect on the runner's performance. With other types of food or drink, a cause-and-effect relationship may be somewhat less clear. For instance, some people have made the allegation that artificial food additives cause children to become hyperactive. Others disagree.

In an attempt to settle the disagreement about food additives, an expensive research study was undertaken to see if the alleged cause-and-effect relationship does exist. This study has just been concluded, and we present its summary report, which appeared across the country in all Scripps-Howard newspapers:

> The controversial claim that artificial food colors and flavors are causing thousands of American children to behavior abnormally has been challenged by scientists at the University of Wisconsin. In a pair of studies costing about $270,000, researchers headed by Wisconsin's Dr. J. Preston Harley have found no evidence linking food additives to seriously hyperactive children.
>
> Dr. Harley based his conclusion on a study of 46 hyperactive children who were given carefully controlled diets for about two months. During one part of the study the youngsters were given diets loaded with artificial colors and flavors and in another segment were given diets containing no additives. Careful observation showed no measurable difference in the children's behavior when they were given additive free diets, Dr. Harley reported.
>
> In the second study, nine of the children were given candy bars, some containing artificial coloring and others free of additives. If there is a link between additives and hyperactivity, the candy supposedly would have shown it, Dr. Harley said. But there was no measurable difference in the children's behavior when they received additives-loaded candy or additives-free candy.
>
> According to Dr. Harley, the two studies performed by Wisconsin's Department of Neurology disprove a connection between food additives and hyperactivity.*

Based upon these two research studies, do you accept the conclusion that no cause-and-effect relationship exists between food additives and hyperactive behavior? Or is there a rival hypothesis to account for the University of Wisconsin's results?

(Turn to page 192 for solution.)

*Copyright 1977 by the Knoxville News-Sentinel. Reprinted by permission.

55. Growing Old

The theory of child rearing to which we subscribe is somewhat to the right of Mark Twain's. He believed that children should be put in a barrel and fed through the bunghole for the first 16 years—at which point he recommended plugging up the hole. Needless to say, this theory is not too popular with our families, and our children are starting to worry about the next ten years. Having just encountered the following study, we are starting to worry about the next thirty or so years ourselves.

The study is described in Wechsler's *The Measurement and Appraisal of Adult Intelligence*[1] along with a number of similar studies on the relationship of age to intelligence in those of us over 16. In this particular study, Wechsler Adult Intelligence Scale (WAIS) IQ Scores are reported on more than 2000 subjects. These subjects were categorized by age at the time of testing (16–17, 18–19, 20–24, and in five-year blocks up to 75 and over). An inspection of data and an accompanying graph lead to the conclusion that intelligence increases slightly from adolescence (where IQs average 103) up into the late twenties (where the average IQ is 113), at which point a steady decline begins that brings the IQ into the 90s between 50 and 60 and then even lower after age 60.

After discounting such rival explanations as the speed factor in such tests (the data suggest there is not one), number of years out of school, and appropriateness of the tests for older persons, Wechsler reached the obvious conclusion that individuals are likely to lose a considerable amount of intelligence during their life span. Based on the findings, should you no longer trust those over 30?

(Turn to page 194 for solution.)

[1] D. Wechsler. *The Measurement and Appraisal of Adult Intelligence,* fourth ed. (Baltimore: Williams and Wilkins, 1958.)

56. Camping Out

Based upon the books you have read, the movies you've seen, the relatives you may have visited, or your own first-hand experience, you are undoubtedly aware of the fact that the daily routine in mental institutions is extremely stifling for the patients. Yesterday, today, and tomorrow are virtually indistinguishable, with weeks, months, and years blending together like cars of a slow freight train seen through an opaque window. Visits to a typical mental institution on any two days of your choice will verify this ironical picture of what life is like for the individuals who are supposedly being helped back to mental stability.

Fortunately, there are some staff members who are sensitive to the ill effects brought about by the same routine day in and day out—and who care enough to try to do something about it. Usually, these attempts at breaking the monotony are not evaluated by means of any sort of formal research investigation; consequently, no one really knows for sure whether the new activity accomplishes its desired goal. But on occasion, data are collected in an attempt to verify scientifically the worth of the innovative program. One such research study recently was conducted in Utah, and the new activity—camping out—was about as different from the daily institutional routine as you could imagine.

The subjects in this investigation were 25 male and female adults aged 19 to 62, who were randomly selected from a state mental hospital located in an urban area of Utah. These individuals were taken to an isolated camp site in the mountains near Flaming Gorge. The patients and staff were on this camping trip for five days (Monday through Friday), and while on this excursion the staff maintained a very low profile. The patients had the responsibility of forming teams for cooking and clean-up, of arranging sleeping accommodations, and of structuring their own free-time activities. Other than busing the group to and from the campsite, the staff took charge on only two occasions—when the group went on a raft ride down the river and when they visited a nearby trading post for Cokes and candy.

The researchers expected this week-long camping retreat to serve as a therapeutic tool, and in particular they hypothesized that the activities would bring about increased social interaction among the patients. To test this hypothesis, two types of data were collected on both the first and final days of the camp-out. According to a prearranged random time sampling scheme, five-minute sessions of group interaction were taped, unobtrusively, on an audio recorder. In addition, photographs were taken of the patients.

One week after returning, all staff members and five of the patients who had gone on the camp-out used the audiotapes and pictures to rate the 25 patient campers in terms of social interaction. These ratings were obtained by using a modified version of the Bales Interaction Matrix. For each of the 25 patients, average ratings from the staff judges and the patient judges were computed. Then, the ratings within each group of judges were averaged across the 25 patients to obtain overall Monday and Friday ratings for the entire group. Since the Bales Interaction Matrix yields 12 subscale scores ("Gives suggestions," "Releases tension," and so one), there were two sets of 12 pretest and post-test composite ratings on the 25 campers, one set from the staff judges and the other set from the five patient judges.

When the pretest and post-test data were tested statistically, the researchers found that there was significantly more social interaction at the end of the five-day camping excursion than there had been at the beginning. The ratings from the patient group of judges showed increases on 11 of the 12 subscales of the Bales instrument, while the ratings from the staff members indicated significant improvement on all 12 subscales. One possible interpretation of these results is that the camping activities and unique environment brought about increased social interaction. Might there be other plausible explanations for the observed differences between the Monday and Friday ratings?

(Turn to page 194 for solution.)

57. Dirty Words

One of our favorite stories is that of the psychologist who asked his client to respond to line drawings of a square, a circle, and a triangle. The client interpreted the square as a window in a house and gave a lurid account of what was going on inside. This was followed by equally lurid descriptions of the activities viewed through a porthole (the circle) and a keyhole (the triangle). When the client was told by the psychologist of his sexual hang-ups, he replied, "Sexual hang-ups! You're the one with all the dirty pictures." This story reminded one of our students of the following study.

Perceptual defense is a term used in psychology to refer to our perceptual system's ability to fend off unpleasant stimuli. It is a way of sticking our heads in the sand without getting our hair dirty. One researcher used seven socially taboo words ("whore," "bitch") embedded within a list of eleven neutral words ("apple," "dance") in order to establish the phenomenon of perceptual defense as one involving the optical system. Sixteen college students (eight male, eight female) were shown each of the 18 words and asked to repeat the word aloud. The measures included latency of response (how long it took), and Galvanic Skin Response (GSR, used here as a measure of emotionality). After excluding the first four words on the list, which were used as a warm-up, differences in GSR were found between the neutral and critical words with greater emotionality associated with the critical words. Recognition thresholds also differed between the two groups of words in the predicted direction. Finally, the male students were able to recognize the words significantly faster than were the female students (no statistic reported).

In view of the earlier discussion, you will not be astonished to find that the researcher viewed the results as supporting the hypothesis that perceptual defense was caused by problems in the recognition of aversive stimuli. Do you agree?

(Turn to page 195 for solution.)

58. Feeling Good and Helping

In the past, researchers have demonstrated that it is possible to increase the likelihood that people will exhibit helping behavior by first inducing a temporary state of feeling good. Based on our own experience, this research finding makes sense, for we are much more inclined to go out of our way in assisting someone else if something nice has just happened to us. (And conversely, we're much more willing to put up with someone else's obnoxious behavior—as when a person attempts to butt in line right in front of us—when we're in a good mood brought about by some happy event.)

Recently, some researchers conducted a study to see whether unexpected good fortune could increase a person's willingness to help, when the opportunity to help and the induced good feeling were separated by a significant period of time. This question was legitimate, since previous research on this topic had presented the opportunity to help *immediately* after the event that supposedly created the unexpected nice feeling.

The subjects in this experiment were pedestrians walking between buildings on a university campus. At intervals of five minutes, a random pedestrian was stopped by the first confederate of the researchers and given a certificate for a free "Whopper" hamburger at Burger King. Supposedly, this event created the feeling of unexpected good fortune. For each of the Whopper recipients, a control subject was identified as the person walking either in front of or behind the individual receiving the free certificate. However, as the term "control" implies, these subjects were given no certificate or anything else that might make them feel happier than they were as they walked along. In fact, in this phase of the study they weren't even stopped. Altogether, 47 Whopper certificates were handed out (to different individuals), and for each of these treatment subjects a matched control was identified.

Approximately 50 seconds after being given the Whopper certificate, each treatment subject and his or her matched control were stopped by two additional confederates of the researchers. Here, they were asked to participate in a social psychology experiment. The designated subjects were simply handed a sheet of paper that communicated two pieces of information: a brief explanation of a planned experiment and an invitation to mail in an attached post card to line up a time for their participation. Later, it was found that ten of the 47 Whopper recipients sent in their post cards, whereas seven of the 47 matched controls sent in their cards. A statistical comparison of these two response rates (10/47 versus 7/47) indicated no significant difference, and the researchers concluded that the certificate for a free hamburger "had no apparent effect upon response to a subsequent, apparently unrelated, opportunity for helping behavior."

In an attempt to explain their results, the researchers provided three possible reasons for why a significantly larger number of the Whopper recipients did not mail in their post cards and thereby demonstrate the hypothesized helping behavior. First, the certificate may not have brought about enough of a good feeling, since it was only a token of reward. Second, the helping opportunity was quite impersonal and may therefore have weakened the tendency for the good feeling to influnce helping behavior. Third, there may have been too much of a delay between the unexpected good fortune and the opportunity to help.

In presenting these three possible explanations for their nonsignificant results, the researchers are suggesting potential cause-and-effect relationships, with the effect here being a lower amount of helping behavior among the Whopper recipients than hypothesized and the possible causes being insufficient good feeling, impersonal helping opportunity, and too much of a delay. Have the researchers exhausted the list of possible causes for their unanticipated results? Or can you think of an alternative explanation for why more of the subjects getting the free certificate did not return the post cards?

(Turn to page 195 for solution.)

59. Head Start

In the early and middle 1960s there was a great emphasis in this country on early education. Two prime examples are the Sesame Street television show and the Head Start preschool program. Both of these efforts, of course, were developed during this period to prepare disadvantaged children for entrance into elementary school.

In the opinion of many, Sesame Street (see Problem 87) has been much more successful in helping middle- and upper-middle-class children than it has been in helping disadvantaged children. Since it benefited the constituents of most congressional representatives, such criticism was not taken as seriously as that made of Head Start—a program that restricted its benefits to those below a certain level of income. By the late 1960s, as Congress was attempting to cut spending on social programs by dismantling Lyndon Johnson's "Great Society," Head Start became a prime target. The chief ammunition was a national evaluation carried out jointly by Westinghouse and Ohio University, in which the results of a number of separate studies were reported and the conclusion drawn that Head Start had not been overly successful in reaching its goals.

In general, studies of Head Start's effectiveness involved comparing the IQs and educational achievements of children in the program to those of a control group made up of children not in Head Start. In the absence of any researcher's ability to assign children at random to poverty, the control groups tended to be constructed by matching. Based on IQ, children in other pre-schools were initially matched with Head Start children. Then, pretest–post-test designs were normally used to compare gains made by the two groups. Needless to say, the finding of no significant difference led to great controversy over continued federal spending for Head Start.

If you had been asked to vote on Head Start, how much weight would you have given this report?

(Turn to page 196 for solution.)

60. Hand Calculators

There are two primary reasons why most researchers prefer to use a computer to analyze their data rather than doing the analysis on their own using paper and pencil. First, the computer is much quicker in getting the answer; second, it doesn't make mistakes. Hand calculators are considered to be (and advertised as) minicomputers, and consequently most of us think of them as possessing the same advantages as the computer: speed and accuracy. With regard to the advantage of accuracy, we assume that hand calculators, if used properly, will always provide correct answers.

Recently, a professional colleague was using his calculator to perform a relatively simple statistical operation, a correlation between two sets of scores. He reported the following series of events. First, he entered his data, pushed the appropriate button, and got the answer. Then, just to be doubly sure of his result, he reentered the exact same set of scores, pushed the same button, and got a different answer! Somewhat perplexed, he than took the same data and entered it into the calculator for a third time, and upon pushing the "correlation" button, he got a result that was different from both the first and the second answer!

After telling us about this experience with his high-quality calculator,[1] he asked us to take a guess as to why he got three different answers from an analysis of the same data. Being sensitive to cause-and-effect relationships, we clearly saw that he was asking us to identify the cause that had produced the effect of three different answers. Our answer was quick and to the point: we suggested that a mistake must have been made in entering the data during two out of the three (or possibly during all three) analyses. Assuming the calculator had been built correctly and had never been dropped, submerged in water, or in any way misused, can you think of a plausible rival hypothesis to explain the differing results that appeared in the display window of our colleague's hand calculator?

(Turn to page 197 for solution.)

[1] A Texas Instruments S-R 51-II.

61. Bumper Stickers

Most of the bumper stickers that we see around town these days tend to be fairly mild in content ("I brake for animals"; "Don't laugh, your daughter might be in this van"). It was not too long ago, however, that bumper stickers were more political and considerably more hostile in their tone, such as "America, love it or leave it" and "Off the Pigs." In the late 1960s this last slogan was associated in part with members of the Black Panther Party—a group that had a history of violent encounters with the police, particularly in California. After receiving complaints of police harassment in the form of traffic citations from black students in his class, one college professor decided to look further into the issue.

Through campus advertising, 45 possible participants were selected and then screened to yield the final group of 15, including five black, five white, and five Chicano students, all with excellent driving records. There were three males and two females in each group. The students' own cars were inspected for safety violations, declared satisfactory, and then used in the study after the application of a Day-glo orange Black Panther sticker. The students all promised to drive safely and went off into the world. Within 17 days they had rolled up a total of 33 citations. Lest you worry unduly, a fund of $500.00 had been set aside to pay the accumulated fines—the depletion of the fund marking the end of the study.

The students made no attempt to talk the police officers out of issuing the tickets, nor did they go to court to protest the citations. According to the author, their encounters with the police "ranged from affable and 'standard polite' to surly" (p. 29), with an occasional search being made of the vehicle. No relationships to race, sex, ethnicity, or personal appearance to number of citations was found.

The professor and the students took the results as evidence of unconstitutional violation of civil rights. How would you judge this case?

(Turn to page 198 for solution.)

62. Debriefing

In the early days of behavioral experimentation, investigators usually chose between one of two popular research designs. One was characterized by a treatment of some kind, a single group of subjects, and a post-test. The other was identical to the first, except that it involved the collection of pretest data prior to the presentation of the treatment. In their typical application, however, it quickly became clear that neither of these strategies could provide valid answers to the cause-and-effect questions posed by the researchers.

Later, researchers saw that they needed to have an experimental group *and* a control group, with post-tests (and possibly pretests) administered to both sets of subjects. However, any old control group would obviously not suffice. It clearly had to be made up of subjects similar to those in the experimental group. So, matching became a popular technique for forming the control group. But not for long. Authors began to write about the subtle problems created by matching, and at the same time they started to underscore the desirable features associated with randomly assigning subjects to the two comparison groups.

The rationale behind the notions of a control group and random assignment of subjects are now well understood by all competent researchers. When a researcher's study has been set up so as to involve an experimental treatment group, a control group, random assignment of subjects to the two groups, and a post-test, the researcher is allowed to sit back and claim that a "true experimental design" has been used. Too often, however, readers of the research report mistakenly assume that the study's results can be accepted as valid as long as the design possesses the four characteristics mentioned above. Let us now take a look at one particular study to illustrate why this is sometimes a mistake.

The investigation we have in mind was recently conducted at one of our largest universities in the United States, and the topic dealt with student achievement and explicit instructional objectives. The researchers' hypothesis was quite simple—namely, that students would profit more from sitting through a formal lecture if they knew at the outset what important questions were going to be taken up and answered. For years, the researchers had always begun each class session with an informal summary of the key points that would be presented. It seemed obvious that the provision of such information at each lecture's start would help the students learn more, but no empirical evidence had ever been gathered to support the practice. Hence, the experiment was set up to provide the documentation.

The study was conducted in the middle of the 1971 summer session within a graduate level statistics course. Before any treatments were applied or any data collected, the 19 enrolled students were randomly split into an experimental group of ten and a control group of nine. When the students arrived for class on the day of the experiment, no one was told that they had been assigned to an experimental group or a control group, nor were they informed that an experiment of any kind was going to be conducted. The instructor simply read the names of the nine control individuals and asked them to go quickly to a nearby room. The activity of these nine subjects in the nearby room was nothing more than a time-consuming placebo—they discussed the results of a previous examination with the instructor. Meanwhile, the ten students left behind in the regular classroom (the experimental group) reviewed a mimeographed sheet listing the primary instructional objectives associated with that day's lesson (two-way analysis of variance).

After the experimental subjects had been given ample time to familiarize themselves with the list of instructional objectives, the control subjects were brought back into the classroom. Before this was done, however, both groups were instructed not to reveal what their activity had been during the time the class was split up. When reunited, all students then heard the same lecture and in a normal fashion were able to ask questions. None of the students had been exposed to the lecture material previously, and questions were asked by members of both groups. At the end of the class session, all 19 subjects were administered an unannounced 12-item quiz covering the main points of the lecture that had just been presented.

The members of the experimental group earned scores on the short quiz that averaged approximately two points higher than scores of control group subjects. This difference, when examined by an appropriate statistical test, turned out to be significant. Therefore, the researchers' hunch had been supported. And because of the utilization of a proper experimental design, the researchers ended their technical report by saying, "The evidence provided by this research endeavor clearly indicates the superior achievement of the students who received the instructional objectives" (Huck and Long, p. 41).

Despite the fact that a true experimental design was used in this study, we feel that there is a plausible rival hypothesis to the researchers' interpretation of their statistical results. In other words, we are *not* convinced that the instructional objectives had a positive impact on the students' quiz performance. Think carefully about the procedures associated with this study, and then see if you can spot a potential flaw that calls into question the researchers' conclusion.

(Turn to page 198 for solution.)

63. Teenagers and Drugs

Although it may sound paradoxical, stimulant drugs have been used successfully with young children in controlling hyperactivity—in particular, the drug methylphenidate, better known as Ritalin. Ritalin has not, however, been recommended for use with hyperactive adolescents. One study had used Ritalin successfully on older children, and the study under consideration here was an attempt to confirm the earlier findings.

An experimental group of 27 was selected from 50 adolescents (12.5 to 19.5 years old) referred by the senior author of the study. Twenty-five of the participants were male, and all 27 were white. None had been given methylphenidate previously. Among the pretest measures used were medical histories, physical examinations, intelligence tests, measures of brain damage, and behavioral ratings by teachers and parents. The adolescents were then given 20 mg of methylphenidate twice a day for 60 days (although four were given 60 mg "in order to achieve optimal clinical results.") Post-testing consisted of the behavioral rating scale, interviews, and changes in school grades over a six-month period.

At the end of the 60-day experimental period, 13 of the adolescents reported "subjective improvement in ability to concentrate and attend," and ten of these 13 reported decreased anxiety. Improvement (as rated by the parent or the teacher or both) was also shown on the behavioral ratings for 15 of the adolescents.

	Experimental Period (60 days)		Follow-Up Period (6 to 14 months)		
P R E T E S T	23 subjects on 20 mg of methylphenidate 4 subjects on 60 mg of mythylphenidate	P O S T T E S T	Improvers (16 of the initial 27 Ss) continued on drug Nonimprovers (the remaining 11) taken off drug	S E C O N D	P O S T T E S T

$$\longrightarrow \text{T I M E} \longrightarrow$$

After examining similar results on the other measures used, the authors concluded that 16 of the 27 adolescents in this study showed improvement. These 16 were then continued on Ritalin for six to 14 months, while the other 11 nonimprovers were not given the drug during this period. Follow-up data showed "impressive gains in behavior control and academic achievement" for those who continued to use Ritalin. This was not the case for the others. The two subgroups of 16 and 11 did not differ significantly in age, IQ, or measures of neurological impairment.

Although, from their data, the authors were unable to predict who would show a positive response to Ritalin therapy, they did recommend a trial period of its use with hyperactive adolescents. Do their data support this recommendation?

(Turn to page 200 for solution.)

64. Being Partial: Not Always a Bad Thing

As you probably know, the correlation between two variables (for example, height and weight) indicates whether there is a tendency for individuals possessing high scores on one variable also to be the individuals who have high scores on the other variable. If there is such a tendency, we can speak about a positive correlation existing between the two variables. If the opposite sort of relationship were to exist (for example, if tall people were light whereas short people tended to be heavy), a negative correlation would exist between the two variables. A third possibility is for two variables to have no systematic relationship. If we were to measure a large group of people in terms of height and intelligence, we would not expect a tendency for tall people to be either smart or ignorant.

Suppose a pair of researchers had evidence that height and vocabulary knowledge were correlated in their sample to the tune of +.96. (This would indicate a very, very strong positive relationship, since the highest value a correlation can ever attain is +1.00.) You might ask the researchers to check their calulations, since you simply find it hard to believe that tall people have better vocabularies than short people. After hearing that the original statistic, +.96, was accurate, and after thinking about the problem for a few minutes, you might ask the researchers to indicate who constituted their sample. To this question, the researchers might reply that they used 100 children selected from grades 1 through 8 in the local community. This piece of information solves the dilemma, for clearly older children have a larger vocabulary than younger children, and older children are usually taller. Therefore, the observed correlation between height and vocabulary is actually reflecting the relationship between age and vocabulary.

There is a statistical technique called "partial correlation" that can be used to prevent this sort of possible misunderstanding from being communicated. With partial correlation, the correlation between the two variables of interest (say height and vocabulary) is investigated at particular values of some third variable (which for us in this example would be grade level). Then, the resulting correlations between the two variables of interest, each assessed at a particular value of the third variable, are averaged together. The correlation between height and vocabulary within any grade level is probably close to zero; and the average of the eight correlations of all the grade levels would also be close to zero. Thus, the correlation between height and vocabulary, partialling out grade level, would lead to a result that makes sense—no systematic relationship.

A partial correlation gives us an index of the type of relationship that exists between two variables when we desire that a third variable be held constant.

Apart from the topic of correlation, we often need to hold something constant when we make comparisons between two or more items. Otherwise, the comparisons made can provide results that are highly misleading and incorrect. For example, consider a sports editorial that appeared in a newspaper during the first week of the 1975 baseball season. The topic was pitchers, the title was "Best of the Best," and a portion of the editorial went as follows:

> How do you judge the best in pitchers? The pitchers who really get your attention are the pitchers who give the team a winning margin, a substantial margin between total wins and losses. Below you will note a chart of all big league pitchers who currently have won 100 victories or more. They are graded on the basis of the margin between the victories and defeats. Old man Gibson [Bob Gibson, of the St. Louis Cardinals] leads the field, which is no surprise.*

The chart that was included in the newspaper editorial had a list of 32 active pitchers along with each man's career total of wins and losses. The 32 players were arranged in order (graded) on the difference between total number of games won and total number of games lost. Bob Gibson had won 84 games more than he had lost, the next pitcher had won 68 more than he had lost, and so on down the list, with the last pitcher having lost two more games than he had won.

The 32 baseball players were arranged in the chart solely on the basis of the won/lost differential. The chart was entitled "Winning Edge? Here It Is," and it gives the impression that Bob Gibson and the other pitchers at the top of the list are the best of the best. We believe that there is a plausible rival hypothesis. In particular, we believe that the sports editor (or whoever set up the chart) failed to partial out an important variable before determining which pitchers were better than others. Any ideas as to what this variable was that should have been held constant or partialled out?

(Turn to page 200 for solution.)

*Copyright 1975 by the Knoxville News–Sentinel. Reprinted by permission.

65. Childless by Choice

Although the human race is in no immediate danger of dying off for lack of reproduction, we have a number of friends who have decided not to have children for one reason or another. These friends are apparently contributing to the nationwide increase in childless families, and it is only natural that someone would choose to study this phenomenon. Two researchers at a university medical center in California gave two-hour psychiatric interviews to 33 young women (under 30) who had decided never to have a child.

Fifteen were using a nonpermanent form of contraception, while 18 others were seen just before having a tubal ligation. The women were also asked to complete a group of attitudinal scales on self-concept, decision making, sexual attitudes, and feminine interests. There was a less formal follow-up interview six months later. All of the women were white, and among the two-thirds of the women who were single were all of those receiving tubal ligations.

The interview data indicated that although a majority of the tubal ligation group did not see themselves as potential mothers and did not differ on the attitude measures, they were strikingly different from normative groups. The follow-up interviews did not yield much of interest to the present discussion.

The authors concluded that "the most striking" finding was the "unambivalent hostility toward babies" of those in the tubal ligation group. Should you believe that this hostility caused the women to seek sterilization?

(Turn to page 201 for solution.)

66. The Price of Beer

As shoppers, we almost always have the option of choosing between various brands of the same product. For example, there are numerous brands of cars in competition with one another. With other products like canned vegetable soup, we may only have the option to choose between two brands (Campbell's and the supermarket's own line). The main point is, however, that we usually are given a choice of brands.

More often than not, the purchase price of a product varies from brand to brand. And since most of us have found out through bad experiences that you usually get what you pay for, there is a definite tendency to think that a particular product will last longer or perform more adequately or taste better if it costs more. Hence, if we have enough money available we probably will purchase the more expensive brand.

But what happens after we make our purchases and take our products home? Do we evaluate the quality of the products that we have bought in a biased way because of their purchase prices? Does an expensive brand seem to last longer or perform more adequately or taste better *because* we spent more money on it, when in fact a less expensive brand is of equal quality? These questions provided the impetus for a recent experimental investigation. The researchers hypothesized that consumers would perceive that a higher-priced brand was of higher quality, even if the quality was exactly the same for all brands. The product they used in this experiment was beer.

The subjects used in the study were 60 married students at Stanford University who classified themselves as beer drinkers. These subjects were led to believe that the experiment involved three different brands of beer. Brand "M" was said to cost $1.30 per sixpack, Brand "L" was said to cost $1.20, and Brand "P" was said to cost 99¢. The subjects knew these price differentials, and the three brands of beer were thought of and referred to as the high-priced brand, the middle-priced brand, and the low-priced brand. What the students did not know was that all the beer in the experiment was really the same, being taken from the same batch number of a California brewer.

The experiment lasted for eight weeks, and during each week the researcher went to each subject's apartment on three occasions. On each visit, the subject got to select one bottle of beer. Each time, the three bottles were presented to the subject on a tray with a card behind each bottle indicating the price per sixpack of each brand and a note taped on the middle- and low-priced bottles indicating the per-bottle savings as compared with the high-priced brand.[1] The label on each bottle simply said "L," "M," or "P." After the subject made a selection, the researcher left the apartment, and the

---

[1] The researcher made sure that the position of the three brands on the tray varied on each visit.

subject could drink that particular bottle or beer at any convenient time before the next visit.

Following the twenty-fourth visit (there were three per week for eight weeks), each of the 60 subjects completed a two-part questionnaire. The first part asked the subjects to rate each of the three brands of beer on a five-point scale: very pleasant, good, fair, poor, or undrinkable. The second part involved a list of 12 words that typically describe high-quality and low quality beers ("full-bodied," "light," "flat," "bitter"). From this list, the subject was required to select the three words that best described each brand. When the questionnaire responses were analyzed statistically, it was found that the high-priced brand was rated significantly better than the low-priced brand, and significantly more favorable words were selected from the 12-item list to describe the high-priced beer.

The researcher interpreted the results as proof that the perceived quality of beer is affected by its price. A definite cause-and-effect relationship was implied—with price being the cause and perception of quality being the effect. Do you accept this interpretation, or are there any plausible rival hypotheses to account for the questionnaire results?

(Turn to page 201 for solution.)

67. A "T" Party

As indicated elsewhere in this book (see Problem 9), we are parents of young children who are reasonably healthy and normal. Not all parents are this fortunate, however, and there is great interest these days in counseling the parents of children with either physical or mental handicaps. The most common approaches to parent counseling involve either a behavioral or a reflective orientation (or some combination of the two); thus, it should not be surprising to find studies comparing these two methods.

One such study in Rochester, New York, had as participants 48 mothers (of 300 who had been contacted) of low-functioning, mentally retarded children who were willing and able to attend the experimental sessions during the spring semester. The 35 who chose to attend during February and March were assigned to one of four groups, two of which used the behavioral approach and two of which used the reflective approach. The day of week on which the group met determined the approach used. The 13 who chose to wait for the April and May sessions were used as a control group, although they received the same counseling after the formal study was completed. No initial differences between the groups were found on a number of demographic variables (maternal age, maternal education, age of child, and so on).

The measures used in this study were collected at three times—baseline, pretest, and post-test—and included a survey of parental attitudes with five subscales and a total score, a checklist of behavioral problems with six subscales and a total score, behavior observations (six scores), ratings of behaviors of concern to the parents (two dimensions), frequency of target behaviors of the child, and parent ratings of the program's worth. Although some other analyses were computed, the bulk of the analyses consised of t-tests between types of treatment on the pre-post difference scores. An additional analysis showed no differences in rate of improvement between groups. The last analysis notwithstanding, the 32 other reported analyses led the researcher to conclude that counseling is better than no counseling and that the behavioral model is superior to the reflective model. Do you agree?

(Turn to page 202 for solution.)

68. Assessing Personality Through Handwriting Samples

In making a casual determination of someone else's personality, most of us base our assessments on what the target person does or says. Although this procedure may work well for deciding who to ask to be in your bridge group, it is obviously quite biased and unscientific. When an *unbiased* assessment of someone's personality is needed, it is highly likely that a written measuring instrument will be used to collect the data upon which the assessment will be made. Hundreds of such personality inventories are in existence, and of course some are better than others. All such inventories, however, share the undesirable features of being costly and time-consuming to administer. If the assessment could be made in some other way—say through a handwriting sample—it would constitute a substantial savings of time and money. But would the conclusions so drawn be valid?

Recently, the "Intelligence Report" division of *Parade* magazine conducted an investigation that seems to indicate that the answer to this question is yes. Their study proceeded as follows. First, they located a handwriting expert. This was Dr. James Bruno, a graphologist and professor at the University of California, Los Angeles. Next they gave Dr. Bruno a handwriting sample from an unidentified person who was described simply as a "government employee." (The handwriting sample was quite short—39 words or abbreviations—and it appeared to be a set of notes for an oral report or political address.) Finally, the graphologist was asked to analyze the handwriting.

Believe it or not, the handwriting analysis ended up being seven paragraphs long and it contained 249 words! Moreover, the personality assessment was amazingly accurate. The handwriting had actually come from President Jimmy Carter, and the graphologist's analysis indicated that the author was probably "a man of strong ego," "a leader of men," "and "a small-town boy in the big city." The last sentence of the handwriting analysis ran as follows: "Given information that he is a 'government employee' prompts the prediction that he can rise to the top of his department, if, in fact, he is not already there."

This little investigation implies a cause-and-effect relationship. The effect is a personality assessment that appears to be incredibly accurate. The causal variable is the match-up of a handwriting sample and an experienced graphologist. In your opinion, do the successful results of this investigation indicate that we all should begin to make personality assessments through

107

handwriting samples rather than standardized personality inventories? Or might there be an alternative explanation for the accuracy of the graphologist's analysis besides a good interpretation of the President's handwriting sample?

(Turn to page 203 for solution.)

69. Yo! Ho! Ho!
and a Bottle of Rum

Whether deserved or not, seafaring men have long had a reputation for drinking spirited beverages in prodigious amounts. Apparently, some members of the United States Navy have decided to continue this tradition as evidenced by a recent upsurge of interest in the development of alcohol treatment centers for naval personnel. It is refreshing to find that the navy is also interested in evaluting the effectiveness of these new programs. One such evaluation is described below.

Three researchers used a battery of personality inventories and a measure of anxiety to examine personality changes resulting from entrance into one of the alcohol treatment centers. The analysis of pretest–post-test differences on the 404 alcholics[1] for whom complete data were available revealed significant positive changes on level of trust, emotional stability, and extroversion. These positive changes were accompanied by significant decreases in both pathology (depression, hysteria) and anxiety. Ratings by the (former) alcoholics' commanding officers indicated the short-term success rate to be over 80 percent. This stands in marked contrast to the 45 percent rate of success reported before the development of special treatment centers.

Based on this study, do you now have reason to believe that the United States Navy is spending our tax money effectively?

(Turn to page 204 for solution.)

---

[1] There were originally 424 participants, but some data were lost as a consequence of "unsystematic testing."

70. Teaching Machines Versus Textbooks

An experiment was recently conducted to see whether students, in general, would learn better from a teaching machine or from a traditional textbook. Moreover, the researchers wanted to find out whether certain *types* of students might learn best from the teaching machine, while other students might learn best from a text. Two types of students were used in the experiment: those having a high interest in mechanical devices but a low literary interest, and those having a high literary interest but a low mechanical interest. As you might suspect, the researchers predicted that the first group would learn best from a teaching machine while the second group would learn best from a text.

Part of the material presented for the subjects to learn was the following fictitious business address:

> Mr. Karl G. Lunden
> Chief of Product Development
> 314 Brewster Building
> 101 Hollyhock Drive
> Mesa, California

Each subject's task was to memorize this address exactly. To facilitate the learning process, all subjects were given the same programmed material; this consisted of 19 frames (that is, separate steps) such that in each successive frame more and more of the address was purposely omitted.[1] The only treatment difference among the subjects related to how they saw the 19 frames. A random half of the subjects used a teaching machine that presented only one frame at a time through a window; the other random half used printed booklets that presented the same 19 frames as a text—down one page, then down the next page, and so on.

The experimental procedure was as follows. After arriving at the experimental room, each of the 60 subjects was given printed instructions describing the task and learning materials. These instructions were identical except for the necessary reference to either the text or the teaching machine. Subjects who were assigned to the teaching machine worked individually, while the text was administered to two groups of about 15 subjects each. The average time needed to complete the 19 frames was about 17 minutes.

The next day, all subjects were tested for their retention of the memorized material. They were asked to reproduce the complete business address, and their performance was assessed by counting the number of individual

---

[1] On each frame, the subject was required to fill in the missing information.

characters correctly recalled in the proper order. A statistical analysis of these scores verified the researchers' predictions: the teaching machine was significantly better than the text for subjects having a high mechanical interest, while the text booklet was significantly better for subjects possessing a high literary interest. When both types of students were pooled together, no difference was found to exist between the teaching machine and the text.

Well, what do you think? If you're a teacher, do the results of this study convince you that a greater amount of learning can take place in your classroom if you measure your students' interest and put your reading assignments into teaching machines for some of the learners? If so, we think that you had better sit back for a moment and think again about the way this study was conducted. In our judgment, there is a problem that interferes with a clear interpretation of the results. Can you identify the methodological flaw?

(Turn to page 204 for solution.)

71. Intelligence and Strangeness

Physicists use a number of constructs such as angular momentum, spin, baryon number, and parity in describing elementary particles. Our favorite construct in physics, however, is that of strangeness. Elementary particles are assigned strangeness numbers that occasionally follow the law of conservation of strangeness, depending upon the type of interaction in which the particles are engaged. We believe that the adoption of this construct in the public schools should be encouraged. Elementary children could be given numbers that would allow teachers to predict the nature of interactions between them. It may be that many of you believe that the IQ score already serves a function similar to that which strangeness serves in physics.

One well-known longitudinal study of this belief was started in 1921 by Lewis Terman. The youngest student in each class (who was relatively likely to have skipped a grade), along with the three brightest (as rated by the teacher), constituted a population that was then tested. The final sample comprised 1528 children with IQ scores above 140—above the ninety-eighth percentile by today's standards. These children were larger, healthier, socially superior, and generally wonderful. As adults this group made remarkable achievements in any number of areas. They also continued to display exceptionally good health, both mental and otherwise.

These data have been used extensively to show that gifted children are not strange creatures who sit in corners and read until their eyes are ruined, but instead are creating a meritocracy. Do you still believe that bright children are a little strange?

(Turn to page 205 for solution.)

72. Dormitory Hours

When we were undergraduates back in the early 1960s, our dates had to be returned to their dormitories or sorority houses by 12:30 P.M. on the weekend and 10:30 P.M. during the week. These dorm hours applied not just to the youngest students but to sophomores, juniors, and seniors as well. (Besides this restriction on our social life, we also were prohibited from drinking and from having cars on campus. Thank goodness for ladders, flasks, and secret garages!)

Soon after we became college alumni, our school and many others like it did away with most of their old-fashioned rules and the *in-loco-parentis* philosophy. But the notion of dorm hours, at least for freshmen, still exists on several campuses. In some places, it is mandatory for all first-year students; in other places, it is an option that parents can choose or not choose for their daughters; and at a few institutions, there are no hours at all but support, among certain parents and administrators, for the reinstatement of such a regulation. A college's position on women's dormintory hours, be it pro or con, seems inevitably to be controversial with some group that is unhappy and desirous of a change.

There are, of course, varied reasons for why many colleges continue to have some form of dormitory hours for first-year women. Prominent among these, however, is the belief that college freshmen need some assistance in learning how to use their time wisely when not in the classroom. After being under the watchful eye of one or two parents for 18 years, the new college student is in obvious danger of "goofing off" to such an extent that academic performance is adversely affected. Requiring students to be in by some reasonable hour, the advocates of the rule contend that the student will be more likely to study, get adequate sleep, and maintain an acceptable grade point average.

Recently, two researchers conducted a study to see if residence hall closing hours do, in fact, have an effect on the grade averages of freshmen women. This investigation took place at the University of Georgia and involved 787 resident freshmen women. In this group, 371 women were required to observe dormitory hours, while the remaining women had parental permission to ignore the closing hours. At the end of their first academic term, grade point averages (GPA) were computed for each of the two groups.

Since it was the parents who decided whether or not their daughters could ignore the dorm hours, there was no chance to assign the students in a random manner to the two treatment conditions Hence, any difference between the two groups in GPA at the end of the fall term could potentially be contaminated by initial differences, thereby making it impossible to tell whether the regulation concerning dorm hours had any beneficial effect. The researchers were aware of this problem, and they attempted, through the use

113

of predicted grade point averages and an advanced statistical procedure, to take this situation into consideration.

Based upon a student's earned grade average in high school, performance on college entrance examinations (the SAT or ACT), and other data, the admissions office at a college or university often predicts how well the incoming freshmen will do in terms of first-term college GPA. In fact, these predicted GPAs are used to help decide which high school applicants should be accepted into the postsecondary institution. As you might suspect, students who have performed well in high school and on the college entrance exam are predicted to earn better grades as college freshmen. Most students do not earn first-term college GPAs identical to their predicted GPAs, but the discrepancies are usually small enough to justify using the predictions in the admissions decision.

In the study on dorm hours, the predicted GPAs were used not to decide which students should be admitted (since all 787 subjects already were), but rather to help equalize the two comparison groups. Instead of contrasting the actual first-quarter GPAs of the 416 women who could ignore dorm hours with those of the 371 women who had to be in at designated hours, the researchers utilized a statistical technique[1] to *adjust* these actual GPAs so as to compensate for group differences in terms of the predicted GPAs. The logic behind this adjustment procedure is relatively simple and straightforward. The group having the higher predicted GPA had its actual GPA adjusted downward, while the group having the lower predicted GPA had its actual GPA adjusted upward. Through this adjustment process, the researchers were simply trying to guess, scientifically, how each group *would have done* in terms of actual GPA if they had started out with identical predicted GPAs. Then, a comparison of the adjusted GPAs becomes free of any bias associated with group differences in high school GPA, performance, or any of the other ingredients used to make the GPA predictions.

The predicted and actual GPAs for the group allowed to ignore the dorm hours were 2.52 and 2.66, respectively (on a 4.00 scale). For the group required to observe the designated hours, these two GPAs were 2.59 and 2.69. Since the predicted GPAs for the two groups were so similar, only slight adjustments were made in the actual first-quarter GPAs: 2.66 was adjusted upwards to 2.68, while 2.69 was adjusted downwards to 2.67. (Had the two groups differed more in terms of the predicted GPAs, larger adjustments would have been made; conversely, if no difference had existed in the predicted GPAs, no adjustment would have been required.)

A statistical comparison of the two adjusted first-quarter GPAs (2.68 versus 2.67) indicated no significant difference. Based on this evidence, the

---

[1] This technique is called the *analysis of covariance.*

researchers concluded that the variable of keeping or ignoring closing hours has little effect on the academic performance of freshmen women. Are you willing to accept this conclusion? Or can you identify some weakness in the logic or procedures associated with this study?

(Turn to page 205 for solution.)

73. Alcoholics in Control

Most of us know people who recognize that they smoke or drink too much. The typical comment of these people is often "I could quit tomorrow if I wanted to," but somehow they do not ever want to. Many studies involving male alcoholics report that they really do believe that they are in control of their behavior, including their drinking. This led two researchers to study the question of control in women alcoholics.

Two scales were used to measure general control orientation and drinking control orientation in 90 women. Data for the alcoholic group were collected on 50 of 62 women in two halfway houses over a six-month period (necessitated by the small population and low turnover of the halfway houses). A control group was used, which consisted of 40 volunteer social drinkers from a local industry and from local chapters of a national association who did not differ significantly in either age or education from the alcoholic group. Statistical tests showed the women in the alcoholic group to be more external[1] on both scales. This is in contrast with male alcoholics, who show greater internality and, thus, greater perception of control over their behavior. The authors give three possible interpretations of their findings: men and women alcoholics differ in their control orientation; women alcoholics in halfway houses may not be representative of all women alcoholics; and in contrast to most other treatment programs, these particular halfway houses did not stress internality. Are there other possible explanations for the findings?

(Turn to page 206 for solution.)

---

[1] That is, believing that their lives were generally controlled by the vagaries of fortune rather than by themselves.

116

74. Disabled Counselors

It is a well-known fact that individuals with physical disabilities are sometimes discriminated against when applying for jobs. Potential employers may be reluctant to hire someone with a disability because of a fear that the disabled person will not be able to perform the job. Or, if it is clear that the applicant *does* have the skills necessary to do the job, there is still a reluctance to hire the individual because of a suspicion that other people—colleagues, supervisors, employees, and customers—will be made to feel uncomfortable by the disabled person.

To see whether potential customers tend to prefer dealing with nondisabled employees, an interesting experiment was conducted. The work setting was presumed to be a counseling center, the "employees" were the counselors, and the "customers" were potential clients who might be going to the counseling center with a problem. Forty-eight students from the University of Missouri at Columbia served as subjects in the experiment, and they were considered to be the customers. They were selected at random from the available student population.

During the experimental session, each of the 48 subjects was seen individually and shown three photographs, one of a male counselor in a wheelchair, one of a male counselor with crutches, and one of a male counselor without any visible disability.[1] To make the pictures realistically depict a counseling relationship, each photograph showed the counselor talking with a client. However, to focus attention on the counselor, only the back of the head of the presumed client could be seen in the picture.

Although each subject looked at just three pictures, there were actually nine photographs involved in this study. In three of these pictures, each of the counselors was paired with the wheelchair; in three other pictures each counselor was paired with crutches; and in the three remaining pictures each counselor appeared to have no disability. Therefore, one of three sets of counselor-disability pictures could be administered to any subject. One-third of the subjects received each of these picture sets, and the sequence of the pictures within each set was predetermined to make sure that all possible sequences appeared an equal number of times.[2]

After the subjects had looked at the pictures of the three counselors, they were given a written list of 20 hypothetical counseling situations. Although briefly described, each counseling situation clearly dealt with an educational

[1] These three counselors had been selected randomly from the staff at the university counseling center.

[2] In other words, there was a complete counterbalancing of counselors and sequences to prevent either of these variables from becoming confounded with the treatment variable—level of disability.

problem, a vocational problem, or a personal problem. For each of these hypothetical counseling situations, the experimental subjects were required to indicate which of the three counselors (from the photographs) they would most like to have for a counseling session if they really had the problem described on the list. The subjects also identified which of the three counselors they would least like to have for each of the 20 problems.

The researchers were concerned that the disability differences among the three photographs were too obvious, and they wanted to "divert attention from the levels of disability." Therefore, at the beginning of the experiment, subjects were given a written explanation of the study, which gave the distinct impression that the research focus was on handsomeness. The bogus explanation of the study stated that previous researchers had not clearly established whether or not certain males are selected more often than others because of their being more handsome. Subjects were further told that the panel of judges had looked at the pictures of the three counselors and been able to rank them from most to least handsome. The final part of these fake instructions said "While we will not give you the rankings, we hypothesize that your selection of the pictures for the hypothetical situations will correlate closely with the rankings of handsomeness we have previously obtained."

Contrary to what the researchers had expected, the results of the experiment indicated that disabled counselors were chosen significantly more often than the able-bodied counselor. A cause-and-effect relationship was suggested, with the cause being the presence or absence of counselor disability and the effect being the client's preference. A very encouraging result—if it weren't for a plausible rival hypothesis. Can you identify an alternative explanation for why the counselors with physical disabilities were chosen more often than the able-bodied counselor, other than the variable of visible disability?

(Turn to page 207 for solution.)

75. The Principle of Least Interest

The principle of least interest suggests that, in a relationship between two people, the person who is least interested is more likely to control the relationship. For example, if a given teacher is less interested than a given student in that student's grade, then the teacher controls the situation through course requirements. However, if the student is the less interested party, then the student controls the situation by skipping classes, exams, and so on. This principle was invoked in partial explanation of some correlates of anxiety in unwed mothers in a study done on the West Coast.

In this study, 25 young women in a home for unwed mothers were interviewed at length on their relationships with their friends, families, the father of the child, and other aspects of their home and community lives. The women ranged in age from 14 to 30, and 23 were from middle-class backgrounds. A scale measuring anxiety was used to classify them as having either high or low anxiety. The authors examined the relationship between anxiety and some background variable such as broken or unbroken home and closeness with the baby's father. They interpreted the results as supporting the hypothesis that "close primary group ties are associated with experiencing low levels of anxiety in a stress situation" (Hauser and Hobart, p. 262).[1] Paradoxically, they also found that under certain conditions, those with a close relationship to the baby's father were less likely to tell the father about the pregnancy than those with a less close relationship. They interpreted this as reflecting an attempt by the more interested party to control the less interested (to increase the probability of marriage), thus going against the principle of least interest as defined above.

Should we increase our "primary group ties" in order to reduce anxiety in stressful situations? It is to our advantage to be more (or less) interested? What should you conclude from this study?

(Turn to page 208 for solution.)

---

[1] "Close primary group tie" being a close relationship with one's family.

76. Popcorn

One of our favorite nighttime snacks is popcorn. The problem, however, is that it never seems to taste quite as good as the popcorn we purchase at the movie theater. When we cook it, one of two things usually happens. Either one-third of the corn kernels end up unpopped at the bottom of the pan, or the bottom layer of the popped corn gets burned and remains stuck to the pan.

In an attempt to solve this problem, we have tried several things, such as using different types of cooking oil, putting the corn kernels into the oil before the oil heats up, putting the kernels in after it heats up, shaking the pan vigorously as the corn pops, not shaking the pan at all, cooking over a medium-hot burner, and cooking over a hot burner. No matter what we try, we are still unable to produce consistently good popcorn. For this reason, a newspaper advertisement (and similar television commercial) really caught our eye.

This ad, for Orville Redenbacher's Gourmet Popping Corn, suggested that our problem was related not to *how* we went about popping corn but rather to *what* we were popping. In other words, this ad strongly suggested that all popping corn is not of the same quality, and more importantly, that high-quality corn kernels will solve the corn-popping problem that we described above. And as you might suspect, the main pitch of the ad stated that Orville Redenbacher's Gourmet Popping Corn belonged in the high-quality category. The interesting thing about this ad was the fact that a little experiment had been conducted to prove the point.

The magazine ad contained a picture of Orville Redenbacher standing behind two seemingly identical see-through popcorn poppers. Both poppers had popped popcorn in them. However, one of the poppers had corn only up to the lid, while the other popper had so much more corn in it that the lid had been pushed up about two inches and the corn was overflowing onto the table. Each popper had a sign positioned in clear view in front of it. As you might guess, the sign next to the barely-full popper said "4 oz. of ordinary" while the overflowing popper was labeled "4 oz. of mine."

The text of the ad gave the distinct impression that the different amounts of popcorn in the two poppers were caused by differences in quality between Orville Redenbacher's Gourmet Corn and the ordinary brand. In part, the text went as follows:

> It's true. My Gourmet Popping Corn will give you a heap more popped corn than you'll get from ordinary kinds. In fact, it pops so light and fluffy, I suggest you start with fewer kernels.
>
> You won't find a bunch of unpopped kernels in the bottom of your bowl either. We harvest and select only my special Number One Quality kernels . . . so every one should pop up perfectly.*

The picture seems to indicate that you get about 50 percent more corn from Orville's brand than from an ordinary brand. Clearly, a cause-and-effect relationship has been implied: the causal variable is the brand of popping corn that you put into the popper, and the effect variable is the amount of popped corn that you get out. Orville's Number One Quality kernels supposedly give you more popped corn. Are you willing to accept this alleged causal claim? Or can you think of any plausible rival hypotheses to account for the different amounts of popped corn in the two poppers shown in the ad?

(Turn to page 208 for solution.)

*Taken from a magazine advertisement,"My Orville Redenbacher's Gourmet Popping Corn Will Blow Your Top Off." Reprinted with permission from Hunt-Wesson Foods, Inc. Courtesy of William H. Hood, President.

77. Cigarette Smoking and Physical Fitness

High school and college coaches advise their athletes to refrain from smoking. There are probably many reasons for this training rule, but we're confident that it exists primarily because of a presumed relationship between smoking and physical fitness. Recently, a researcher put this hypothesis to an empirical test. The study was quite simple, with the subjects being required to perform a series of tasks. The researcher's hunch was also quite straightforward—that individuals who smoked heavily would perform less well on tasks that involved the circulatory and respiratory systems, while smokers and non-smokers would perform about the same on tasks involving minimum physical activity.

The subjects in this investigation were 88 military personnel who ranged in age from 19 to 39, and they had been performing moderate calisthentics for two hours a week for six weeks prior to the actual experiment. On the day of the study, each subject was required to perform five physical-fitness tests. The three that definitely involved the circulorespiratory system were crawling 120 feet on the ground as fast as possible, running through a 49-yard obstacle course as fast as possible, and running a mile on a grass track. The other two tests—those that involved minimal stress—involved swinging from rung to rung on a horizontal ladder as far as possible without touching the ground, and throwing five grenades (from a kneeling position) toward a target located 90 feet away.

All 88 subjects had the crawling test first and the one-mile run last. The other three tests were administered in different orders to different subgroups of the total subject pool. After completing the five tests, each subject was required to write down the number of cigarettes smoked per day. Upon analyzing the data from the five fitness tests and the smoking frequency question, the researcher discovered that his hypothesis had been confirmed. On the three tests involving physical stress (crawling, the obstacle course, and the 1-mile run), the people who smoked more were found to perform significantly worse than those who smoked infrequently; and on the two tests that involved minimal stress on the circulorespiratory system (climbing and throwing), no significant differences were observed between those who smoked heavily and those who smoked infrequently or not at all.

The implication of this study is clear: smoking impairs your ability to perform well on fitness tests involving stress to the circulatory and respiratory systems. Do you accept this conclusion? Or can you offer any plausible alternative explanation(s) for the results that were obtained?

(Turn to page 209 for solution.)

78. To B-Mod or Not To B-Mod

One of our neighbors recently instituted a system using gold stars as reinforcers for her 7-year-old son in order to increase the time he spent reading and decrease the time he spent engaging in unacceptable behaviors. Since the neighbor's 9-year-old son naturally wanted to be involved in this family project, there was little choice but to include him. The outcome was about what any cynic would have predicted; that is, the older child read more and behaved even better than usual, while the younger child gave up completely in the face of the competition. As their mother bemoaned the abject failure of behavior modification to modify the behavior of the child whose behavior need modifying, we were tempted to give her a copy of the study described below.

This study had as its purpose a comparison between a behavior modification treatment technique and a placebo treatment. Particular attention was paid to the problems of both differential expectancy of success between the two groups (often confounded with treatment in previous research), and of ensuring that both groups received equal time from the status figures (persons at the doctoral level).

The participants in the study were twelve families with more than one child. In each case the target child was a male (between 5 and 14) who had been engaging in one or more highly undesirable behaviors (such as setting fires or stealing). Since the treatments were centered on groups of three families, the first three families referred for treatment were assigned to the behavior modification group, the next three to the placebo group, and so on for the second six families. The treatment group received training from a programmed text in addition to a weekly group session in the presence of two experienced therapists, while the placebo group spent their nongroup time making tape recordings of their problems and holding group sessions without the therapists. Both groups received daily phone calls in order to maintain contact with participants. A coding system was used by trained observers to describe the family interactions (particular attention was paid to deviant behaviors) on a pre-post basis. The observers were unaware of the families' group assignments. The parents completed a symptom checklist and an expectancy questionnaire given each week. Finally, the amount of approval each parent received from the therapists during the group sessions was calculated, as was the amount of contact time each family received from the staff.

Although both groups were supposed to receive equal professional contact, a significant difference was found in favor of the treatment group in the amount of telephone time received (118 minutes versus 57 minutes). No significant group differences were found on the expectancy questionnaire—it appeared that both groups held consistently high expectations for success throughout the study. A second analysis indicated that parents in the treatment group received significantly more approval (mostly from the therapists) in the group sessions. A number of other measures failed to show differences and the authors concluded that, overall, the social settings of the two groups were equivalent. As for the targeted deviant behaviors in the child, the treatment group showed a 61 percent decline (significant) while the placebo group showed a 37 percent increase (nonsignificant)—two-tailed[1] *t*-tests were used in each case. A series of one-tailed[2] *t*-tests were used to show decreases in child symptoms for the treatment group and either no change or increases in the placebo group. A graph appeared to show differences in expectation of success, but statistical analyses failed to confirm their existence. Finally, a two-tailed test showed no difference on the one of the 29 family interaction observation categories (mothers' commands) that seemed clinically relevant. The authors concluded that the treatment was dramatically successful in reducing targeted deviant behavior.

One finding the authors found difficult to explain was the response of the placebo group parents to the question, "Has your child improved?" Despite reporting no change in the child's symptom behaviors, parents invariably answered yes. Two possible explanations were given: the question was too general, or the parents were being polite. Are there other explanations? Would you recommend behavior modification to a friend on the basis of this study?

(Turn to page 210 for solution.)

---

[1] Two-tailed tests are used when the researcher is not sure which mean should be larger.
[2] One-tailed tests are used when the direction of the difference is known in advance.

79. Student Resignations at West Point

For obvious reasons, any organization is hurt by the voluntary resignation of individuals who have demonstrated the ability to perform successfully while on the job. However, the organization becomes especially concerned when the people who resign have been carefully screened to begin with, when there are far more applicants than available positions, when it is costly to train the ones selected, and when it is impossible to substitute in midstream a new person for the one who has resigned. Such is the case at the United States Military Academy at West Point, for in this situation the students are admitted, as a class, only once per year. When one resigns after beginning the program, not only are time and money wasted on the lost cadet, but more importantly, that slot remains vacant until graduation.

Presuming that the screening process has provided a batch of new students who are committed to the military service and capable of successfully completing the training program, the staff at West Point would like to do anything it can—without lowering its standards—to decrease the number of voluntary student resignations. Occasionally, research projects are undertaken to find out what is likely to help out in this regard. Not too long ago, one such project was conducted to see whether a rather simple technique might serve to decrease the number of resignations. This technique involved mailing each prospective student a booklet that described, in a realistic way, the day-to-day conditions associated with the student's future life at West Point. The booklet included descriptions of both stressful and mundane experiences, and the researchers hypothesized that it would bring about realistic expectations and consequently decrease the number who left soon after arriving because they "really didn't know what they were in for."

This particular study was conducted in the summer of 1971, during which time the new cadets were involved in an intensive training program designed to familiarize them with fundamental military discipline. As you might imagine, this two-month program necessitated some quick adjustments on the part of the new students. The new cadets learned in a speedy fashion that their life at West Point was frequently going to be more stressful—in both physical and psychological terms—than what they had previously experienced.

About a month before the start of the rigorous summer program, a sample of 246 was randomly selected from the 1230 individuals who had indicated that they were going to accept their appointments. These 246 individuals constituted the experimental group, and each person was mailed a copy of the descriptive booklet. Presumably, the individuals receiving this information would arrive at West Point a month later better prepared for the training program.

A control group was randomly selected from among the new cadets who were not sent the experimental booklet. Since one of the 246 booklets wasn't delivered because of a change of address, and since 11 other members of the experimental group did not report for the training program, 234 of the nonbooklet individuals who showed up on the first day of the program were identified and comprised the control group. Students in the two groups were not told about the experiment, and it can be assumed that those in the experimental group thought that all of the new cadets had been sent the informative booklet, while those in the control group were simply not aware of the fact that something had been withheld from them that other students had received.

Records were kept of all the voluntary resignations that took place between the beginning of the summer training program (July 1) and the first day of classes in the fall. During this time period, only 14 of the 234 experimental students resigned, while 27 of the 234 students in the control group dropped out. When tested statistically, this difference—14 versus 27 resignations—was found to be significant. In the words of the researchers, these results "supported the hypothesis that candid information presented after the decision to participate but before entering the organization reduced the probability of voluntary resignation" (Ilgen and Seely, p. 453).

Are you convinced that the informative booklet served to decrease resignations? Or is there something about the methodology of this study that argues against the implied cause-and-effect relation?

(Turn to page 211 for solution.)

80. Miss America

For anyone who wants to advertise a product, service, or any other message, there are six basic types of media available: newspapers, magazines, radio, television, direct mail, and outdoor billboards. Before agreeing to use any of these media, the person paying for the advertising should be interested in knowing whether a cause-and-effect relationship exists between the ads and sales. We are confident that representatives from each of the six media would say "Yes, our medium does bring about increased sales." Moreover, each representative would probably boast that his or her medium did a better job than the other five media.

Not too long ago, the Institute of Outdoor Advertising (IOA) conducted a research study aimed at proving the superiority of billboards. The goals and results of this empirical investigation were reported in two IOA promotional brochures, and we here reproduce the full report from one of these brochures:

> We've long believed that Outdoor can outperform other media in getting across a message to the public. What we needed, here at the Institute of Outdoor Advertising, was a way of proving it. Last year we thought of a way. We would see if our medium, by itself, could increase public awareness of the name of Miss America 1975.
>
> We approached the Outdoor companies with our plan. We asked them to donate space not already sold or earmarked for public service announcements. They gave us 10,000 panels—or about $1.5 million worth of Outdoor at the going rate.
>
> Our poster[1] was to go on display for two months beginning January 1, 1975. But before it did, the Outdoor companies sponsored a series of studies to determine public awareness of Miss America's name prior to posting. Random sample surveys were conducted during November and December, 1974 in 44 metropolitan markets by 25 colleges and universities and 12 independent research organizations. Over 15,000 adults were questioned.
>
> Despite all the exposure Miss America had received (previously) on TV and radio and in print,[2] *only 1.6% of the respondents* gave the correct answer when asked, "What is the name of Miss America 1975?"
>
> Then our posters went up. And in February and March 1975, a second wave of over 15,000 interviews was conducted by the same research teams. This time, *16.3% of the respondents*—about one of every six—knew who Miss America was. That's a 10-fold increase in awareness. Projected nationally it would mean that Outdoor had communicated a new and difficult name to more than

[1] This poster showed a large picture of Miss America with her crown, scepter, and roses; the only message on the poster (in large letters) was "Shirley Cothran, Miss America 1975."

[2] The IOA reports that over 50 million Americans saw the coronation of TV on September 7, 1974, that her name appeared in hundreds of newspapers and magazines between September and October, and that she appeared on five network television stations and was interviewed on dozens of local television and radio stations during this three-month interval.

20 million adults. Through a two-month posting, Outdoor made Shirley Cothran the best-known reigning Miss America in history.*

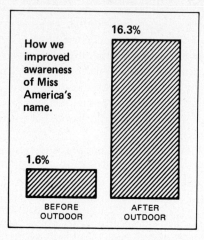

Clearly, this large-scale study was undertaken to demonstrate a cause-and effect relationship. Phrases such as "to see if our medium, by itself, could increase public awareness"; "Outdoor had communicated a new and difficult name"; and "Outdoor made Shirley Cothran the best-known . . . Miss America" definitely imply a causal interest and a causal interpretation of the data. The promotional material put out by the IOA gives the distinct impression that outdoor advertising was the causal agent that brought about the tenfold increase in public awareness of her name. Can you think of any competing explanation(s) for why the percentage of individuals familiar with Miss America's name went from 1.6 percent on the pretest to 16.3 percent on the post-test?

(Turn to page 212 for solution.)

81. Groups for Parents

Since we have young children who are occasionally less than perfect in their behavior, we are naturally attracted to studies that deal with behavior problems in children. Groups for Parents is a packaged method that offers parents both a support group of other parents and didactic information on an integrated humanistic behavior modification approach. The authors of "Groups for Parents" (along with a few others) published a study evaluating the effectiveness of their approach in "improving both general child behaviors [and] individually targeted ones." They also reported success in increasing the parents' rates of positive reinforcement along with the rates of compliance in their children.

The method of evaluation was quite simple. Thirteen groups of parents (a total of 277) met once a week for two and one-half hours over an eight week period. About one-half of the parents had been referred by various community agencies; the rest had heard about the program from friends or other informed sources. The pre- and post-test measures used included a problem behavior checklist, positive reinforcement rates (measured by the parents), compliance rates (also measured by the parents), and client satisfaction (self-report). Approximately two-thirds (180) of those enrolled completed the entire eight-week course.

The data analyses were equally straightforward, consisting of analyses of the differences between pre- and post-test means. Significant results that concern us were reported on the problem behavior checklist, reinforcement rates, and compliance rates. In addition, a very high rate of client satisfaction at the end of the study was reported. On the basis of these results, should we enroll in these courses the next time they are available?

(Turn to page 213 for solution.)

82. Unequal Egalitarianism?

Within the college and university setting, faculty vacancies are sometimes created when a department is given additional money to increase its staff size. When financial resources are in short supply, positions become open only when a current faculty member resigns to go elsewhere, retires, or dies. In any event, job descriptions of an available position typically conclude with a statement to the effect that, "Our institution is an equal opportunity employer; we do not discriminate on the basis of race, color, creed, national origin, age, or sex." The implication of such a statement, of course, is that the institution does not discriminate at the time people are considered for employment—*or after they are hired.*

Once faculty are employed, overt discrimination could manifest itself in several ways: in promotion and tenure decisions, in teaching and field service assignments, and in yearly salary increments. With respect to the consideration of raises, the following presents interesting statistics:

> Colleges are supposedly enlightened and egalitatian institutions. But, according to a recent report released by the Department of Health, Education and Welfare's National Center for Education Statistics, [NCES] the gap between salaries of full-time men and women college faculty members is widening.
>
> The report shows that the average salary of men on 9 and 10-month contracts rose 6.7% last year; in that same period the average salary for women rose 6.1%. "The dollar gap between men's and women's salaries is now greater than in 1974–75 at all faculty ranks," says Marie D. Eldridge, NCES administrator.*

Assuming that the NCES statistics are correct, it is quite legitimate to ask, why did male salaries increase 6.7 percent while female salaries increased only 6.1 percent, with this inequity existing at all faculty ranks? The implied answer contained within the article is that college administrators have continued to discriminate against female faculty members. Certainly this notion was conveyed by the title attached to the article ("Unequal Pay," which was probably interpreted by most readers as meaning "unfair pay") and by the phrasing of the first two sentences (*"supposedly* enlighted and egalitarian institutions. *But . . ."*).

Is the discrepancy between the average male and female raises—6.7 percent versus 6.1 percent—attributable to continued discrimination against females? Although the above article gives this impression, we feel that there is a very plausible alternative explanation.

(Turn to page 214 for solution.)

83. Adopting the Sick Role

In 1961, D. Mechanic and E.H. Volkard developed a measuring instrument that attempts to assess one's tendency to "adopt the sick role." This instrument is made up of three hypothetical situations of a medical nature, and to each situation the respondent indicates how likely it is that he or she would go to see a doctor. Each situation has four response alternatives (scored 0, 1, 2, and 3); hence, total scores on the instrument can range from 0 to 9, with a low score indicating a greater willingness to seek medical assistance.

People vary in the scores earned on this instrument, presumably indicating that they also vary in their tendency to adopt the sick role. Recently, a researcher hypothesized that first-borns (oldest children) would score lower as a group than siblings on the three-item questionnaire about seeking medical assistance. The rationale behind this hypothesis was quite simple, and it had to do with differential parenting. In the researcher's opinion, the first-born child has parents who are less knowledgeable about rearing children and more sensitive to, and nervous about, any abnormality in health (such as a slightly runny nose or a mild fever). Consequently, so the theory goes, the first-born is taken to the doctor more often than younger siblings and thereby encouraged in subtle ways "to expect and accept contact with medical authorities and subsequent entry into the role of being sick under conditions of minimal symptoms" (Franklin, p. 437).

To test his research hypothesis, the researcher administered the three-item questionnaire to 152 volunteers attending school at a midwestern university. The mean score among the first-born respondents was 5.37, while the mean score among the remaining subjects was 6.00. These means indicated that the first-borns would be more inclined to seek medical assistance for the three hypothetical problems on the questionnaire than would siblings. And a formal statistical analysis of the data showed that a significant difference existed between the two means. Hence, the researcher's hypothesis seemed to be supported.

The cause-and-effect relationship being investigated in this study can be summed up as follows: first-borns, because they are treated differently by their parents, are more inclined to want a medical opinion when a minimal symptom appears. We can't argue with the statistical results of the data analysis—first-borns *did* indicate a significantly greater tendency in the predicted direction. But we can (and should feel obligated to) question the causal end of this alleged relationship. Was it really differential parenting that brought about the different mean scores on the three-item questionnaire? Or might there be some other reason why the two groups had dissimilar tendencies to adopt the sick role?

(Turn to page 215 for solution.)

84. School Adjustment Problems

One of our local pediatricians firmly believes that children should not begin school until they are at least 7 years old. This conclusion is based on his experience with the hordes of 6-year-olds who pass through his office with emotional problems (mostly bedwetting) during the first two weeks of school each September. After his views received wide publicity in a newspaper article, we felt compelled to challenge him on methodological grounds. An earache suffered by one of our children soon gave us the opportunity to point out that, for one thing, the pediatrician only saw the children with severe problems (selection bias) and, that for another, there was no guarantee that school was causing the problems. But the likelihood that any change from an unstructured to a structured existence for the child could be the cause of the problems was lost on him.

The relationship between school adjustment problems and family size was the focus of a study that recently came to our attention. An attempt was made to determine whether children in large families differed from children in small families in either the number or kind of problems exhibited in elementary school. The participants were selected from a group of 1056 children who had been identified by their teachers during the 1972–73 school year as having adjustment problems. An initial screening resulted in the selection of 189 children from small families (one or two children) and 137 from large families (five or more children). Since these two groups were found to differ on five of six demographic variables (such as socioeconomic status, having repeated a grade, sex, geographic area of residence), the researchers made the groups more comparable by selectively dropping participants from 56 small families and 11 large families. The resulting subsamples were quite similar on all six variables.

Teacher ratings and an adjustment inventory were used to classify children according to the type of problem exhibited. Statistical analyses revealed that although both groups of children had about the same number of problems, there were significantly more behavior problems in those from small families, and significantly more learning problems in those from large families.

The researchers' explanation for these findings included the ability of parents in small families to spend more time with each child as well as the possibility of the child's having more study space and fewer distractions. They also speculated that parents in large families would place greater emphasis on family harmony and, thus, be less tolerant of disruptive behavior in their children.

Can you think of other possible causes for the group differences?

(Turn to page 216 for solution.)

85. Typed Papers and Grades

Most students like to receive high grades. Most parents like their children to receive high grades. Therefore, most students and parents would probably be willing to invest a modest amount of money in a service or commercial product if it were causally related to better grades. Some might even be willing to invest a great deal of money, depending upon how low one's grades have been in the past and how much value is attached to the higher grades that might be earned. Not surprisingly, college students have collectively paid thousands of dollars—possibly millions—to unethical businesses that write research or term papers for the students to turn in as their own work.

Grades are a powerful motivator. Realizing this, the people who market Smith-Corona typewriters have put out an advertisment in news magazines that implies that a student's grades are likely to go up if the student turns in research papers that are typed rather than handwritten. The ad is entitled "Students Who Type Usually Receive Better Grades," and the evidence comes from a national survey of 400 high school and college instructors. Each instructor was presented several statements, and the task was to choose one of five responses for each statement: agree strongly, agree somewhat, have no opinion, disagree somewhat, disagree strongly. Over 50 percent of the sample agreed (either strongly or somewhat) with the statement, "Students who type usually get better grades." The high school and college instructors also tended to agree that typing helps students improve their spelling, punctuation, and organization.

The clear implication of this advertisement is that students will raise their grades if their papers are typed. A definite cause-and-effect relationship is suggested: typed papers cause higher grades. If this message came through to high school and college students and their parents, we suspect that many people marched right out and bought a new typewriter, for surely the $200 investment would be worth it if the typewriter brought about better grades! However, we are not convinced that the survey evidence supports this cause-and-effect inference. In other words, we believe that there is a plausible rival hypothesis to explain why typed papers receive higher grades than papers that are not typed. Any ideas?

(Turn to page 217 for solution.)

86. Loneliness

Results of many health studies over an extended time period have indicated that disease strikes married people less often than those who are divorced, single, or widowed. For example, divorced individuals are twice as likely as married individuals to contract lung cancer or to suffer a stroke. Further, the coronary death rate is five times as high among widows between 25 and 34 than among married women of the same age.

But *why* are married people less likely to be the target of disease and physical impairment? According to a specialist in psychosomatic medicine, the answer is loneliness. In this doctor's theory, social isolation brings about a feeling of loneliness, and the feeling of loneliness then produces emotional deterioration followed by physical deterioration. Dr. James J. Lynch's theory and the reasoning behind it are contained in a recent book entitled *The Broken Heart: The Medical Consequences of Loneliness,* but we are concerned at the moment only with a summary of the doctor's evidence, which appeared in a national news magazine.

The article about loneliness reported several items that allegedly support the isolation-loneliness-death hypothesis. Among these pieces of evidence were the following: Irishmen living in Boston have a higher coronary death rate than their brothers who are still living in the "closely knit culture" of Ireland; Nevada—a "freewheeling singles-oriented state"—has a higher death rate from heart disease than neighboring Utah, which has close family ties brought about by the Mormon tradition; and there are only one-third as many heart attacks in Roseta, an Italian-American community in Pennsylvania, as there are in the surrounding towns which are more culturally diversified.

We certainly do not disparage Dr. Lynch's attempts to reduce the frequency of heart attack (or other disease) among the young, nor do we wish to down-play his attempts to eliminate the terrifying feeling of loneliness. But we do have some difficulty accepting the "evidence" reported above as proving his theory. Is it possible, we wonder, that the high rate of heart attacks among Boston Irishmen and Nevadans and people living near Roseta can be explained by something other than loneliness? In other words, are there any plausible rival hypotheses to account for the presumed cause-and-effect relationship identified by Dr. Lynch?

(Turn to page 217 for solution.)

87. Sesame Street

Most studies involving television seem to focus on its potential to do harm (see Problem 99), particularly where children are concerned. Even those parents who use television as a babysitter try to monitor the shows their children watch. Given the powerful social force that television has become in the last 20 years, it was inevitable that an attempt would be made to use television for the social good. In particular, Sesame Street served as the focus of a wide-ranging series of studies of its effectiveness in preparing children for entrance into the first grade.

In 1970 and 1971, the Educational Testing Service undertook an evaluation of Sesame Street that included both disadvantaged children (in Boston, Durham, N.C., Winston-Salem, N.C., Los Angeles, Phoenix, and rural California) and advantaged children (in Philadelphia). Since it was initially thought that a show on a noncommercial station would not be very popular, periodic visits (weekly in 1970, monthly in 1971) were made to randomly selected families in each city. During these visits, verbal encouragement and Children's Television Workshop buttons and pennants were dispensed in order to promote viewing of Sesame Street.

Using the analysis of covariance in conjunction with a pretest–post-test design, the researchers reported differences between those who watched and those who didn't on a series of cognitive and attitudinal measures. In addition, encouragement was found to increase viewing. The researchers concluded that all preschoolers benefited from watching Sesame Street. Although advantaged children watched more often, the researchers did not find differential effects of encouragement as a consquence of the race, sex, IQ level, age or social class of the child.

Did we spend our money wisely on the televisions we bought so that our children could watch Sesame Street in color?

(Turn to page 218 for solution.)

88. Financial Woes of Colleges and Universities

As individuals, most of us don't seem to be doing as well financially as we would like. The cost of living goes up too fast, our salaries don't, and our investments never seem to turn into the pot of gold at the end of the rainbow. But we're not the only ones who are having trouble. Many businesses are in financial difficulty, and we just heard about one in San Francisco which had to shut down because of lack of profit. Even the banks are complaining because they can't, in at least some states, charge a higher interest rate on the money they lend.

Recently, colleges and universities have announced that they, too, are having difficulty making ends meet. As a result, students frequently find that their tuition and other fees are being increased. However, a recent editorial challenged this claim on the part of educational administrators. The complete editorial went as follows:

> Educators talk dismally about the financial woes of colleges and universities, but the latest figures on the subject seem not to support their complaints.
>
> The National Center for Educational Statistics in Washington reports the number of colleges, universities, and branch campuses increased from 3055 to 3075 during the school year just ended. The number of public colleges increased by 13. The number of private colleges—many of which are said to be struggling—increased by seven. Which seems to show that higher education may not be quite as anemic as we've been led to believe.*

The implication in this editorial is that the financial condition of colleges and universities has an effect upon the number of institutions that fold or start up anew. Furthermore, the editorial seems to argue that by looking at changes in the effect variable (number of institutions) we can determine what is happening with respect to the causal variable (financial condition of the institutions). Do you agree with this implied cause-and-effect interpretation of the statistics? Or might there be some alternative explanation(s)?

(Turn to page 219 for solution.)

136

89. Moral Development Across the Life Span

The increasing emphasis on examining developmental processes across the life span has led to many studies in cognitive as well as noncognitive areas. One recent study by D. Bielby and D. Papalia examined development along a dimension that is linked to both cognitive processes and moral development as delineated by Lawrence Kohlberg's stage theory.[1] In that case individuals supposedly progress through stages and do not regress to an earlier stage. The researchers decided to see whether the relationship of moral development to age followed this pattern.

The 72 middle-class participants in the study were sampled from each of six age groups (six males and six females from each) and asked to respond to stories presenting moral dilemmas. The age groups (I to VI) used were 10–14, 15–19, 20–34, 35–49, 50–64, and over 65 years of age. Those in poor health or under custodial care were excluded from the over-65 group. Since an age-by-sex analysis of variance showed no main effect of sex and no interaction of sex with age, subsequent analyses did not include sex as a factor. One of the results, based on a one-way analysis of variance of the six age groups, was significant. Follow-up tests were then used to compare the specific mean levels of moral development for the six age groups. Significant differences were found between each of the age groups III ($\overline{X} = 3.75$), IV ($\overline{X} = 3.96$), and V ($\overline{X} = 3.58$), and age groups I ($\overline{X} = 2.50$) and II ($\overline{X} = 2.50$); as well as between IV and VI ($\overline{X} = 2.92$). Further analysis of these means showed the existence of a nonlinear relationship between age and moral development. (Additional analyses were performed on other variables, but those are not relevant to the present discussion.)

Essentially, the authors concluded that there were age differences and that age and moral development were nonlinearly related.[2] Although they did acknowledge the problems of using cross-sectional methodology (confounding age and cohort) to look at a longitudinal question (see Problem 55) we still consider this to be a serious objection to this study. Are there other objections that might be raised?

(Turn to page 220 for solution.)

[1] A stage theory states that as we develop we move through a series of stages or developmental steps. According to stage theorists, it is not possible to skip a stage.

[2] A linear relationship would have indicated that moral development showed a constant increase (or decrease) with each succeeding year. A nonlinear relationship indicates that changes in moral development are not constant and that these changes may be both positive and negative (that is, they may increase and then decrease).

90. A Hypothetical Basketball Game

Since so many Americans are sports enthusiasts—either as participants or observers—we have attempted to include in this book a few rival hypotheses from the field of athletics. As you will recall, we have previously exposed you to problems dealing with golf balls (an experiment to see which brand could be driven the furthest off the tee) and major league pitchers (a comparison of winning records to establish who was the "best of the best"). Now, let us turn out attention to a winter sport—basketball.

Recently, a highly respected and nationally read newspaper carried a short article about the success of some first-year members of the National Basketball Association (NBA). Entitled "Pro Basketball's New Hotshots."the complete article was as follows:

> The National Basketball Association has cornered a healthy share of rookie marksmen this season. Tops among these first-year men are New Jersey's Bernard King (24.2 points a game) and Phoenix's Walter Davis (22.6), both of whom appear ahead of established stars such as Julius Erving, George McGinnis, Jo Jo White, and Earl Monroe in the scoring department.
>
> Behind King and Davis, the next most productive rookies are Milwaukee's Marques Johnson (18.6), Kansas City's Otis Birdsong (15.5), and LA's Norm Nixon (12.4). Add their averages together and you have a high-powered unit hitting at 93.3 points a clip, or exactly 20 more points per game than Portland's starting line-up.*

This article was written halfway through the 1977–78 season, and at this time the Portland Trailblazers had the best won-loss record in professional basketball. They were the only team in the NBA that had won more than 50 percent of its games on the road, and on their home court the Trailblazers were undefeated. Their record of 33 wins against only five losses was by far the best in the NBA, and even by midseason they had built up a seemingly insurmountable lead within their division.

This information about the fantastic success of the Portland Trailblazers is needed in order to grasp fully the impact of the newspaper article's last sentence. The five rookies mentioned in the article had a cumulative scoring average of 20 points per game *more* than the cumulative average of Portland's starting line-up. And as we interpret that final sentence, it seems as if the

---

author is suggesting that the data on scoring averages could be used to predict who would win the basketball game if the five NBA rookies played against the five Portland starters. From the last sentence, we suspect that many readers would infer not only that the five rookies would win such a game (were it to be played), but also that the final score would be, from the perspective of basketball, quite lopsided.

We do not doubt for a minute that the five rookies named in the short article are truly outstanding athletes. And we suspect that some of them—or maybe even all of them—will achieve the status of the established stars who were also named in the article. However, we're not sure whether or not we should accept the implication that the rookies would win the hypothetical game brought to mind by the comparison of the two cumulative averages. Can you think of any alternative explanation(s) for why there is a 20-point differential between these two averages, other than the implied explanation that the rookies are better players and would win?

(Turn to page 220 for solution.)

91. Do Snowstorms Increase Absenteeism?

We moved from the Chicago area to Tennessee in 1970 and found that in the south a snowstorm is labeled "massive" any time there is more than 4 inches of accumulation. Since 1 inch is enough to close the schools for three days, you can imagine the impact of larger amounts. In Chicago, however, we had many opportunities to watch snow accumulate by the foot rather than by the inch. Thus, it was only natural for us to be attracted by a study that used a Chicago snowstorm as the independent variable in a study of work attitudes and attendance among managerial employees.

About a year before the snowstorm, the researcher had collected data on work attitudes among 3010 workers in the national headquarters building of a large corporation. The participants had responded to the questionnaire anonymously, but the 27 functional groupings in which each belonged could be identified. Additional data were available on 340 similar employees in the firm's New York headquarters. The onset of a "severe and unexpected" snowstorm in Chicago prompted the collection of data in order to see if work-related attitudes were able to predict job attendance in the face of adversity. The New York sample was used to provide a baseline for any correlations found in the Chicago sample.

The researcher found that various job-related attitudes *were* predictive of differential rates of job attendance across the 27 groups in Chicago. There were no significant relationships found in New York. After assuming that it was up to the individual to make an attempt to get to work, he concluded that attitudes could be used to predict job-related behavior in cases where the behavior was clearly under the employee's control. We wonder whether the researcher's conclusion is warranted?

(Turn to page 222 for solution.)

92. Acting Like an "A" Student

Several years ago, an author by the name of Nelson N. Foote suggested that an individual's socially defined identity may explain why the individual is or is not motivated to perform a task. In a different arena, a social scientist named Stanley Milgram has collected evidence to show that people tend to comply with an authority figure's request, even if the request involves doing something that normally wouldn't be done. Putting these two thoughts together, a researcher recently hypothesized that students would be motivated to excel on a test if they were told by an authority figure to assume the role of someone who is typically thought of as having a highly motivated social identity.

The subjects were 39 college freshmen enrolled in an introductory social psychology class. The experiment was conducted as an in-class activity, with mandatory participation. The procedures were as follows:

> Subjects were randomly assigned to an experimental (n = 19) and a control group (n = 20). The former was read the following instructions: "This is an experiment to determine the effect of a lecture that is read. At the end of the lecture there will be a test. This test will not in any way affect your grade. The lecture is on youth and society; please try to listen as if you were an 'A' student." The control group was given the exact same directions excluding, ". . . as if you were an 'A' student." After these directions were completed, subjects were read, in a monotone voice, an intentionally dull lecture lasting approximately 15 minutes. At the completion of the lecture, a brief multiple-choice exam was administered.*

After the multiple-choice exam had been scored, the resulting data were subjected to a formal statistical test. This statistical comparsion verified the research hypothesis, for the experimental group achieved significantly higher scores than the controls. The researcher ended the published paper with this statement: "Since both groups were asked specifically to listen to the directions, but only the experimental group was asked to assume a motivated social identity, it is concluded that these data suggest support for Foote's (1951) theory as well as extending Milgram's (1963) work on compliance."

A cause-and-effect relationship was investigated and allegedly identified in this experiment with the 39 college freshmen. The effect variable was the earned score on the multiple-choice exam, and the causal variable presumably was the presence or absence of the phrase "as if you were an 'A' student" at the end of the directions. Can you think of any alternative explanation(s) to account for the significant difference between the performances of the two groups on the exam other than this slight difference in what the subjects were told prior to the dull lecture? Or do you accept the conclusions as valid?

(Turn to page 222 for solution.)

*Reprinted with permission from John B. Cullen, "Social Identity and Motivation." *Psychological Reports,* 1973, *33,* p. 338.

93. Wrong Number

One of our least favorite events is to have the phone ring at an inopportune moment, especially when we find that the caller has dialed a wrong number. Occasionally such callers infuriate us even more by hanging up with little indication of remorse on their part—undoubtedly auguring the ultimate decline of modern society. Nonetheless, we wonder what our reaction would have been as participants in the following study.

In an attempt to study the helping behavior of blacks and whites towards members of their own and the other race, two psychologists called people in Brooklyn and said that the caller's car had broken down on the highway and that the caller ("George Williams") was attempting to reach his garage mechanic with his only dime. The recipient of the call was then asked to call the mechanic and report the caller's location. Helping was defined as the participant's actually calling the mechanic's number (really the number of a research team member). The caller was either obviously white (Brooklyn accent) or obviously black (Southern black accent). Five hundred forty participants were categorized as black on the basis of their having common black last names, as well as on the basis of the neighborhood in which they lived. Five hundred sixty-nine whites were classified only on the basis of geographic location. Voice characteristics were used to confirm the other selection criteria, and fewer than 1 percent were eliminated on this basis.

Statistical analysis showed a significant relationship between the race of the participant and the race of the caller in helping, with blacks helping both blacks and whites equally, and whites helping whites more often than helping blacks. Although other analyses were also performed, this one is sufficient for our purposes. The general conclusion of the researchers was that "race of the victim (inferred from his dialect) has a small but detectable influence on helping behavior" (Gaertuer and Bickman, p. 169).

Given that the researchers recognized socioeconomic differences between the two samples as possibly confounding their results, are there other plausible rival hypotheses to be considered?

(Turn to page 223 for solution.)

94. Are Reading Problems Inherited?

Learning to read the English language is undoubtedly one of the most difficult tasks we face in our lives. It is, therefore, more surprising that most children manage to learn than it is to find that there are some children of normal intelligence who have great difficulty in this area. Much interest has been shown in the latter group recently, and rather than classifying them under "miscellaneous," the current trend has been to use the term "learning disabled (LD)." Unfortunately, there has been little distinction between the two labels as used by those most concerned. A friend of ours who heads a major LD research and service project goes so far as to use the term "school-certified learning disability," since he is not convinced that LD is other than in the mind of the beholder. Nonetheless, one recent study made an attempt to differentiate subgroups among young LD children with reading problems.

In this study, 63 children (7 to 12 years old) who had been referred to LD clinics constituted the target group, while 23 children with grade-level or above reading ability were used as controls. All target children were at least one year behind in reading, had IQs above 90, and showed no visual or hearing losses. The target children were then classified as familial (56 percent) or nonfamilial (31 percent), based on the presence or absence of a severe reading problem in a family member (sibling, parent, uncle, aunt, or grandparent).[1] Twenty behaviors were then rated for each child, followed by testing on their ability to pay attention to an auditory stimulus and measurement on skin conductance. Nineteen of the 20 items on the Behavior Rating Scale showed differences (t-tests) between the LD and control groups. Within the LD group, familials and nonfamilials differed on seven items. The auditory vigilance tasks yielded significant LD/control differences but failed to show subgroup differences. Finally, the skin conductance measure showed subgroup differences but no LD/control differences. Among other conclusions, the authors found the familial/nonfamilial distinction useful and recommended further study in this area.

If you were doing research in this area, would you use this distinction?

(Turn to page 223 for solution.)

---

[1] Not everyone was classified, for reasons such as adoption.

95. Ethics of Random Assignment

Given the number of diet books that are available in our local bookstores, as well as the number of advertisements for diet foods of one sort or another that assault us through the media, it is easy to forget that undernourishment in children exists in the United States. A few years ago, two researchers at the University of Colorado Medical Center set out to find the effects of severe undernourishment on the early development of children. They also examined the social factors that were correlated with undernourishment.

Although by now you have probably picked up enough knowledge about experimental design to realize that the ideal study in this area would include the random assignment of children to a nourished or undernourished group, ethical considerations obviously preclude such an approach. Needless to say, the authors of the Colorado study took a slightly different approach. They compared 19 children (under 1 year of age) who had been hospitalized for undernutrition with 19 control children from a similar socioeconomic group who were matched with the target group on birth date, weight, sex, and race. Although the control group averaged 14 days older and 27 g less than the target group, neither difference was statistically significant. Among the measures used over at least a two-year follow-up period were medical histories, physical examinations, heights, weights, and head circumferences. In addition, developmental quotients and maternal intelligence were also assessed. Other measures were taken on the families, but these are not of methodological concern. In making most comparisons t-tests were used.

The results of the physical measures indicated a negative correlation between physical development and duration of undernourishment. This same trend was found in the area of mental development, with language development yielding the most striking results. Finally, parental separation, alcohol-related problems, and number of siblings under 2 years of age were among the social factors associated with undernourishment of the child.

The authors suggested that "undernourishment in the first year of life is detrimental to later development." They go on to speculate that repopularizing breast feeding might well go a long way towards solving this serious social problem. What conclusions should you draw?

(Turn to page 224 for solution.)

96. Japanese Women and Business Profits

At one time or another, most American adults purchase stock in a business organization. Before you decide which company to invest in, it is obviously a good idea for you (or your stock broker) to examine closely the current and past financial standing of the company. By considering such things as gross earnings, diversification, and recent record of dividend payments, it is possible to make a somewhat scientific assessment of the advisability of purchasing the stock.

But what about examining the company's history on employing women? Not many investors pay much attention to this variable. However, a recent Japanese study suggests that maybe we all should start doing this—assuming that United States and Japanese businesses are similar. If they are not similar, the study at least says something about Japan to the foreign investors. Here's a summary of the study as reported in a national magazine of the United States.

> Nomura Securities has made a study of Japanese stock companies which proves that Japan's most successful firms employ an above-average number of women. According to the study, 25 highly profitable companies employ at least 40% women. The 48 companies at the bottom of the Tokyo stock market employ only 17% women. Nomura's simple explanation: Japanese women are paid about 40% less than Japanese men.*

In the United States, such blatant sexual discrimination in terms of salaries would lead quickly to legal suits, and consequently we do not believe that the results of the Japanese study should be generalized to our country. But suppose you (or someone else) were interested in Japan—not from the standpoint of buying stocks, but rather from the standpoint of writing a paper about why certain Japanese companies earn more profit than others. Here, a cause-and-effect relationship would be a primary interest, with differential profits being the effect and lots of possible things being the causes.

The Nomura study summarized above gives the clear impression that one of the variables that causes high or low profits is the percentage of women employed. Since women are paid less, the company that employs women rather than men pays out less in salaries and therefore ends up with a larger amount in the profit column at the end of the fiscal year. This line of reasoning suggests that it would not make any difference which sex were hired if women had to be paid as much as men for the same type of work. This, as we see it, is the clear message of the Nomura study's conclusion. Women are nice to have around as employees because they can be paid less.

*Copyright 1977 by Parade Publications, Inc. Courtesy of Lloyd Shearer.

We want you to imagine that you just became chairman of the board of one of those 25 high-profit Japanese companies that have been employing 40 percent women. We also want you to suppose that a new Japanese law is going into effect stating that women must be paid salaries equal to those earned by men for doing the same type of work. Under these conditions, would you want to hire (for new positions or vacant old positions) more men than women, more women than men, or an equal number of men and women? The new law requiring equal pay for both sexes would take care of Nomura's simple explanation, since the new law would imply that sex doesn't matter any more. This would mean that the three possible answers to our question are equally good from the standpoint of end-of-year profit. Do you agree?

(Turn to page 224 for solution.)

97. Stop Signs

According to recent projections, the population of the United States is continuing to shift from the North and the East to the South and the West. Not surprisingly, many cities have been unable to cope with rapid growth when sustained over a long period of time. For example, inadequate planning has led to overwhelming traffic problems in both large and small towns throughout the South. Although our home state of Tennessee is not immune, we realized how well off we were after reading the next study about driving behavior in Nigeria.

According to the researcher, most Nigerians consider traffic accidents to be the work of vengeful gods. As a consequence, charms and amulets are used as the chief means of avoiding automotive mishaps and maintaining the physical well-being of the drivers. Since accidents were increasing every year, a study was undertaken to determine whether Nigerian driving behavior could be modified by external cues. In this case two different types of stop signs were used—one sign "written on the ground" and one "visibly exhibited standard stop sign."

The first set of observations were of 440 drivers, of whom 270 did and 170 did not use a turn signal upon encountering the stop sign written on the ground. After three standard signs were installed at the same intersection, further data collection showed 524 drivers indicating turns and 247 not doing so. Statistical analysis revealed a significant positive effect for the standard signs.

If you were in Nigeria, would you feel safer as you approached an intersection with standard stop signs?

(Turn to page 225 for solution.)

98. A Student-Designed Graduate-Level Course in Business

In the 1960s studies conducted in business and industrial settings showed that employee performance and satisfaction could be increased by giving the employees a greater voice in the decision-making process. More recently, a researcher at the University of Pittsburgh wondered whether this technique of "participative management," if used in the college classroom, would lead students to rate their courses more highly in terms of how much they felt they learned and instructional effectiveness. To answer this question, an experiment was conducted at Pittsburgh's Graduate School of Business.

The subjects in this experiment were the 99 students enrolled in four sections of a required graduate-level course. All four sections were taught by the same instructor, two in the daytime session of the 1972–73 winter quarter and two in the evening session of the same year's spring term. Since two sections of the course were available each of these terms, it would have been possible to assign one section each term to the two instructional strategies (treatments) that the researcher wanted to compare. However, there was a concern that such an arrangement would permit students in the two treatment conditions to interact and thus "discover differences between the instructor's methods for each class" (Kilmann, p. 337). To avoid this potential problem, both classes offered in the winter quarter were assigned to the experimental treatment, while both of the classes in the spring quarter were assigned to the control condition.

In the two experimental classes, the students were told on the first day of class about some basic constraints in the course. But within these broad limits, the students were given a voice in the "classroom issues" that they considered important and were thereby allowed, in the words of the researcher, to determine the "basic design" of their course. Unfortunately, the technical report of this study did not go into any detail whatsoever as to what these classroom issues were or what the basic design ended up being like. Our guess is, however, that the experimental students decided how to utilize class time, what the out-of-class assignments would be, how many tests to have, and maybe even what type of test questions (essay, true-false, or multiple-choice) would be administered.

When the spring quarter arrived, the students who enrolled in the two sections of this same business course were given absolutely no opportunity to help set up the course. Instead, the instructor dictated the course design. The requirements and procedures utilized in these two sections were identical to those developed by the experimental students during the previous quarter. By holding the course design constant across the two academic terms, the researcher was clearly trying to set up his experiment so that any observed differences between the two treatment conditions could be attributed to the issue of who set up the course, not what was in it.

One week before the end of each term, the students enrolled in the business course were asked to fill out a teacher and course evaluation form. This evaluation form, administered by a student representative (not the course instructor), contained 22 items dealing with the two outcome variables of interest: student perception of instructional effectiveness and of how much had been learned. Each item resembled a multiple-choice test question, with the five possible answers varying in point value from 1 to 5, depending upon how satisfied the respondent was. After these forms had been filled out by all four sections of the business class, the experimental groups' average response to each item was compared to the average rating from the control group subjects.

As it turned out, the experimental subjects provided higher ratings than the control subjects on 21 of the 22 items. And on eight of these items, the difference between the two average ratings was statistically significant.[1] On only one item, dealing with the contributions of lectures to learning, did the control subjects supply a higher average rating than the experimental subjects. But this difference was not significant. Taken together, this set of results was interpreted as providing support for the hypothesis that participative management would cause business students to react more favorably to their courses—if not to all their courses, then at least to the one required graduate-level course associated with this study.

Are you willing to accept the researcher's conclusion? Was the real causal variable of this study simply the presence or absence of student involvement in the classroom issues and course design? If your answer to these two questions is no, then what rival hypotheses do you feel can adequately account for the obtained statistical results?

(Turn to page 225 for solution.)

---

[1] These items dealt with the extent to which the instructor increased student interest; presented worthwhile material; encouraged initiative; stimulated thinking; showed respect for student opinions; was sensitive to student differences; the extent to which class discussion contributed to learning; and the extent to which the respondent would recommend the course as an elective.

99. The Effects of Television

Along with most parents, we have a difficult time keeping the television watching of our children under control. After the daily watching time exceeds four hours, there is a crackdown; for example, our current restriction is ten hours a week. Of course, as time passes we expect the television to ease back into prominence, quickly followed by another attempt on our part to control its encroachment on the lives of our children. Rightly or wrongly, our attitudes are based on the assumption that almost any other activity is better than sitting passively in front of the television.

Although the study we are about to report does not involve children, it does hit close to home. In this study, three researchers investigated the effects of television on agression in "normal adult males"; that is, people similar to the stalwart authors of this book. The initial pool of participants was comprised of 725 volunteer couples (husbands and wives). Through the use of matching *and* randomization, 260 of these couples were assigned to one of five groups differing in the content of the television shows watched. These groups were prosocial or "helpful" (51 couples), violent or "hurtful" (45 couples), neutral (19 couples), mixed (both prosocial and violent; 25 couples), and natural (43 couples). Content was controlled through the use of cable television. Although the researchers state that the groups were similar on pretest measures, no explanation was given for either the unequal sample sizes or the reduction of the number of couples from 260 to 183.

In all of the groups, the husband was the target of the study, with the wife being used as a "knowledgeable and sensitized observer" of the husband's behavior. The husbands were *not* told they were being watched more closely than usual by their wives. The wives, in order to stay more objective, pledged not to watch the shows with their husbands. All viewing took place in four-hour blocks during a seven-day period.

The two findings we wish to discuss were that the prosocial group showed a decrease and the violent group an increase in aggressive mood, and that group differences in "hurtful behavior" as reported by the wives was related to group membership in the expected direction. The researchers concluded that "ordinary dramatized television entertainment produced meaningful and measurable psychosocial effects on normal adult males" (Loye *et al.,* p. 215).

Should our children be restricting our television viewing to shows with prosocial content?

(Turn to page 226 for solution.)

100. Exercise, Heart Attacks, and Buses

As you have probably noticed, more and more people each month are beginning to engage in regular exercise programs. In particular, the numbers of tennis players and joggers have increased by leaps and bounds during the last few years. In general, many people seem to be spending more time as participants in sports activities and less time simply watching professional and collegiate athletes on television.

Although some people have begun to integrate exercise into their daily activities solely because it is now the fashionable thing to do, most individuals are probably motivated by the research evidence that has come out of the exercise physiology laboratory. This research has shown that a regular program of exercise is likely to bring about, among other things, better cardiovascular efficiency, lower blood pressure, increased coronary circulation, and loss of unnecessary body weight. These effects of exercise usually make the individual feel better, in part because there is the belief and hope that these outcomes will reduce the risk of heart attack and thereby increase longevity.

It is easy for researchers to show a cause-and-effect relationship between exercise and variables (such as weight loss) that can be measured immediately after the exercise period. But establishing a definite causal relationship between exercise and heart disease is much more difficult. Several attempts have been made to document the possible connection between these two variables, but in most instances a scientific examination of all relevant data reveals facts that make the proof less than absolute. And sometimes, as you will now see, it is the researcher himself who points out an aspect of a study that calls for a different interpretation of the original results.

In 1953, Dr. J. N. Morris of London Hospital's Medical Research Council conducted what has turned into a classic study of exercise and heart disease. His subjects were the drivers and conductors of London's double-decker buses, and he found that the drivers had one and one-half times the incidence of heart disease as the conductors and twice the coronary death rate. Since the drivers simply sat in their seats all day while the conductors ran up and down the stairs to collect the fares, Dr. Morris asserted that exercise was the causal variable that brought about the observed health differences between the two groups.

Three years later, Dr. Morris published a second paper in which he pointed out an alternative explanation for his original results. Following his first paper, Dr. Morris had examined the records maintained on the uniforms issued to the bus drivers and conductors, and he discovered that upon beginning their respective jobs, drivers were consistently given larger uniforms than conductors. Thus, in his 1956 paper entitled "The Epidemiology of

Uniforms," Dr. Morris pointed out that the differential amount of exercise associated with the two jobs may not have been the cause of the differential rates of heart disease and coronary death. Instead, it could have been that the heavier, more coronary-prone men chose the job wherein one could sit while working, whereas the thinner men (who were less coronary-prone to begin with) chose to become conductors.

We wish to commend Dr. Morris for pointing out, in his second paper, a rival hypothesis that was associated with his initial interpretation of the 1953 data. It is difficult for most researchers to see that an alternative explanation exists for their presumed cause-and-effect discovery, but to announce such an insight publicly requires an incredible amount of professional self-confidence. Nevertheless, we feel there may be yet *another* rival hypothesis or two. Can you think of any other reason(s) for the differential rates of heart problems between the drivers and conductors, other than the original claim (exercise) or the revised explanation (initial health condition)?

(Turn to page 227 for solution.)

SOLUTIONS

1. The Common Denominator

While the local newspaper states that age is the "common denominator," there are several rival hypotheses to account for why these four elections turned out the way they did. It is quite possible that the four winning candidates spent much more money for advertising in the local newspapers, on the radio, and on television. Or possibly each winner had a larger group of more energetic campaign workers. Perhaps the winners were more conservative in political ideology than the losers. Perhaps they were taller. The simple fact is that the four winners, as a group, probably had numerous things in common that separated them from the four unsuccessful candidates.

In order for Mill's method of agreement to work, the various occurrences of the phenomenon (here, winning any of the four elections) must have *one and only one* circumstance in common. If there is more than just one common denominator, then there is no logical way to claim that one of them was the causal agent that brought about the observed phenomenon. However, upon seeing a common denominator, people often jump to the conclusion that they have identified *the* cause, when in fact they have overlooked other commonalities that might also be the explanation. For this reason, G. C. Helmstadter has warned that Mill's canons of logic (including the method of agreement) "must not be applied automatically or carelessly. Without thoughtful attention to the requirements of each approach, inappropriate conclusions are all too easy to come by."[1]

2. Sensory Deprivation

As we see it, a very plausible rival hypothesis connected with this investigation is "experimental mortality." This term does not mean that anyone died (although we are somewhat surprised that 21 of the experimental subjects actually made it through the week-long experiment without any auditory or visual stimulation along the way). Instead, mortality refers to the fact that unequal subject dropout may make it look as if a treatment worked when it really didn't.

Whereas almost all of the control subjects remained in this study for the full seven-day period, barely half of the subjects in the experiment condition stuck it out for the full week. If the ones who dropped out were similar to those who remained, then the results may be valid. But we doubt that they were similar. It is our guess that the 21 subjects who stayed in the study had, on the average, a superior ability to think creatively in the absence of external stimuli. And maybe this type of individual is better able to concentrate on simple tasks, such as hearing a beep, than people who need lots of stimuli—possibly *loud* stimuli—to keep them going.

The main question here, of course, is whether the data for the experimental group would have remained the same if the 19 dropouts had not voluntarily left the study but had stayed in their cubicles and taken the various vigilance tests. We're not sure of the answer. But that's just the problem with mortality (or any other plausible rival hypothesis)—we're left in a quandary as to the proper conclusions to draw. The only

---

[1] G. C. Helmstadter. *Research Concepts in Human Behavior.* (New York: Appleton-Century-Crofts, 1970), p.95.

thing we're fairly confident of is the fact that the researchers *anticipated* differential mortality. Note that twice as many subjects were assigned at the outset to the experimental group as to the control group (40 versus 20.) A better study, in our opinion, would be one set up so as to decrease or even eliminate this confounding variable, rather than simply anticipating it.

3. A Painful Look At Hunger

Although Cannon and Washburn's theory of hunger is no longer with us, we do have as a legacy two recurrent methodological problems. First, as we should all now be aware, correlation does not imply causation. In this case it is not clear whether stomach contractions cause hunger, hunger causes stomach contractions, or some third variable causes both.

A second problem involves the researchers' failure to distinguish between stomach contractions' being necessary to create the subjective feeling of hunger, and their merely being sufficient to produce hunger pangs. In other words, this is the difference between producing a symptom associated with the construct of hunger and producing hunger itself.

A dietary hint—eating slowly allows time for the chemical content of the blood to change enough to "fool" the hypothalamus into stopping the eating response. Eat quickly and you will eat more!

4. Beer: Brand Differences In Image

As far as we can tell, there are *no* rival hypotheses associated with this research investigation. We can think of no plausible explanation to account for the significant differences among the three groups besides the study's manipulated independent variable—the seventh item on the shopping list.[1]

Because the conclusions from this study appear to be based upon a respectable research design and methodology, we feel that you are justified in passing it along to your acquaintances who put their untouched intellectual magazines out on the coffee table to impress their guests. Maybe they can start putting certain brands of beer in their refrigerators to impress even further the people who come to visit.[2]

---

[1] Recall that we gave you a warning in the Foreword that some of our rival hypotheses would have no discernible design or logical problem. Be on guard for a few more of these sound studies. But in most of what you encounter as you read about additional research endeavors or other less formal types of alleged cause-and-effect relationships, there *will* be blatant or subtle rival hypotheses that we feel are plausible.

[2] However, a few of our beer-drinking friends have really raised their eyebrows in surprise that Pabst was the "high-image beer." On our campuses, it evidently would not fare so well—in spite of the blue ribbon.

5. Seasonal Variation In Personality

The main problem associated with this study is the phenomenon of testing. When tested twice, examinees tend to do better the second time, even if there is absolutely no feedback concerning performance on the first test or any activities between the two tests that would logically cause the second set of scores to be different from the first set. This phenomenon has been observed when there is a long interval between the two testings, when alternate forms of the measuring instrument are used (instead of the exact same instrument), and also when the assessment being made deals with personality rather than with factual knowledge. With personality testing, people tend to show up as "more normal" at the second measurement.

In the study on the MMPI, the examinees' average spring scores were significantly lower—indicating better adjustment—on three of the eight clinical scales. On the other five scales, the spring mean was also lower than the winter mean (but not significantly lower.) And we suggest that these differences between the two sets of scores may be a function of the phenomenon of testing rather than a function of seasonal variations.

We wonder what would have happened if the order of the tests had been reversed, with the April test done first, followed eight months later by the December testing. Isn't it possible, due to the phenomenon of testing, that the examinees would score significantly better in December? And wouldn't these results make it look as if springtime has some sinister effect on mental health?

To control for the phenomenon of testing in studies such as this, we suggest that the pool of available examinees be subdivided, with different subgroups tested in different sequences. In this particular study, half of the college students could have been tested (as they were) first in December and then again in April, while the other half could have been tested first in April and then a second time the following December. Such a plan for data collection would mean that it would require a year longer to collect the data than was actually the case, but the results would be more interpretable. For if the first subgroup did better in April and the second subgroup performed better in December, the notion of seasonal variations might not appear too plausible— while the phenomenon of testing would. On the other hand, if both groups were to perform significantly higher (or lower) in April, then more confidence could be placed in causes other than the phenomenon of testing.

Our next concern with this study has to do with the fact that seasonal fluctuations cannot be identified accurately by taking measurements within a one-year period. Instead, data must be collected over several years, with the same pattern of results becoming evident each year, before one can claim that seasonal variations have been discovered. In any given season of any given year, unusual events may cause people to perform differently when tested from the way they normally do at that time of year. For example, think about the MMPI study and assume that there really is a seasonal effect, with people feeling better in the spring. Isn't it possible that one year, people might show up as feeling worse in the spring because they have just seen a national figure assassinated, the stock market drop substantially, a television exposé on poor teaching in the public schools, reports of a mass murder, or a review of a new book that advocates revealing (rather than concealing) personal problems? We are not exactly sure how these five events would affect *your* score on the MMPI—or ours—but we are confident that you see our point: exceptions can sometimes occur in the general trend of any seasonal variation. And unless we have data coming from several consecutive cycles, it is impossible to know whether data at any given point in time are typical of what usually happens at that time.

Finally, we want you to assume for a moment that neither of our first two rival hypotheses were operating. In other words, suppose that the students' scores on the second testing (in the spring) were known not to be affected by the phenomenon of testing or some atypical historical event. Would this mean that spring-related events—warm weather, new flowers, the sound of birds singing, and the like—cause people to feel less troubled than they do during the winter? When we put this question to a couple of our doctoral students, they quickly responded, "No." They defended their position by pointing out that many college students feel good between April and June because they have deliberately set up less rigorous course schedules for their spring terms and can see that summer vacation is just around the corner. As we think back to our own undergraduate days, we clearly recall feeling good in the spring for both of these reasons.

6. Mind Your Ms and Qs

After seeing the results of the Pepsi experiment, the Coca-Cola Company conducted the exact same study, except that Coke was put in *both* glasses. Participants preferred the letter "M" over the letter "Q," thus creating the plausible rival hypothesis that letter preference rather than taste preference could easily have accounted for the original results. Since no statistical tests are given, another plausible rival hypothesis is that of instability; that is, we don't know whether "more than half" means 51 percent or 99 percent or how much confidence we should place in the finding. Flipping a coin 100 times is almost sure to result in either heads or tails occurring more than half the time.

Strangest of all was the fact that the same design error of using one letter exclusively for each brand was repeated in a second study conducted by Pepsi. In a feeble attempt to demonstrate that their initial results were not biased by the use of an "M" or a "Q", Pepsi duplicated their first study, this time using an "L" for Pepsi and an "S" for Coke! Clearly, these three studies indicate that there is sometimes more in advertisements than meets the eye (or the taste buds).

7. Immediate Feedback

The major problem with this study concerns the activities that took place after the answer sheets associated with each quiz were collected. As you will recall, at this point 18 of the 35 quiz questions were shown again while the instructor pointed out which answer was correct and why. These were the "feedback" questions, and students performed better on them at the time of the final than on the group of "nonfeedback" questions.

Unfortunately, there are two ways in which the feedback and nonfeedback questions differed from one another in this study. The first and most important way is in terms of feedback, that is, knowledge of the correct answer. This was the variable that the researchers wanted to manipulate in the study, and as such it constitutes the treatment variable. However, the two groups of questions also differed in terms of a second variable—how long the subjects got to see the questions before the final examination. While the nonfeedback questions were seen once (for 45 seconds during the quiz), the feedback questions were seen twice (once during the quiz and once during the postquiz feedback session.)

We are not certain what specific effects might be associated with seeing a question twice, rather than once, prior to a final exam. However, it seems as if one could argue that this difference between the two types of items (and not feedback) might have been the true cause for the differential examinee performance on the final. We wonder why the study wasn't set up to control this variable. This could have been accomplished easily by presenting feedback for only a random half of the items that were reshown immediately after the quiz papers had been collected.

A second problem of this study is associated with the person used to provide the feedback. This person was the course instructor! Hence, the course instructor knew which quiz items were classified in the feedback and nonfeedback categories and could conceivably have consciously or unconsciously dealt with the feedback questions in lectures and individual discussions with students between the quiz and the final. In other words, the instructor may have helped the students prepare for the feedback part of the final more than the nonfeedback part. We feel that it would have been better to have someone other than the instructor present the feedback after each quiz, and also to have the instructor kept in the dark about which quiz questions were being put in the feedback and nonfeedback categories.

8. Wilt Thou Take This Plant...

The fact that one of the two coleus plants wilted after one and one-half weeks could have been caused by an initial difference between the quality or healthiness of the two plants. Even if the two plants had been grown under the same auditory conditions (either 100 decibels of noise or no noise,) it is altogether possible that one of them would have wilted after a 10-day period. This is certainly the case in our vegetable and flower gardens each year, when we put in several new plants that all look similar at planting and that receive equal soil, sun, and water treatment; in spite of these similarities, some of the plants grow while others do not.

Randomization—flipping a coin, pulling names out of a hat, or using a table of random numbers—is an important characteristic of good experimental design. But if there are potential differences in the units of experimental material (in this experiment, the coleus plants,) then randomization has a much better chance of equalizing the comparison groups prior to treatment application if the sample sizes are large. With small samples, randomly assigning the units of experimental material to the treatment and control conditions may not work very well. And when there is only one unit of material to be assigned to each of the comparison groups, randomization cannot achieve its desired goal at all. If the two coleus plants did, in fact, differ in healthiness, then the chances are even that the healthier plant would be assigned to the quiet growing condition. Had there been four plants, the chance that the two healthiest would end up being assigned to the quiet conditions would be only 1 out of 4. Had there been 20 plants, the chance that the ten healthiest would end up in the nonnoise group would become 1 out of 1024. Within the context of any single experiment, randomization is much more likely to equalize the comparison groups on all variables except the manipulated treatment variable when the sample sizes are large.

Let us attempt to make our point about the coleus plant experiment by using an analogous hypothetical study about children and language development. Suppose we wanted to see whether first-born children begin to talk earlier (or later) than second-born children within the same family. Since the sex of a child is determined pretty much at random, we might think that sex, as an extraneous variable, is controlled in our comparison of first-born and second-born children. But what if the study involves only a single family that has just two children? And what if the first child is a boy and the second a girl (or vice versa?) Has the randomization of sex to the two "comparison groups" really equalized the two groups on sex, thereby permitting any observed difference to be attributed to order of birth?

9. Imaginary Friends

We believe that there are two possible flaws in this study. First, the use of retrospective self-report seems suspect. We find it plausible that the researchers have measured willingness to report an imaginary companion, or even simply memory, rather than the actual presence of such a companion. It would be easy enough to argue that those who had been punished for telling their parents about their imaginary friends would be less likely to remember them. Or, if they did remember, they would be less likely to tell others about them. Perhaps this parental punishment is the causal variable in the present study.

Our second concern is that, in the absence of experimental manipulation, the researchers have engaged in the logical fallacy of *post hoc ergo propter hoc* ("after this, therefore because of this.") That is, the fact that current creativity is mildly correlated with the reporting of past imaginary companions in no way allows the conclusion that a causal linkage exists. It is as if we were to argue that if most heroin addicts drink less milk as children than do nonaddicts, lack of milk drinking causes heroin addiction (when it would be much more likely that some third variable, such as poverty, led to both.)

Despite the temptation, we will refrain from putting any of our editorial friends on the spot.

10. Pre- and Postreward Delay

As we see it, there are no plausible rival hypotheses associated with this study. Because of the tight scientific controls imposed by the researcher (randomization of subjects to conditions, a counterbalanced order of putting the 60 rats through each trial, collection of data by electronic machines rather than by humans,) we feel relatively comfortable in accepting the cause-and-effect conclusions.

With respect to the dispute between the contiguity and reinforcement theories, we would recommend (as does the original researcher) that the results not be interpreted as conclusive proof that one theory is right and the other wrong. Were this experiment to be replicated with a more homogeneous set of rats (or simply a larger number of them), one might obtain a significant difference between the no-delay and postreward contiguity position. However, the potentially heterogeneous nature of the rats used in this study and the relatively small sample size do *not* constitute alternative explanations for the significant findings that were obtained.

11. Air Force Officer School and Dogmatism

Of the five subgroups involved in this study, the ones having higher pretest means ended up with means that were still above average, but not so far above average as they were at the start. On the other hand, the groups that began with lower pretest means finished the 14-week program with means that were still below average, but they weren't nearly so low as they had been to begin with. Although such an outcome tends to make it look as if the SOS program had a moderating effect on the subjects' dogmatism levels, the researcher felt that a plausible rival hypothesis might be the phenomenon of regression toward the mean. We agree.

Whenever a group of people is measured twice, the ones with extremely high (or low) scores on the first measurement will still tend to have high (or low) scores on the second measurement, but they will be less extreme than they were initially. In other words, extreme scorers (based on the first measurement) will "regress" toward the overall mean of the second set of measurements. This phenomenon will be observed no matter how close in time the two measurement periods are, even when the intervening activities have no influence at all on the measured characteristic. The only time regression will not exist is when the correlation between the two sets of measures is $+1.00$ (which isn't very often!). To the degree that this correlation moves from $+1.00$ toward zero, the amount of regression increases to the point, at $r=0$, where the high and low scorers (based on the first measurement) tend to perform equally well on the second measurement.[1]

The observed correlation between the Rokeach pretest and post-test dogmatism scores for the 250 subjects in this particular study was $+.71$. Based on this correlation, the researcher made a prediction about how high each of the five subgroups would have scored on the post-test, assuming that the SOS training program had absolutely no impact on the participant's dogmatism levels and that any pre-post changes were caused entirely by the phenomenon of regression. These "estimated" post-test means for the five subgroups turned out to be almost identical to the actual post-test means (which are presented on page 20) with the biggest discrepancy being only 1.34 points. Given the amazingly close similarity between the actual and estimated post-test means, the researcher concluded that the "significant interaction is most likely due to regression to the mean" (Gleason, p. 38.)

---

[1] This brief discussion of statistical regression may leave the impression that people only regress in one direction—from the first to the second measurement. In actuality, regression operates in both directions. Hence, high scorers on a post-test tend to regress toward the mean of the pretest.

Before leaving this topic, let us attempt to make one final point about the regression phenomenon. This point concerns the fact that regression exists in terms of subgroup means, not in terms of individual scores. A subgroup of high scorers on the pretest will have, on the post-test, a subgroup mean that is less extreme, but some of the members of this subgroup, as individuals, will probably end up with post-test scores that are equal to (or even higher than) their pretest scores. Were this *not* the case, the dispersion among the post-test scores would have to be less than the dispersion among the pretest scores. But regression has no effect whatsoever on the variability of the scores in the full group at either measurement period, as evidenced by pretest and post-test standard deviations in the SOS study of 22.41 and 22.50, respectively.

12. A Penny for Your Thoughts

Although the researchers were creative enough to include personality factors in their model, they neglected the possibility that those same factors would also confound their study. That is, it seems plausible to us that the participant's color preferences have been confounded with their classification as either "competitive" or "cooperative." In other words, those whose favorite color is red are classified as more competitive than those who favor black. Thus, had the reward schedule been switched so that red was "cooperative" instead of black, the same differences would have appeared, but in the opposite direction!

13. Pretest Sensitization

Ironically, this study, which attempted to investigate a possible threat to *external* validity, presents us with results that are uninterpretable because of a very plausible threat to *internal* validity! In other words, we cannot accept the researcher's claim that the phenomenon of pretest sensitization has been identified, because there is a clear rival hypothesis to account for the significant finding on the Mt Scale data. As we see it, the phenomenon of testing could have brought about the observed results.

When people are tested twice, they tend to do better on the second testing, even if there is no feedback provided following the first testing or any intervening activity that might improve performance. When the tests administered deal with achievement, the phenomenon of testing causes people to appear as if they know more on the second test; when the group is measured by a personality instrument, the examinees tend to look better adjusted at the second testing. This phenomenon has been found to exist when alternate forms of the measuring device are used at the two testings, and even when the two measurements periods are close enough in time to prevent any intervening activities from explaining the change in performance.

In the counseling study, one of the groups was pretested, counseled, and then post-tested; the other group was simply counseled and then post-tested. We contend that the significant difference in adjustment on the post-test may be entirely attributable to testing, and not at all brought about by pretest sensitization. Or the significant finding may be partially attributable to each of the phenomena, with both operating in concert. Or maybe the results are a function of pretest sensitization by itself, as the researchers imply. The nature of the two-group design of this investigation leaves us in doubt as to which interpretation is correct, and we wonder why the Solomon four-group design (specifically set up to isolate the pretest sensitization phenomenon, if it exists) was not employed in the Massachusetts investigation.

Before concluding, we would like to point out that the phenomena of testing and test reactivity would have drastically different implications for the way we interpret this particular counseling study. If the significant difference between the two groups was actually due to pretest sensitization, then we could assume that the treatment (counseling) used by the researchers would be just as effective for your clients, so long as you administer pretests prior to administering the treatment (and also presuming that other barriers to external validity do not exist.) But if the post-test difference between the two groups was caused by testing, then we are left with absolutely no idea as to the worth of the treatment. Perhaps you could "improve" your client's level of adjustment by measuring them twice with no counseling at all between the two testings.

14. Brainstorming

A possible problem in this study is related to the point in time at which the four-man groups were run through the experiment. Recall that the regular brainstorming sessions were run during the first half of the academic term, whereas the synectics sessions were run during the last half of the term. Couldn't someone argue that the synectics groups generated more ideas on the nine problems because they were working on these problems during the last half of the academic term, rather than because of a beneficial effect associated with the role playing?

Since some of the nine problems that the subjects had to work on were somewhat unusual (like devising brand names for a bra), it seems possible that a report of the experiment might have been transmitted from those students who participated early in the term to those students who were scheduled to participate later on. And if this sort of discussion did take place, then the second set of subjects might well be expected to generate more ideas because they had been "primed" for the task. And who were the second set of subjects? The ones who got the synectics treatment!

But even if there had been no discussion of the experiment at any time during the academic term, we still feel as though the groups being run through the experiment late in the term might be expected to perform better. Students get to know one another as an academic term progresses. And as people become better acquainted, they become less inhibited. Therefore, students who were participating in this study earlier in the term may have internally screened ideas for one or more of the problems because they seemed stupid or risqué, while students participating later in the term may have been completely open with their ideas.

If the synectics groups had been run through the experiment during the first half of the term, would the results have been the same? We don't know. And because of our inability to answer this question, the variable of the time of the term must stand as a plausible rival hypothesis.

15. Model Drinking

At first glance it seems as though science has discovered the B-girl—one who sits with customers and drinks watered down drinks at a rapid rate. However, the findings of this study cannot be dismissed so lightly. The design of the study should pose questions other than those already raised by the researchers. For example, how can they get by with only three subjects? Did a reputable journal really publish this study? Why weren't statistical tests used? These were some of the questions asked by one of our graduate students when she brought this study to our attention. In response to these questions, we explained that the *Journal of Applied Behavior Analysis* (JABA) was probably the most prestigious journal dealing with what are known as single-subject designs, that it was indeed reputable, and that this was typical in that no statistical tests were used to analyze the data. While we might cavil at some aspects of the study—the use of volunteers, the order of conditions, the variable number of sessions used for each participant, the lack of statistical analyses—it is important to realize that the basic research paradigm is used widely in clinical research in psychology and special education.[1]

Although we respect the philosophical position of those who use single-subject reversal designs, we do have a concern about the drinking study we have considered. The researchers found that the subject's drinking level increased and decreased in relation to manipulated changes in the model's consumption level, and they concluded that the model's drinking behavior brought about (caused) changes in the subject's rate of drinking. Maybe their interpretation was right. But as we see it maybe the subjects altered their drinking behavior in response to the two new confederates who sat down at the bar during the B and C phases of the study. Since the drinking rate of the model was the opposite of that of the other two confederates, and since these two activities were completely confounded, we think it is impossible to tell exactly who had a causal effect on the subject's behavior.

16. Required Textbooks in College Courses: Are They Needed?

In our role as faculty members, we spend a great deal of time trying to select the best possible text to go along with each of the courses we teach. And although we do not check up on our students to make sure that they buy the required texts that we adopt, we do strongly encourage them to purchase—and read—the assigned material. Our feeling is that students are better off (at least at the undergraduate level) if they have a required text in their courses. Hence, our bias is to feel good about the results associated with the Marquette study. Nevertheless, we *do* think that there are a couple of very plausible rival hypotheses.

---

[1] The position of those who use this paradigm is simply that individual differences should be considered important in a group design. Although adherents often project a certain religious fervor, it is well worth reading Murray Sidman's *Tactics of Scientific Research* (1960), which still serves as the most comprehensive statement on this position. It provides an important counterpoint to the more common group design approach.

For one thing, we wonder whether the instructor (who taught the two sections of the statistics course) and the researcher were the same person. If this were the case, then we would argue that the researcher's hunch—that is, his hoped-for results—may have caused him to teach differently in 1975 from the way he did in 1974. We suspect that the researcher desired his data to show that the textbook did have a beneficial effect; this desire may have caused him to try a little harder with the 1975 students.

But what if the statistics instructor was not the same person as the researcher, and what if the teacher was kept blind to the treatments associated with the two classes? We would still argue that the results must be accepted with a grain of salt, for teaching experience is clearly confounded with treatments. The instructor may have done a better job teaching the 1975 group, the class using the required text, simply because he had been through the material once before during the fall of 1974. This rival hypothesis would be especially plausible if the instructor began teaching the psychological statistics course for the first time during the 1974–1975 school year.

Finally, we wonder whether the two groups of students came to the course quizzes with equal opportunities to do well, apart from any difference that may have been introduced by the formal treatments. We suspect that the ability levels of the two groups really were about the same. However, isn't it possible, even likely, that some of the test questions appearing on the 1974 quizzes made their way back to student-operated test files? And isn't it possible that some of the sophomores in 1975 came to the quiz sessions with a fairly good idea of the questions that might be asked? If the students at Marquette are at all similar to those who attended our undergraduate institutions, the answer to both of these questions is yes.

Before closing, we should probably say something about the fact that 17 of the original 68 students were not included in the final data analysis because they withdrew from the course. It is possible, we must admit, that this mortality rate, (nine from the 1974 class, eight from the other) could have been the cause of the observed group differences. While it is possible, we consider this rival hypothesis to be somewhat implausible—at least in comparison with the other problems that we have mentioned.

17. Claustrophobia

The first (and more obvious) rival hypothesis is related to handling the puppies. The members of the all-at-once group were handled once, as they were put into the small box at the start of their continuous ten-minute exposure to the traumatic environment. Members of the small-dose group were handled every time they went in or out of the box; that is, at the beginning and end of each of their ten minute alternating minutes in the cramped quarters. Hence, the small-dose group was handled 19 times more often than the all-at-once group. This handling, even if it didn't involve prolonged cuddling or petting, could very well have lessened the trauma of the situation for the small-dose group, and this handling may have been the true reason for the difference between the two groups in terms of yelping behavior.

A second (and less obvious) problem of this study is related to the fact that the puppies in the two groups were in the experiment for different lengths of time: Ten minutes for the all-at-once group versus 19 minutes for the small-dose group. It is possible that puppies (or any other subjects) experience more trauma when initially put into an experimental setting than after they've been there a while. Apart from the handling variable discussed earlier, the small-dose group had nine extra minutes to adapt to the experimental room, lights, odors, and people. Maybe the members of both groups emitted most of their yelps during the first eight or nine minutes that they were in the *experiment* but stopped yelping thereafter. If this had been the case, the average number of yelps for the all-at-once group would have been greater than for the small-dose group, simply because the latter group was measured only during the odd-numbered minutes (first, third, and so on.) If the all-at-once group had been left in the box for 20 minutes (rather than ten) and if both groups had been measured during the odd-numbered minutes of the experiment, it is possible that the frequency of yelping behavior would have been the same in both groups. Such a result would imply that exposing subjects to a traumatic environment in small doses does not lessen the trauma that is experienced.

18. Hypnosis and Biofeedback

The researchers' answer to our query at the end of the study's description is given in the title used for this write-up, namely, that auditory feedback and hypnosis were confounded during all of the experimental sessions. We believe that there were additional problems. For one thing, it seems likely that previous experience with meditation could easily have provided the training necessary, since the relaxation sought in meditation changes the peripheral skin temperature. Also, we find it reasonable to believe that the purposely biased sampling procedure used in this study may have come up with participants who already possessed the ability being tested.

It seems as though the author's goal was to create optimum conditions for establishing that it was possible to control peripheral skin temperature. In this they succeeded. It remains for future researchers to seek out the processes involved.

19. How to Stop Smoking

In our judgment, the first question that you should have had in relation to this experiment concerns the validity of the data. All of the data were self-reported, and it is not at all inconceivable that the subject was actually doing more smoking between sessions than she admitted. Especially if the subject sensed that the researchers were highly expectant of positive results, she might have felt embarrassed about acknowledging the true extent of her smoking behavior. Hence, you probably wondered if the good-looking data were an accurate reflection of what was actually going on.

The researchers were also aware of the potential problem with their data. Fortunately, they attempted to eliminate the rival hypothesis through a reliability check on the subject's reports of smoking behavior. At five times during the follow-up phase of the study, one of the subject's fellow workers was contacted and asked whether she had seen the subject smoking. This report from the co-worker corresponded with the self-reported data from the subject, thereby reducing the plausibility of this first rival hypothesis. (Of course, it is possible that both the co-worker and the subject supplied false information to the researchers, but we consider this to be extremely implausible.)

The second rival hypothesis that we suspect you thought of is *history*—defined in general as something outside the experimental setting that takes place concurrently with the treatment and makes an ineffective (or detrimental) treatment appear to work. In this particular study, the subject may have voluntarily sought out, between the baseline and follow-up periods, some other sort of treatment that had the potential to help her decrease her smoking behavior. And possibly it was this something else that actually brought about the dramatic change in the daily number of cigarettes smoked. Maybe the subject saw a television documentary about smoking and cancer; maybe she read a book on how to quit; maybe she attended a group session for nicotine addicts who desired to kick the habit. Or, the historical event may have been something that the subject did not seek out but rather had thrust upon her, such as the discovery that a close friend or relative who smoked heavily had lung cancer and a short time to live.

Despite the fact that the rival hypothesis of history does constitute a possible explanation as to why the subject stopped smoking, we consider it to be relatively implausible as an alternative explanation. Although it is possible that the subject, while receiving the experimental treatment, sought out or had thrust upon her some activity or event that had a more potent effect on her smoking behavior, it seems to us that such a coincidence is somewhat remote. Furthermore, we are confident that the vomiting (which took place during the litter-handling activities) was completely unrelated to any historical event—rather, it was clearly brought about by the awful experience of putting one's arms up to the elbows into 5 pounds of cigarette filth.

We acknowledge the possibility that something other than the aversive treatment *may* have been the true cause of the change in smoking behavior. But we do not consider such a possibility to be very probable. Hence, we accept the researchers' claim for the implied cause-and-effect relationship. Of course, the same treatment procedures might not work as well (or at all) for a new subject.[1] But they *did* appear to work amazingly well for the 27-year-old female volunteer in this investigation.

20. Class Attendance Plus Study Versus Study Versus Nothing

If the researchers really wanted to see whether the addition of the in-class activities could improve performance beyond that obtainable through an out-of-class reading of Mager's text, then the follow-up analysis should have involved a direct comparison of the first two treatment conditions. In other words, if this were the goal (as the researchers said it was), then the performance of subgroups I and IV should have been contrasted with the performance of subgroups II and V. Subjects receiving the third treatment (that is, subgroups III and VI) should not have been involved in this comparison of the follow-up analysis.

The mean score for subjects receiving both the text and instruction was 25.06. The follow-up analysis should have compared this mean against 21.66, the mean for subjects who read the text but didn't receive the in-class training. However, by the

---

[1] The issue of subject generalization is a portion of external validity, a topic with which we are not concerning ourselves in this book.

researchers' "pooling" of the data from subjects in the second and third treatment conditions, 25.06 was actually compared against a point halfway between 21.66 and 13.41. Hence, the pooling of the data from Subgroups II, III, V, and VI stacked the deck in favor of the researchers, giving a signficant difference in the follow-up comparison. Possibly, 25.06 and 21.66 are not far enough apart to be called significantly different; were this to be the case, the major conclusion drawn by the researchers would be unjustified in light of their own data.

21. Charity Begins at Home

In our description of the study we did not exclude the possibility that the order of presentation of the information might have had an influence. For example, perhaps information about the percentage of neighbors donating was always the last information given the participant. In that case, the percentage information might have had an effect only because it was the last information heard by the potential donor. Fortunately, the researchers eliminated this flaw by constructing all possible sequences of verbal information so as to control for any effects of order of presentation.

Our main objection to this study is that the first author was apparently the only experimenter used in the study. Since we assume that she was aware of the study's purpose, it seems plausible that her tone of voice, the time spent with each participant, and assorted other behaviors might have been the cause of differential giving across experimental conditions.

Since we are unable to eliminate a possible experimenter effect, we do not feel confident in recommending the researchers' findings to you in the event you do any charitable solicitation.

22. Professional Socialization in Nursing School

To some extent, we suspect that the phenomenon of professional socialization *does* exist. (In fact, we wish that more of our students would begin to see things our way!) Nevertheless, there are two aspects of this study that make us unwilling to accept the conclusions drawn from the statistical results. One of our concerns is about the way the instrument was built—specifically, the way the item analysis was used to select the final 60 items. Our other concern has to do with the cross-sectional nature of the research design.

Regarding the issue of item analysis, we feel that the researchers began with a hypothesis and then proceeded to use their hypothesis as the criterion in deciding which items to retain or throw out. Little wonder that the data ended up supporting the original hypothesis! In case our point isn't immediately obvious, let us review and comment more fully on the item analysis portion of this study.

The 112-item scale was initially administered to 488 students. This group was randomly split, and then data from the first half were used to decide, for each item, whether it should be retained or deleted. And as you recall, 60 items were retained.

However, the criterion for keeping an item was "a significant shift toward agreement with faculty perception of the trait's importance as the students rose in class rank." Hence, the 60 items selected for the final form of the scale were items that were known to support the professional-socialization hypothesis. Consequently, the fact that the other half of the subject pool provided data in support of the hypothesis is not too startling an outcome. It's exactly what we would expect!

Our point is simply this: the instrument was built in such a way as to guarantee support of the hypothesis. Such a technique for building a measuring instrument is all right as long as the initial hypothesis is not really a hypothesis but rather a known fact. But in this study, the notion of professional socialization seems to be regarded as a hypothesis since previous research on the topic had not always shown the freshman-to-senior shift toward faculty views, and one of this study's *findings* was that "students adopt faculty professional views in direct relation to length of training."

Our second concern has to do with the cross-sectional nature of the research design. None of the nursing students were measured successively as they progressed through their undergraduate programs. Instead, groups of freshmen, sophomores, juniors, and seniors were all measured at the same point in time. Based upon the responses provided by these four groups, a developmental trend was inferred from the data by the researchers. Even if the instrument used to collect the data had been built so as to test (rather than confirm) the hypothesis of professional socialization, we question whether the cross-sectional design would have allowed the goals of the study to be achieved.

If the statistical finding of class differences in amount of agreement with faculty were valid, it would not necessarily mean that students become more similar to faculty in their views as they spend more time in training. Possibly attrition is the explanation. Maybe none of the students are changing their views at all over time, but the students who don't see eye-to-eye with the faculty are tending to leave the program as time goes on. If some of these students left during each of the three final years of the under-graduate program, results similar to those collected by the researchers would be obtained.

Or possibly the apparent trend in changing attitudes is simply an artifact of per-manent cohort (age group) differences. The students who were freshmen at the time of this study, if given the new scale during each of their next three years in school, might respond in the same way as they did when freshmen. Maybe that group of students represents a "new breed" of nursing students (as compared with the older upperclass-men who went through high school earlier,) and possibly they will not move at all closer to the views of the faculty. In fact, maybe over their four-year program they will develop more self-confidence and security to disagree and therefore end up with lower scores as seniors than they did as freshmen!

Before concluding our analysis of this study, we should point out one final flaw in the data collection and analysis portions of the investigation. The full 112-item scale was administered to all 488 students, but only the 60 "good" items were scored for the 244 students who were in the second half of the subject pool. Previous research using other measuring instruments has shown conclusively that people will often respond dif-ferently to a subset of items when that subset appears by itself rather than as a part of a longer instrument. Therefore, we're not at all sure whether new nursing students would respond similarly to the students used in this investigation, even if our theories about attrition and cohort differences are inaccurate.

23. Counseling Practicum

There are, in our judgment, two alternative explanations that might account for the changes that took place between the pretest and post-test responses to the OCI. One of these has to do with nonpracticum experiences taking place during the eight-week duration of the study, while the other has to do with the phenomenon of testing.

The subjects of this study spent four half-days a week in a public school throughout the eight-week practicum. Unfortunately, we have no idea what these individuals were doing during the rest of the time. Were they taking a half-time load of graduate courses? Or working on their master's theses? Or working at a part-time job to support themselves and their families? Since we don't know what the 36 subjects were doing besides the practicum during the eight-week period, it seems quite possible that the significant changes on 11 of the 12 OCI scales were brought about by some activity *other than* the field-based practicum. Perhaps during the eight weeks many of the subjects read a book about counseling. And possibly it was this activity (or something like it, say a television program on school counselors) that served as the true cause of the observed pre-post changes.[1]

The second rival hypothesis associated with this study is related to the phenomenon of testing. Research has shown that people often perform differently on the second administration of a test from the way they did when it was initially administered, even if there is no training or feedback provided after the first testing. This phenomenon of doing better the second time has been found to operate on both achievement tests (where people appear to be smarter on the second test) and personality instruments (where they appear to be "more normal" the second time tested.) And the phenomenon can exist even if two different versions (parallel forms) of the test are used at the two testings.

Because of the proven phenomenon of testing, we wonder whether the 36 subjects in this study might have changed from pre to post even if 'there had been nothing happening during the eight weeks to prompt a change—in other words, no practicum, no television shows, no courses, no work on the master's thesis, nothing. And the fact that significant changes were found on 11 of the 12 OCI scales (rather than just one or two) does not make this suggested rival hypothesis any less plausible. It is possible that a group of graduate students might show similar changes if tested on each side of an eight-week interval with nothing in between (or, more realistically, if tested on two consecutive days.)

In summary, the results of this study would be more believable if a control group had been built into the investigation. If this had been done properly, the two suggested rival hypotheses discussed above could be ruled out entirely.

---

[1] Some authors use the term "history" to describe the possibility that some other activity, besides the presumed causal activity, that takes place *between* the pretest and post-test may actually be the true cause of observed changes.

24. Where the Wild Goose Goes

This study is a classic in ethology and, as far as we can tell, quite well done. In other words, we can't think of any rival hypotheses for why the two groups of birds showed an escape reaction only to the long-necked silhouette.

However, an ethologist colleague reports that one somewhat jocular criticism of the study has been that the study only showed that geese were alarmed when they saw other geese flying backwards. We consider this to be an implausible rival hypothesis.

25. Crashing into the Rear of a Taxi

Although we *do* feel as if there are three possible problems associated with this study, we must first commend the researcher for devoting his time, energy, and money to such an important topic of investigation. And as we stated earlier, the concern for accident prevention (rather than simply accident survival) gets our full endorsement. In this regard, we wish that more people in the area of traffic safety would follow Dr. Voevodsky's lead.

We have, however, three questions about this study that cause us to wonder whether the new warning light was truly as effective as the data seem to indicate. First of all, we are somewhat concerned about the way in which the drivers were assigned to the two groups of cabs. Were the drivers of the equipped cabs equal in driving ability to the drivers of the unequipped cabs? We are not sure. The person who made the assignments was the dispatcher, and we have been told that he disregarded the expressed preferences of the drivers. But did the dispatcher have any preferences? Assuming that he knew which cabs had the warning lights mounted on the back, isn't it possible that —in an attempt to help the researcher obtain good results—he assigned the better drivers to the equipped cabs and also assigned the equipped cabs (with the better drivers) to the areas of San Francisco that are less accident-prone? In our opinion, the best procedure would have been to assign the drivers at random to the two groups of cabs.

The second question we have concerns the researcher's logic about cautiousness on the part of the drivers. Isn't it possible, we ask, for a driver to be more cautious in terms of potential accidents involving following cars, yet equally (or less) cautious in terms of cars that are in front? The data presented by the researcher indicate that drivers of the equipped cabs had about the same number of front-end accidents as the drivers in the unequipped cabs.

Nevertheless, we are simply unwilling to accept this "evidence" as proof that the drivers were not more careful when driving equipped cabs. (And most assuredly, we reject the notion that rear-end collisions are due to the driver of the second car. Maybe they are in a legal sense but we've seen some brake-happy drivers who definitely cause people to hit their rears.)

Finally, we are a bit concerned about the validity of the data. Did the drivers report to the cab company all of the accidents they had? Isn't it possible that when in the safety-equipped car, the cab drivers were more reluctant to report that they had been involved in any traffic mishaps? If we were driving a cab that had extra equipment on it specifically designed to prevent accidents, the occurrence of an accident might make us feel as if we had driven less carefully than we could have. And to keep our jobs, we might be tempted simply not to report the accident, especially if it was a minor one. Surely one's job is considered to be more important than someone else's research.

26. Angina Pectoris

By considering these two research studies together, you will recall that there were three groups. The patients in all three groups were operated on, but only two of the groups actually received the treatment of bilateral ligation of the internal mammary arteries. Since there was equal improvement among the three groups in terms of relief from angina pectoris, we agree that the surgical technique of ligation appears to be unnecessary. However, we cannot accept the claim made by the authors of the second study that the likely cause of the postoperative improvement was psychological expectancy.

Yes, the three groups were the same in that all patients were operated on and probably did expect the surgery to work. But they could very well have been the same with respect to other variables (besides this psychological expectancy of improvement) that changed in all three groups concurrently with the operations. In particular, we wonder whether the patients might have voluntarily altered, on account of the operation, their diets and/or patterns of rest and exercise.

Angina pectoris is known to be associated with heart attacks. So is the condition of being overweight, a characteristic of most Americans. We all know that our hearts would be better off if we would lose some unneeded poundage, but most of us continue to eat with somewhat reckless abandon. (It is the same thing with people who know that smoking is bad for one's health but light up several times each day anyway.) But what if it became obvious that a heart attack was just around the corner and that an operation was necessary to help avoid the impending disaster? Wouldn't that cause the individual to take seriously the advice about weight loss? As we see it, the answer is yes.

Maybe the equal improvement among the three groups *was* brought about by psychological expectancy. We really don't know for sure. Nevertheless, it seems to us that an equally plausible explanation for the clinical improvement is a change in diet and rest and exercise among the patients in all three groups, a change brought about by the operation. By eating better food, by getting more adequate rest, by establishing a pattern of appropriate exercise—by doing these things for the first time right before or right after the operation, the patients, we believe, may have caused the angina pectoris to go away because of what they put into or did with their bodies rather than because of what the operation created (in terms of expectancy) in their heads.

27. Psychotherapy Revisited

The rival hypothesis illustrated in this study is that of experimental mortality; that is, ten of the original participants had been lost to the researchers by the time follow-up data were collected. It is possible that their reason for dropping out was related to the goals of the study. We don't know for certain in which direction (if at all) the results are biased, but we do have a recommendation for researchers who find themselves in a similar situation. We suggest that they report descriptive data on those who have dropped out. In the absence of such data, we are unable to reject experimental mortality as a biasing factor.

28. Passing Out

The two explanations provided for the differential rates of fainting both have to do with what males bring to the dentist office versus what females bring. The breakfast explanation says that men faint more because they bring stomachs that are not filled up as much as they should be. And the exposure explanation suggests that the male rate is higher because men bring with them an inadequate ability to deal with pain since they have not dealt very much with their childrens' pain. Either of these explanations may be partially or totally true. However, we would like to suggest that the fainting rate among males may be higher because of differences that exist *after* the patient gets into the office.

As we all know, an old stereotype has it that males constitute the stronger sex. Isn't it possible that the treatment given to males by dentists and their assistants differs from the treatment given to females? For example, isn't it possible that male patients are encouraged to have their dental work done without novocaine or gas (with the dentist saying, "It's just a little cavity"), whereas females are encouraged to take some sort of pain preventer–because the dentist perceives the female to be weaker and less able to withstand pain? Or, possibly there is more of a tendency to hide the novocaine needles from a female patient than from a male, again because the dentist or assistant presumes that women are fragile and do not like to see that long needle that looks big enough for horses. And when extracting teeth or drilling for cavities, does the male patient receive the same treatment as a female with an identical problem?

Besides this concern about the treatment given to the patient once in the dentist's chair, we must also raise the question whether males and females tend to visit the dentist at different times of the day. We suspect that males, because of work schedules, are normally given appointments early in the morning, late in the afternoon, or over the lunch hour. If it were true that people tend to faint more often at certain times of the day than others, then maybe the differential sex rates have nothing whatsoever to do with what the patients bring with them to the dental office or how they are treated once there; possibly the different rates are purely attributable to differences in when the visit is made.

29. Nine Out of Ten Better in One-Fourth the Time

Dartmouth College—being in the Ivy League along with Harvard, Princeton, Yale, and other prestigious institutions—has exceedingly high entrance requirements. Students have to be very bright to be admitted, and they would probably earn a far higher percentile rank (on the average) than students at other institutions, regardless of the instructional method! We also believe that it is quite possible that students at Dartmouth or other highly selective institutions might perform better after one year than students elsewhere do at the end of four—even though the teaching approach at all institutions was the same.

We must reiterate that our concern is not with the intensive language model—it sounds excellent. Instead, our concern is with the implied cause-and-effect relationship between the teaching model and the test results. Did Rassias' model cause Dartmouth students to perform better, in one-fourth the time, than 90 percent of the students in the other 199 colleges? We believe the admissions office at Dartmouth deserves a little credit for these results too!

30. Flexible Time

We wish that the researchers had told us a little more about the "experimentally designated" control groups. Was random assignment used, or were employees allowed to volunteer for one group or the other? Without additional information, we cannot rule out the possibility of a selection bias.

The rival hypothesis of history must also be considered. For example, the researchers indicated that certain "organizational changes" took place during the study that might have caused differences in the third group. Since differences were only found in the third and fourth groups where one-group pretest–post-test designs were used, these differences may have reflected seasonal variation in the work load of the groups. They may simply have had more work to do at the end of the study than at the beginning.

Finally, we don't know whether the employees were told that they were participating in an experiment. If they were then it is possible for any significant effects to be attributed to their knowing about the purpose of the study rather than to the experimental manipulation

We cannot accept any conclusion from this study—too much information is missing.

31. Fore!

Every golf ball has identification information on it, usually on two sides of the ball, and it's almost impossible to place a ball on a tee such that the label is hidden from view. (We've tried to do this, since we get distracted by almost anything when on the first tee—blades of grass, noises, and the ball's label.) Hence, our first rival hypothesis is that the 51 golfers knew which brand of ball they were hitting. Surely they caught on to the fact that the experiment dealt with a comparison of different balls, and it's possible that they also became knowledgeable about who was conducting the study—Rawlings. If the golfers had this information, then every time they placed the Toney Penna DB on the tee they may very well have been motivated (possibly unconsciously) to hit Rawlings' ball a little harder. We doubt that the Nationwide Consumers Testing Institute allowed the 51 golfers to know who manufactured the different balls they were hitting or who was footing the bill for the experiment, but we're not told this in the ad. Hence it must stand as an alternative explanation for the obtained results.

The second, more plausible rival hypothesis has to do with the known fact that any golfer varies in the distance he or she hits the ball and the absence of any statement about the six balls being compared with an inferential statistical test. The average distances for the six balls are very similar (ranging from 244 to 255,) and it seems to us that the Toney Penna DB could have ended up on the top of the list *simply by chance*—that is, simply because the golfers (at least some of them) had a better-than-average swing when the Rawlings ball was sitting on the tee. In order for us to be confident that the obtained differences between the six balls were not attributable to chance, the six distances should have been contrasted with an appropriate statistical test. If such a test had been applied and if the results had indicated that the six average distances were more divergent from one another than would be expected by chance *and* that the Toney Penna DB average of 254.57 was significantly different from the other five average differences, then under these circumstances we could have had some confidence that the new ball developed by Rawlings would again show up as the best if these same 51 golfers were again to hit three balls of each brand. But without such a statistical comparison, we are left with the distinct possibility that a replication of the experiment might result in the Toney Penna ball having the worst average distance.

Should you assume that Rawlings or the Nationwide Consumer Testing Institute (or other companies who are pushing different products) performed the necessary statistical comparisons but simply failed to mention this in their published advertisement? We feel that this policy is not a wise one for the consuming public to follow. The phrase "significantly different" doesn't take up too much space in an ad, yet it is an especially important indication of well-trained, unbiased experimenters. (By the way, a more detailed explanation of the golf ball study mailed to us by Rawlings did not mention anything about a statistical treatment of the data.) A better policy, in our judgment, is for you to demand that the advertiser indicate that chance outcomes have been ruled out (at least at some given confidence level) as the causal explanation for why the printed test results turned out the way they did.

The third rival hypothesis that we have in mind concerns a possible order effect. Suppose the 51 golfers all hit the three Rawlings balls last, after they had hit the 15 balls associated with the other five brands. In addition, suppose that the golfers were asked to begin hitting the 18 balls of this experiment without any practice swings. If this had been the case, then it is quite plausible that the observed mean differences between the six brands (even if significant) were caused by a warm-up effect. (Or maybe changes in the wind velocity had a systematic effect on the distance measures.) Since Rawlings did not tell us whether or not the six brands were counterbalanced in their order of being hit, we cannot rule out the possibility of such an order effect.

Does the Toney Penna DB go farther when hit because of its weight distribution point, its centrifugal action, and the other alleged engineering characteristics? Maybe it does. But then again, maybe it does not. Until Rawlings provides us with more detailed, complete information about how they conducted their test and how they analyzed their data, we'll simply have to suspend judgment. And as a little warning to our golf ball-buying friends who have seen Rawlings' ad and are about ready to buy a new set of Toney Penna's, we feel compelled to yell "Fore!"

32. Six Weeks on Nothing but Bread and Water

We really don't know, of course, what laboratory rats think about while they eat. However, we suspect that they, like humans, have taste buds that cause certain foods to be preferred over other foods. And quite possibly, rats prefer certain types of bread more than other types. Maybe they like the whole grain kinds, which have tiny seeds in them, or maybe they prefer the fluffy white types, which have a spongy texture. Clearly, we do not know *which* type of bread the rats prefer, but it does seem reasonable to consider the possibility that certain brands of bread taste better to rats than other brands.

If the 33 brands of bread utilized in the CU experiment do not taste the same to rats, then a plausible rival hypothesis for the obtained results concerns the amount of bread consumed. As you will recall, each of the 35 groups of rats (except the control group given milk) was allowed to eat *unlimited* amounts of the food assigned to it during the six-week duration of the study. Possibly the group given Thomas' Diet Rite Bread liked its taste better and consequently ate more of it. As a result of simply having eaten more, this particular group could have made a better showing in terms of the growth and health criteria. This could have been the case if all 33 brands were actually equivalent in nutritional value, or even if some other brand had a higher nutritional value but poorer taste.

In a subsequent issue of *Consumer Reports,* the editors responded to a barrage of letters that protested the use of rats as subjects for a study dealing with human food. In this follow-up article, it was acknowledged that the various rat groups did *not* eat the same amount of bread over the six-week period of the study. We were not told which groups ate the most, but if there were a relationship between amount of food consumed and consequent standing on the criterion measures, then our suggested rival hypothesis would become all the more plausible.

The experiment could have been conducted in such a way as to control the variable of amount of bread consumed, thereby causing it to lose its rival hypothesis status. Instead of giving each group an unlimited amount of bread to eat, the researchers could have given them a standard amount that would be the same for all 33 breads. Maybe the standard amount would be something like three slices per rat per day, or maybe it would be based upon the weight of the bread, say 1 ounce per meal. The point is that the study could have been set up such that taste differences among the breads would not influence the amount eaten, which in turn might affect growth and health.

33. To Insure Promptness

In the discussion of their findings, the researchers do raise the possibility that people who dine in groups may tend to be less generous or to eat at times when restaurants are crowded and thus get poorer service. Although these possibilities may be rival hypotheses in their study, neither we nor the researchers see them as very plausible. Nonetheless, we should consider the plausibility of these factors as subject to empirical study; for example, what is the relationship of generosity to income?

Melvin Snyder of Dartmouth College raised a more serious objection to the original interpretation of the findings.[1] Rather than accepting the conclusion of diffusion of responsibility, he devised an equity explanation. That is, as Snyder put it, "two customers can be served with little more effort than one person" (p. 308). Snyder interviewed ten waitresses and one waiter on this point and found that all preferred to serve one party of four rather than four parties of one. Hence, people in groups may tip less, not because they can hide among the crowd, but because they want the total tip from the table to be commensurate with the effort taken to serve the table.

The researchers' hunch was right: people tip less in groups. However, their explanation (diffusion of responsibility) is, if we believe Snyder's reasoning, incorrect. Even in science, therefore, it is possible to be right for the wrong reason.

34. Do the Blind Sometimes See?

The rival hypothesis associated with this experiment is related to the fact that the data were collected not by scientific recording devices, but rather by human observers. In experiments such as this, there is a possibility that significant differences between comparison groups will be produced by an observer bias, not by true treatment effects. Since so many research efforts utilize observers to record what the study's subjects are doing, it is important for you to see how observer biases can become confounded with treatment effects. So, let us reexamine the Wisconsin rat experiment, this time with a focus on the possibility of an observer bias.

The two observers sat 4 feet from the front of the operant-conditioning chamber and watched each rat as it was shocked through the grid floor. Following each shock, the observers independently classified the rat's motor response into one of four mutually exclusive categories (no response, flinch, and so on) and also recorded whether the rat produced a verbalization. These recordings, which lead the data of the experiment, were based upon subjective impressions of how each rat responded to each shock that was administered. Even though the data were characterized by relatively high inter-rater reliability, it is still possible that the observers' subjective impressions of the rats' responses were influenced by something else they saw within the lighted chamber. To be more specifiic, the observers may have been influenced by the physical character-istics of the rats prior to (or between) the administration of the various shocks.

As you will recall, research prior to the Wisconsin study had demonstrated that hormonal injections during infancy produce changes in a rat's body weight and coat texture. Therefore, it is conceivable that the two observers noticed that the 78 rats they were watching did not look alike. Furthermore, it is possible that the observers un-consciously (or maybe even consciously) used these side effects of the treatments to classify the rats into subgroups having common characteristics. And if they did that, then it is also possible that the observers became biased in what they saw; for example,

---

[1] Melvin Snyder. "The Inverse Relationship between Restaurant Party Size and Tip Percen-tage: Diffusion of Responsibility or Equity?" *Personality and Social Psychology Bulletin*, 1976, 2, p. 308.

they may have recorded that the big healthy rats *didn't* jump when they were uncertain about whether or not all four feet left the grid, and they may have recorded that small, anemic-looking rats *did* jump when the same ambiguous postshock behavior was emitted. In summary, the observers may have been able to determine which treatment groups the rats belonged to (even though they weren't told this,) and this self-discovered information may have biased their perceptions.

We suspect that you see the point about observer bias that we're trying to present, but we also suspect that you have doubts as to the plausibility of this possible phenomenon as a rival hypothesis for the significant results obtained in the Wisconsin study. However, the idea of observer bias as a possible problem in this rat experiment did not come from the authors of this book. Rather, it was suggested by one of the two researchers who conducted the original study. The following is an excerpt from a follow-up article that appeared two years after the technical report of the rat study:

> In this experiment, the sensitivity to electric shock of 78 female rats that received one of eight different combinations of neonatal and adult hormone treatments was measured by a modification of the Evans (1961) procedure. Although the observers were nominally blind, the hormone treatments produced changes in body weight, phallic length, and in the texture and appearance of the animals' coats that could have provided clues for the identification of the treatments that the subjects received.
>
> To assess this possibility, one of the observers was asked to guess the exact combination of treatments each subject received. By chance alone the observer would be expected to correctly identify the subjects' experimental condition one out of eight times in general, or 9.75 times in this case. In fact, the observer guessed correctly 18 times (23%). Thus in this case the observer correctly identified the treatments received by subjects significantly more often than would have been expected by chance ($X^2 = 7.97$, df $= 1$, p $< .01$,) and the possibility that observer bias influenced the results must be considered (Beatty and Beatty, p. 71).

The title of the follow-up article was "How Blind is Blind?" The author's main points were that the people who administer treatments or record subjects' behavior are often presumed to be ignorant of ("blind" to) the subjects' treatment group affiliation, that these people are actually not so blind, and that the results of the study can be distorted when it becomes possible for these people to ascertain which particular treatments were given to each of the subjects. We conclude with a final quotation from this follow-up article—a general comment that many researchers and the readers of their research should think about:

> Since most observational techniques require sophisticated observers, it is not unlikely that "blind" observers may discover the treatment conditions of the subjects through some leak in laboratory security. Moreover, sophisticated observers are likely to be aware of the purpose of an experiment even if they are not explicitly informed of it, and, by observation of side effects of treatments on the appearance or behavior of subjects, they may be able to identify the treatments that the subjects have received (p. 70).

35. Humor, Curiosity, and Verbal Absurdities

As we see it, there are two possible rival hypotheses associated with this study. One has to do with variables *not* used as part of the matching process. The other has to do with the phenomenon of statistical regression—that is, with regression toward the mean.

Since the average verbal and nonverbal IQs (and their distributions) were nearly identical in the two comparison groups, intelligence cannot be offered as a possible reason for one group being able to detect more verbal absurdities than the other group. Intelligence was controlled. But other variables were not. Many of these remaining variables would not logically be related to the observed performance on the verbal absurdities test. However, some might be so related. For example, what about reading ability? Isn't it possible that children with above-average curiosity are also above-average readers? If so, the matching on IQ did not at the same time control for reading ability, for intelligence and reading ability are not perfectly correlated.

Hence, the two comparison groups may have differed significantly on the verbal absurdities tests for reasons associated with variables other than curiosity or intelligence. However, our main concern is related to the second rival hypothesis with this study: statistical regression. We feel that the two comparison groups were almost bound to differ in terms of their mean score on the verbal absurdities test because of the imperfect correlation between the IQ scores and the verbal absurdity which, in turn, brings forth regression to the mean. Since this form of regression is somewhat subtle and since many researchers use matching in their research, let us explain in detail why we think the phenomenon of regression is of concern here.

As you will recall, the total subject pool of 191 was measured in terms of curiosity and then split into an upper half and a lower half. Then all children were measured on IQ. Since the correlation between curiosity and IQ was $+.55$, there was a tendency for the children with high-curiosity scores to be the same ones who had high IQ scores. Now, if this correlation had turned out to be $+1.00$, it would have meant that the high-curiosity group had all of the high IQ scores, and therefore no matched pairs would have been possible. However, since the correlation was $+.55$, the distribution of IQ scores associated with the high-curiosity children overlapped with the IQ distribution associated with the low-curiosity children. While the two curiosity distributions did not overlap at all (since it was divided into top and bottom halves,) the two IQ distributions must have overlapped—or else it would have been impossible to end up with mean IQs for the two groups as similar as they were.

Now when we say "overlap," we do not mean to imply the geometric notion of congruency. The distribution of IQ scores associated with the high-curiosity subgroup was not the same (in terms of IQ *range*) as that associated with the low-curiosity subgroup. Because of the moderately·high positive correlation between curiosity and IQ scores, when the total group of 191 was split on the basis of curiosity scores, more of the high-IQ children went into the high-curiosity group. And more of the low-IQ children went into the low-curiosity group. This had to be true because of the correlation between the curiosity and intelligence measures. Therefore, the mean IQ of the 95 or so high-curiosity children was necessarily higher than the mean IQ of the 95 or so low-curiosity children.

The matching process selected, for each matched pair, a child from the high-curiosity (and high-IQ) group who had an IQ similar to that of a child from the low-curiosity (and low-IQ) group. In any one of these matched pairs, it is likely that the child coming from the high-curiosity group had an IQ that was *below average* compared with the IQs of other members of the high-curiosity half of the total subject pool. Conversely, the other member of this matched pair most likely had an IQ that was *above average* compared with the IQs of other members of the low-curiosity half of the total subject pool. Had the 102 children forming the 51 matched pairs been given the same IQ test for a second time, it is a cinch that their mean IQs on the second measurement would not be identical, as was the case with their first IQ scores.

On the second IQ testing, the 51 high-curiosity subjects would end up with higher scores than they did on the first testing. This would happen because these 51 children are a nonrandom subgroup of the high-curiosity subject pool—nonrandom in the sense that their mean IQ score is below average. On the second testing, these 51 subjects would tend to regress upwards toward the overall mean of the full group from which they have been selected. For similar reasons, the 51 low-curiosity subjects would tend to perform less well on the second IQ test because they constitute an extreme group with above average scores on the first test (as compared with other low-curiosity children;) hence, their mean performance on the second IQ test would regress downward toward the mean that all 95 low-curiosity children would have earned had all of them been given a second IQ test.[1]

But in the actual study on curiosity, no one was given the IQ test twice. So, you may wonder why we consider regression to be a problem. The reason is simply this. As long as the correlation between IQ and some other variable is less than +1.00, the phenomenon of statistical regression will operate to cause the two groups of 51 subjects to end up with different mean scores on that other variable. Had the other variable been a second intelligence test, regression would have occurred. (Test-retest correlations for IQ tests are *not* +1.00.) Had the other variable been scores on a verbal absurdities test—as was the case—regression would still be expected to influence the data. Only if curiosity and intelligence had correlated 0.00 (which wasn't the case) or if intelligence and verbal absurdity scores had correlated +1.00 (which we seriously doubt was the case) would regression not have been associated with this study.

36. Quantity? Versus Quality

Although Cox and Catt clearly made an heroic effort in their comparison of departmental productivity in APA journals with Roose and Andersen's reputational rankings, we are not convinced that their index of productivity is representative of the quality of a given doctoral program. There are many prestigious journals that publish articles in psychology besides those published by the APA, and many individuals no longer consider the APA journal representing a particular area as necessarily the leading journal in that area. In addition, there have sprung up in the past few years new areas of research not well served by the APA journals—psychology of women,

---

[1] For the sake of clarity in this explanation, we have presumed that the phenomenon of testing did not exist.

environmental psychology, and population psychology—and new journals have been created to meet the needs of those in such areas.

Finally, it seems that Cox and Catt have equated quantity of scientific knowledge produced with quality of training. We see these as two quite different constructs. We suggest that a more appropriate list would be based on ratings of graduates of the various programs on teaching, scholarly success, and other such criterion behaviors. Do we intend to take this on as our next project? Definitely not!

37. Speed and Death on the Highway

The yearly fatality rate changes from 1973 through 1976 may have been attributable to the number of people driving cars on the highway or the size of their cars, not the speed at which they drive.

The national speed limit of 55 miles per hour was put into effect in 1974 because there was an oil embargo imposed on the United States by the Middle Eastern oil-producing countries. It was hoped that the new speed limit would help conserve the gasoline that was available. However, the supply of gas following the embargo in 1974 was insufficient, and people had to line up for hours at gas stations to buy fuel—usually with a 5- or 10-gallon limit that precluded "filling it up." At best, it was a hassle to get gas in 1974; at worst, it was dangerous (due to fights that broke out when someone tried to butt into the line.) As a consequence, many people did not drive so far or so frequently or did not drive at all (riding public transportation or forming car pools instead). Thus, the 20 percent decrease in fatalities in 1974 was probably caused, to a large degree, by a reduction in the number of people driving and the number of miles driven.

The oil embargo only lasted about six months. However, people most likely had become accustomed to driving less and they probably did not immediately return to their preembargo driving frequency. Increased gasoline prices in the postembargo period made many people think twice about driving as far as they used to. But after a while, we think that people became adjusted to the higher prices and gradually returned to their preembargo driving habits. Thus, the total number of miles driven by all Americans may have decreased sharply in 1974 and 1975, then increased in 1976. This variable—miles driven—could be the true explanation for the fatality statistics, not reduced speed.

And what about the size of the cars that people drive? During times of gasoline scarcity, small cars become much more popular because it's possible to go more miles in them on any given amount of gas. But small cars normally do not come through accidents very well. Therefore, isn't it possible that the fatality rate increased in 1976 because the gas shortage in 1974 had convinced people that their next new (or used) car should be a small one? Maybe the switchover to small, gas-conserving cars took place in late 1975 or early 1976, and maybe the lower protection of these cars was the true cause of the unfortunate rise in car-related deaths.

Most likely, all three variables (speed, car size, and miles driven) operated together to produce the observed trend. Therefore, since these three variables are confounded, the reported statistics cannot be used to argue convincingly for any one explanation. Without further data, we cannot accept the newspaper's claim that driving speed was the cause of the initial decrease and then of the later increase in traffic deaths.

This particular example allows us to make an important point about cause-and-effect relationships. Suppose there are two variables, A and B, and let us assume that it is known that A is the cause while B is the effect. Further suppose that A is the only cause of B, with no other variables being related to B in a causal manner. Given this sort of situation, if we observe changes in B, then we can correctly assume that prior changes in A have taken place. For example, if we glue a pencil to the ground such that it is standing upright, we could measure the length of a shadow formed by the sun's rays. Let this variable (shadow length) be variable B, the effect. Of course, variable A, the cause, would be the time of the day. If we observe a change in B, then we can say with confidence that variable A has changed as well.

But more often than not, an effect has multiple causes. We could symbolize such causes as A_1, A_2, and so on. In this situation, an observed change in variable B cannot be tied to one and only one of the known causes (say A_2) unless it can be verified that all other A's have remained constant. Getting back to the issue of traffic fatalities, we know that the death rate is an effect that has multiple causes. Thus, an observed decrease (or increase) in the yearly fatality rate cannot be attributed to one of the known causes, unless we have confidence that the other causal variables have not changed. To be even more specific, couldn't someone from the Women's Christian Temperance Union have taken the yearly statistics that were reported in the newspaper article and used them as evidence that people drink less while driving immediately following an increase in gasoline prices? Yes, but we do not accept that claim since we know that drinking and driving speed and several other variables are all causally related to the yearly fatality rate on our highways. Given a change in the latter, accompanied by no other data, we cannot validly claim that people are drinking more or driving faster or anything of the kind.

38. Getting a Bank Loan

Yes, we *do* feel there is an alternative explanation for the results. In short, we think that the sequence of events in this study may have created a bias in the attitude inventory filled out by the 53 "loan officers." And this bias, we believe, would cause the similarity index to be positively correlated with the amount of money approved for the loan.

Recall the activities in this study. Each subject first looked at the applicant's formal application and responses to the attitude inventory. Next, the decision was made regarding the amount of money to be approved. Then, after those materials were turned in, the subjects filled out the attitude inventory on their own. In our opinion, the subjects' responses to the attitude inventory very possibly were influenced jointly by the applicant's attitude responses and by the loan decision.

The 53 loan officers in this study varied tremendously in how much money they were willing to approve. We contend that this level of nonagreement could potentially be a function of different interpretations of the relevant information on the loan application, and it might not have been produced at all by the attitude information in the applicant's packet. (If the loan application, by itself, had been distributed to the 53 subjects, would they have been in agreement on the level of appropriate support? We doubt it.) Whereas the researchers seem to be arguing that the degree of attitude similarity causally influenced the loan decisions, we feel that the true causal relationship may have operated in the opposite direction.

For the subjects who chose to approve a large loan, there may have existed an unconscious motivation to agree with the attitudinal position of the applicant. Since the approval of a large loan constitutes an assessment of someone as a good financial risk, the subjects making highly favorable decisions may have found it difficult, immediately thereafter, to take an attitudinal position in opposition to the person who had just been supported financially. For similar reasons, among the subjects who chose to approve small loans or no loan at all, we think there may have been an unconscious motivation to disagree with the applicant. Since the subjects in this latter group had announced that the applicant was a poor financial risk, they may have found it somewhat difficult to turn around and also announce that they were in the same boat—even though the "water" was now attitudes rather than finances. Rather, these subjects may have experienced a psychological desire to separate themselves from the risky applicant.

In this study, events took place at three points in time. At time one, the subjects examined the formal loan application and looked at the applicant's attitudinal responses; at time two, they decided on the amount of money to be approved; and at time three, the subjects filled out the attitude inventory themselves. Maybe the second of time one events (the applicant's attitudes) did affect the time two event, as the researchers imply. But possibly the true causal relationship is from the time two event to the time three event. Without further evidence from a subsequent study, it is impossible to determine with assurance whether one of these explanations is right and the other wrong (and if so, which one is right,) or whether both are correct and operating in concert to produce the outcome discovered in the investigation.

39. The Four-Day Workweek

We consider there to be two possible flaws in this study. The first involves the comparability of the experimental and control groups. It seems to us that the differences in the geographic location of the plants might serve as a plausible alternative cause for observed differences in the dependent variables. There may have been other events that took place in either the plants or in their surrounding communities that were unrelated to the changeover and yet were reflected in the data. For example, the shutdown of a nearby major employer might have made everyone in the experimental group happier to have a job—no matter what the hours were. Thus, the threat of history seems inescapable in this study.

The second flaw seems to be reflected in the findings. Perhaps there was an initial positive reaction to having a four-day workweek and a three-day weekend, but perhaps this wore off after a year of finding that the net result was an additional day in which to spend the same amount of money. In any event, the lack of differences at the end of 25 months certainly adds to the plausibility of the theory that novelty, rather than the changeover, caused the first year's differences.

We believe that you should be even more tentative than the researchers in drawing your conclusions.

40. Newspaper Advertising

There are, in our judgment, three problems associated with this study that potentially invalidate the conclusions. The first problem has to do with the question that was asked of subjects as they came through the checkout counter. The second has to do with the personnel used to collect these answers. And the third problem has to do with the honesty of responses.

The main problem with this investigation relates to our inability to tell how many of the subjects would have bought a sale item even without the newspaper ads. Surely some of the subjects made plans to visit the grocery store on what was actually the fifth day of the study and read the local newspaper during one or more of the four preceding days. Although these subjects responded affirmatively to the question about having seen the newspaper ad, this does not necessarily indicate that the ad caused them to go to the store or to buy any of the 28 sale items. Very possibly, they were planning to visit the store to purchase (among other things) a subset of the 28 "critical" products *before* they saw the advertisement. Did they see the ad before shopping? Yes. Did the ad cause them to buy advertised products? Possibly not.

To get around this problem, a different sort of question could have been asked. Instead of inquiring whether or not the consumer had read about the sale items in the newspaper, the clerks could have asked, "Would you be buying these sale items if they had not been advertised in the paper?" Or, "Did our newspaper ads about these sale items cause you to purchase the items you have selected?" However, we feel that an alternative strategy would have produced more valid data and also made the questioning unnecessary. Without too much difficulty, the printed advertisement could have taken the form of an insert and been included in a random half of the home-delivered newspapers. A record could have been kept concerning who got the ads and who did not, and then the data could have been collected regarding the presence or absence of the 28 sale items in the market basket on day five of the study.

The second problem of this study relates to the personnel used to collect the data. These were the store clerks at the checkout counter. They examined each subject's purchases to see if any of the 28 advertised items were present, and if any were they asked their question about having read the newspaper ads. However, since the store clerks were also the ones who assessed each subject's socioeconomic status, we wonder whether the clerks' knowledge of customer SES might have biased the way in which they interacted with the subjects as the subjects came through the checkout counter. Possibly more (or less) time was spent talking with the lower SES subjects *because* the clerks knew they were in this category. We feel that the personnel used to classify subjects into SES categories should not have been the ones to collect the data regarding the effects of the newspaper ads.

Finally, we wonder about the honesty of responses to the question: "Did you read about these sale items in the newspaper ads?" A significantly greater number of lower-class subjects than middle-class subjects answered affirmatively. This almost gives the impression that lower-class consumers read the paper (or at least the ads about sales) more than middle-class consumers. Maybe this is true. However, a rival hypothesis is that middle-class consumers are embarrassed to admit that they are buying items simply because they are on sale. A partial (but not complete) way to get around this problem would have involved a cut-out coupon in the paper that had to be presented at the checkout counter before the consumer could get the sale price.

41. The Dentist's Drill

Was it the sound of the drilling that led to the significant hearing loss among the dental students over the three year time span of this study? Maybe it was. But then again, we feel as if there may be some plausible alternative explanations to account for the observed impairment in hearing ability. To be more specific, we feel there are several other possible activities or events involving the dental students during the three-year period of this investigation that may have been the true cause of the hearing loss.

For example, suppose the dental students—who as a group are not very wealthy at that point in their professional careers—did not eat very many well-balanced meals while in dental school. Were this to be the case, as it probably is, couldn't one argue that poor diet was the true cause of the decrease in hearing ability? Or suppose the dental students took jobs during the summer months to help pay for the expenses incurred by attending dental school. And further suppose that some of the students were working on ground crews at the airport terminal or with a jackhammer breaking up cement sidewalks. Might not these noisy activities be the true cause of the hearing loss, rather than the drilling in the dental office?

Our suggested explanation of diet may be plausible; the explanation concerning the airport and jackhammer is not plausible (although it is possible.) The rival hypothesis that we consider to be most plausible concerns music. It has been our observation that young men and women between the ages of 20 and 30 enjoy listening to records, the radio, and tapes. And in general, what they listen to is not soft classical music. Rather, the preferred choice of music among these individuals is loud rock music, and in many cases, acid rock music. Since previous research has demonstrated that an extended exposure to loud music can bring about a hearing loss, we suggest that the auditory abilities of the dental students may well have decreased over the three years of the study because of the music they listened to at home, rather than the drilling that took place near the dental chair.

To be able to accept confidently the conclusions of this study utilizing simply one group of dental students, we need to be able to rule out logically any possible cause of hearing impairment other than the drilling. Since this is nearly impossible to do, a different research strategy could have been employed so as to give us more faith in the results. The available group of dental students should have been randomly divided into two subgroups. One of the two subgroups would work for a period of time (possibly three years) with earplugs or earmuffs whenever they were drilling in the dental office. The other subgroup would not use these preventive measures while they were in the dentist's office. With this strategy, activities such as diet, jet noise, jack-hammer vibrations, and rock music would be expected to affect one subgroup just as much as the other. And a difference between the two groups at the end of the study could be attributed confidently to one and only one causal variable—the drilling noise.

But once again, let us put in a plea that the poor patient in the chair not be forgotten. If drilling really does bring about hearing loss among dentists, won't it do the same thing among dental patients? And even if the noise created by drilling teeth does not bring about hearing impairments, we still like the idea of earplugs or earmuffs for the patient. At least for some of us, that grinding noise of metal against teeth is one of the most horrid sounds we know. It sure would be nice to eliminate that auditory experience even if it is not permanently damaging.

42. Psychotherapy Revisited Again

One rival hypothesis (discussed by the researchers in the original article) is that of experimental mortality; that is, the test scores of those participants now located by the researchers might alter the statistical analysis substantially. Furthermore, we can only speculate on the direction of any effect to be found if we were able to locate those missing. Perhaps they have all had severe mental problems resulting in institutionalization, or perhaps they all left Chicago after a severe winter and are living happily ever after in southern California. Short of hiring a large number of private investigators, we have no way of finding out.

Furthermore, we hope that you have noticed that the presence of a control group would have improved the study. At the very least we could have assessed the effects of the weather on the dropout rate in the study. In order to be comparable, the control group would probably have to be comprised of other college students who had sought psychotherapy but had been placed on a waiting list. Of course, it would be nice if random assignment could be used to assign students to either psychotherapy or the waiting list.

43. Animadversion

We cannot accept, on the basis of this particular study, the claim that students are biased in their evaluation of instructors and that the animadversion error is associated with teacher evaluations from poor students. In our opinion, the primary flaw associated with this study is related to the expected distribution of ratings from unbiased raters. A second flaw, connected with the first, has to do with the conspicuous absence of a control group.

Regarding the major flaw, the researchers made the assumption that we should expect, in the case of *unbiased* raters, similar ratings from each of the student subgroups. We disagree. It is our experience that students vary tremendously in their reasons for being in a college course, in their ability to handle the materials, and in their "style of learning." With respect to this last characteristic—learning style—the professor who chooses to employ a single format for everyone (say a formal lecture approach or a completely student-oriented discussion approach) will unavoidably be using a teaching style that is not optimal for all students. Consequently, some of the students may do poorly on tests because the instructor utilized a format that was inappropriate for them, and their low ratings of the instructor may be a perfectly unbiased assessment of how they felt about the instruction which they received. At the other end of the continuum are the students who do well on the course exams. They probably score well, at least in part, because the instructor's style fits their needs. And we would expect these students to rate the instructor more positively than the other group which failed to receive the type of instruction it needed.

Hence, the empirical verification that students who get poor grades give the instructor low ratings does not, by itself, demonstrate that the low ratings were biased by the low grades. To find out whether prior information on grades does, in fact, influence ratings of teacher effectiveness, a control group is needed. Suppose a random half the students (the experimental group) receives feedback concerning their grades prior to rating the instructor, while the other half (the control group) is required to evaluate the instructor before finding out what grades they earned. If the low-scoring subjects in the experimental group gave lower ratings than the low-scoring subjects in the control group, than a claim for the animadversion error could legitimately be made. But if the two groups of low-scoring students gave the teacher the same type of rating—even though such ratings might be lower than those given by high-scoring students—then it would not be possible to assert that the information on grades created a bias in the teacher evaluations. Without the control group (or some other form of baseline comparison point), it is simply impossible to interpret data from a single group that gets information on grades prior to evaluating the teacher.

44. The Ultimate Martini

Having a preference for straight rum (as opposed to straight vodka or straight gin) does not necessarily mean that an individual will prefer a rum martini over a vodka or gin martini. Since the olive, lemon twist, and vermouth were left out of the drink, the test comparisons that were made cannot, in our judgment, be considered to be a martini test. As occasional drinkers, we prefer rum to vodka or gin. But when we order a Bloody Mary, we do not want any rum in it!

Since we are not heavy martini drinkers, we considered it important to have an authority examine the Bacardi advertisement and evaluate the implied logic. Here is his response:

> As a waiter and part-time bartender, I might assume from this advertisement that I would be doing the best for my customers if I served them a martini made with Bacardi rum the next time I received an order for a (noncall liquor) martini. Yet, through my two years' experience in my present occupation, it is my unsubstantiated observation that true martini drinkers do not want a martini to be smooth, but rather they want it to have a bit of a bite with the desired effect of stimulating their taste buds—something that gin does very well by itself and vodka does adequately with a twist of lemon or lime but rum? Why not bourbon?
>
> The Bacardi company's results lead me to believe that the 21 cities in which the tests were conducted are located in Puerto Rico with 550 tee-totalers who probably couldn't distinguish between 7-Up and gin. I will conclude by stating the only similarity between a white rum martini and a gin or vodka martini is the color of the liquors and alcoholic content.

As lovers of food and drink, we commend any researcher who attempts to discover how to make better consumable items for meals or parties. But in the research on any one item (such as a martini), if one ingredient is varied for comparative purposes, the other ingredients should be left in. And the name of the item should not be kept a secret. What if we gave adults milk, iced tea, and coffee and found that 41.4 percent preferred coffee? Would it be fair to conclude that the ultimate milkshake should be made with ice cream and coffee?

In addition to our first and major concern discussed above, we have (and suspect that you also have) three other questions about Bacardi's advertisement. How were the

550 drinkers from the 21 cities selected? In what sequence did the subjects taste their three "martinis"? What does the word "leading" mean in terms of the gin and vodka brands? We certainly hope that a random sample of drinkers was used (and not just a preselected group who were known to prefer rum), that the sequence was varied (and not such that everyone tasted the rum martini first), and that the gin and vodka were leading in the sense of prestige (and not just sales). But even if these three facets of the study were as we hope they were, our first and major concern still causes us to feel that a true martini taste test was not conducted.

45. Modeling Clay

While we are generally sympathetic towards social learning theory and its methods (including modeling,) we have difficulty accepting this study as evidence in its favor. While the authors are to be commended for the design (true random selection and assignment) and analysis (appropriate use of the analysis of variance,) we do wonder about the effectiveness of English instructions being given to children for whom Spanish is a first language. We would have recommended that the entire experiment be conducted in Spanish to eliminate the very plausible rival hypothesis that the nonmodeling instructional group received its instructions in a foreign language.

46. Procrastination

Is there really a tendency for people who procrastinate to produce profile drawings of the human figure? Maybe there is. But somehow, we are not convinced of this possibility by the results from this study.

We cannot disagree with the statistical results of this investigation—there *was* a significantly larger number of profile drawings produced by the group of late applicants than by the early-applicant group. However, we can and do question the validity of the researcher's assumption that the late applicants were procrastinators. Isn't it very possible, we ask, that the late applicants were actually individuals who earlier had applied to—but were denied admission to—one or more other schools of nursing? If so, then neither of the two comparison groups would be made up of procrastinators.

But if the two groups of applicants did not differ in terms of the variable of procrastination, then what was the reason for the statistically significant difference between the two groups regarding number of profile drawings produced? Our first inclination was to point to intelligence as the explanation; in other words, maybe those who applied late (after being denied admission elsewhere) were not as smart as those in the early group, and maybe there's a tendency for profile drawings to come from people who are not too smart. However, upon a careful rereading of the technical report, we noticed that the 61 subjects selected from the late applicant pool were matched, on the variables of IQ and age, with the 65 early applicant subjects. Thus, our explanation of intelligence would not seem to solve the puzzle.

To be quite honest, we are left in sort of quandary in trying to come up with a good reason for why the two groups differed in the number of profile drawings generated. We can't accept the researcher's explanation of procrastination, and our thought about intellectual differences seems to have been controlled by the matching process. Our only remaining suggestion has to do with possible seasonal variations in the way people respond to the Human Figure Drawing Test. When the test is administered in the summer months of May through August, maybe the examinees tend (for some unexplicable reason) to produce profile drawings; in the winter months of November through February, maybe they tend to produce full-face drawings.

The explanation of seasonal variations, even to us, does not seem to be a very plausible explanation for why the two groups differed. Maybe you can come up with a better reason. But since we're sort of stuck, in light of the title we have given to this discussion we think that it is fitting and proper that we put off any more attempts to solve the puzzle for at least a couple of days.

47. Grip Strength and Sleep

We have already indicated that we (and most of our friends and relatives) feel quite weak in the morning when we first wake up. Nevertheless, we are somewhat reluctant to accept totally the implication of the grip-strength study because of two rival hypotheses. Our alternative explanations for the obtained results have to do with the subjects' stomachs and bladders, and we believe that either one or a combination of both may explain why the 20 male subjects squeezed the dynamometer harder in the afternoon than in the morning.

The afternoon measurements, you will recall, were taken sometime between 12:00 noon and 2:00 P.M. on the first and sixth days of the study. Most of the subjects, if not all of them, probably had eaten one—or possibly two—meals during the six-hour interval prior to each afternoon's session with the dynamometer. On the other hand, none of the subjects had anything to eat prior to the strength test on the second through the fifth mornings. Hence, a possible cause for the observed difference between the morning and afternoon measurements was food intake prior to performing the test. People may have felt weaker and performed less well in the morning not because of residual drowsiness, but rather because of a famished feeling in the midriff.

A second rival hypothesis concerns the bladder. Most men wake up with a full bladder—and a dire need to head first thing for the bathroom. But in this research investigation, upon hearing the alarm go off each subject was required to stand up and squeeze the dynamometer. When one's bladder is full, it is simply impossible quickly to exert maximum energy without having a little accident. Even though most subjects claimed, in a postexperimental interview, that they tried just as hard in the morning as in the afternoon, we seriously wonder whether they held back a little bit when squeezing the dynamometer in the hopes of holding everything in their bladder. And in support of this concern, it is interesting to note that three of the subjects admitted that they *did not* try as hard during the morning sessions.

48. An Object Lesson

Since the analyses were based on the total number of social interactions, we have no assurance that each child contributed equally to the results. That is, two or three of the children might have been involved in 80 to 90 percent of the interactions. In this case, the results would not be representative of the behavior of the average 2-year-old. Fortunately, a statistical analysis eliminated this plausible rival hypothesis.

We might also speculate on the effects of an intervention program that attempts to facilitate social interaction in 2-year-olds through the introduction of appropriate objects into their environment. Maturation would clearly be a problem, as indicated by the second finding of the study. It would be necessary to control for the fact that as toddlers get older they become more social. In our case, the principle might be that as toddlers get older, we are more likely to believe in their existence.

49. Teaching Experience for Counselors

In this particular group of 21 student counselors, was it really teaching experience that brought about a large number of evaluative statements? Maybe it was. But we think that there is a plausible rival hypothesis that might also explain the results. To be more specific, we contend that the observed differences between the three groups may be attributable to the variable of age, not the variable of teaching experience.

In the formal report of this research study, the authors did not present any information about the ages of the 21 subjects. Therefore, we don't know for sure whether the mean ages within the three groups were similar or different. Nevertheless, we feel fairly confident in guessing that the student counselors having no teaching experience were younger than those having two years' experience and that the subjects having at least seven years' experience were oldest. If this was, in fact, the case, then age might very well be the causal agent underlying the differences in interviewing behavior.

Maybe people become more judgmental as they become older and get more experiences under their belt. If this is true, think what would happen if we made a comparison between experienced counselors and new counselors, all carefully selected such that none had any previous teaching experience. Might not the older group be more evaluative in their comments? And wouldn't this result make it seem—at least to the uncritical thinker—that we could prevent counselors from becoming more evaluative by having them perform some job other than counseling?

In short, we feel as if the three comparison groups in this study should have been comprised of individuals of equal age. Suppose we had two groups of current on-the-job counselors, all of whom went through the same graduate training program at the same time. Further suppose that in one of the two groups, students left school and took counseling jobs, and that in the other group, students took teaching jobs first and later switched to counseling positions. A comparison of these two groups would not allow us to rule out all possible rival hypotheses, but it would give us a much better feel for the true effect of teaching experience with the potentially critical variable of age being controlled.

50. Caffeine, Alertness, and Visual Monitoring

As far as we can tell, there aren't any rival hypotheses associated with this study. It is a methodologically "clean" experiment, providing results that have an unambiguous message.

At first, we thought there might be some sort of problem associated with the toggle switches. Since five of the subjects were watching the same display board and responding at the same time in the same room, we initially wondered whether subjects might hear one another depressing the button on the toggle switch. If so, a sleepy subject with tired eyes might be able to perform well simply by listening. However, the experimental room had soft music piped into it that probably decreased or eliminated any audible cues for responding. And even if the music had not been present, the effect of any of these audible cues would have operated to make the five groups show up as similar, not different.

So, we accept the results. And on our next cross-country driving excursion, we fully intend to drink lots of coffee with the expectation—now supportable by empirical evidence—that it will help us to keep alert, awake, and ready to hit the brake pedal when the car in front begins to slow down. Our only concern is for being able to find enough rest rooms along the way!

51. Barricade Your Opponents

Rather than having a number of reasons for not following Kelsey's advice, we have numbers *for* reasons. Some of these numbers are 800, 1100, 1400, and 1700, along with similar numbers that represent the points accruing to your opponents when they are able to "double" your contract and defeat it by three or more "tricks." In the colorful parlance of tournament bridge, this occurrence is known as "going for telephone numbers" (four-digit penalties).

Kelsey's methodology is as suspect as his advice. The one-sided presentation of examples proving his point is certainly an example of selection bias. Are there no examples in which scientific bidding won the day? Putting aside the question of statistically significant differences, we also believe there is a rival hypothesis to the conclusion drawn from the World Championship deals. Our experience leads us to believe that some deals are easier to play than others. It may be that the deals easier to play are also simpler to bid. The hands that are difficult to play may be more difficult to bid.

Although barricade bidding is often a lot of fun, we hesitate to recommend it unless you are an advanced player (or else very wealthy). We, unfortunately, are neither.

52. Some Shocking Nonsense

The most obvious rival hypothesis concerns the five shock-associated nonsense syllables: "jul," "sab," "hij," "yur," and "cil." These were the affective items for all 55 subjects, regardless of which of the three list arrangements was used. Simply stated, it is possible that these five items were easier to learn than the remaining ten. Maybe the shock had no bearing whatsoever on the learning of nonsense syllables, with the difference between 18.6 and 16.8 being solely attributable to syllable difficulty. (To get around this plausible rival hypothesis, each of the subjects should have had a random set of five items off his or her list selected for pairing with shock.)

The second rival hypothesis concerns the fact that there were five affective items versus ten neutral items. If we are correct in making a guess as to how the two averages were computed (see the footnote on p. 84), then we feel that sublist length could have been the true reason for the observed difference between 18.6 and 16.8. Surely we would expect a subject to be more likely to make an error on the ten-item portion of the list simply because this part is twice as long as the other part. Therefore, even without any shock at all, a difference between the two averages would not be too surprising.

53. Affirmative Action
Has Been Too Successful

As convincing as the data may appear to be, we believe that a few obvious rival hypotheses were overlooked. For example, it seems quite probable that women's colleges (almost all small, private, and expensive) have traditionally attracted a different kind of student than have the coeducational colleges (many of which are large, public, and inexpensive.) Also, we would be willing to bet that the negative correlation between the number of achievers and the number of men students is in large part a consequence of those few women who attended colleges with technological orientations (such as engineering and architecture). That is to say, if only ten women attend such a school, graduate, and are successful, this will push the correlation in the negative direction since the women would be vastly outnumbered by the men (even though, according to the author, the temptation to act in a traditionally feminine manner would have been present).

Thus, while in favor of the existence of single-sex institutions to provide a choice of educational settings, we do not accept this author's causal link.

54. Food Additives and Hyperactivity

In spite of the way the two research studies turned out, we feel that there still could be a causal relationship between food additives and hyperactivity. There are two reasons, in our judgment, why such a relationship might not have shown up in either of the two studies.

First of all, the studies only lasted two months. And during at least a portion of this time period, the 46 hyperactive children were on a diet that included food additives.

Therefore, they were off additives for less than two months. Since we don't know too much about physiology, we can not say exactly how long a hyperactive child would have to be on an additive-free diet before a change might show up in the child's behavior, presuming that a relationship did in fact exist. But isn't it possible that a much longer time period would be needed than the time provided in the Wisconsin study? A nutritional expert will have to decide whether this rival hypothesis is plausible, but it certainly seems possible.

But what if the 46 hyperactive children had been taken off food additives for an indefinite time period (say five years) to eliminate our first concern? And what if there *still* was no observable difference in the childrens' behavior before or after the diet change? Would such a set of results disprove a cause-and-effect relationship? We do not think so. We will explain our reasoning in general terms in the hopes that our point can be applied to any study, and we have little doubt that you will be able to apply it to the pair of studies conducted at Wisconsin.

Suppose that a cause-and-effect relationship does, in fact, exist between X and Y, where X is the cause and Y is the effect. If X shows up, then Y will occur at some later point as a result of the initial cause. Furthermore, let us assume that if Y occurs then it is possible to look back in time and always find a preliminary occurrence of X. In other words, to get Y we need X, and if we see Y it means that X has already taken place.

Now, suppose we take a group of people who possess characteristic Y. And further suppose that we somehow make sure that none of these people experience X′, a possible cause of Y (the prime sign here means that X′ may or may not be the cause of Y.) If our group continues to exhibit characteristic Y, does this prove that X′ is not a cause? The answer is no, for two reasons.

First of all, Y may be an irreversible characteristic. Once developed, it may stay with people forever, even though we take away the true X that brought about Y. For example, the ability to perform long division is a skill, which we can consider to be Y; this skill is brought about by demonstration and practice, which constitute X. X must precede Y. But once a person has Y, we can stop X without altering Y. If we didn't let you see any sample long division problems (say for a year) and if we didn't let you practice any of these math problems, would it prove that demonstration and practice are not the cause of this math skill if you still could solve long division problems at the end of the year? Of course not, simply because math ability (at least on this simple level) is an irreversible skill.

But what if Y *is* reversible? Even here, we feel that the elimination of X′ without an observable change in Y does not prove that something other than X′ is the cause. Once Y is produced—at least in humans—a whole host of expectations from other people may encourage, in subtle ways, the continued expression of the Y characteristic, even if Y is undesirable. If this is the case, even a removal of X may not affect the strength, frequency, or pervasiveness of Y. Think of hyperactivity as Y and presume, for the sake of argument, that food additives are the true X. Once hyperactivity in a child becomes evident and significant, others adjust to it, and the reasons for the hyperactivity may shift from the original X to one or more new X s. The original X (food additives) could be taken away and yet Y (hyperactivity) could very well continue to manifest itself.

If someone wanted to spend $270,000 to see if food additives are causally related to hyperactivity, why didn't they use normal children as their subjects? In other words, if X were the true cause of Y, and if we begin with a group of subjects who don't possess Y and give each subject X, then Y should become apparent sooner or later. Working backwards, as the Wisconsin researchers did, makes it far more difficult—if not impossible—to establish clearly that any particular X is the true cause of Y, or that any particular X' is *not* causally related to Y!

55. Growing Old

The problem with this study is common and easy to overlook. Cross-sectional methodology should not be used to draw longitudinal conclusions. Since the data were all collected during the same year, the younger subjects might well be presumed to have grown up under different environmental conditions (primarily nutritional and health-related) than did the older subjects. In order to draw conclusions about the changes in intelligence brought about by advancing age, we must take repeated measures on the same individuals at different times and *not* on differently aged individuals at the same time. Naturally, this takes a little longer (about 40 years or so.)[1]

If the same approach were taken to study the relationship of age to height, our surprising conclusion would be that people shrink 5 to 6 inches as they grow older. The impact of improved environmental conditions on height was demonstrated in the classic study by F. Boas,[2] in which he found that the height of children of immigrants was directly related to the amount of time they had spent in the United States. A more recent study[3] showed similar results for American-born Japanese, with these findings being attributed to more adequate diet and better environmental conditions.

56. Camping Out

We are confident that the week-long camping excursion to the mountains near Flaming Gorge helped to break the monotonous daily routine of the staff mental hospital. And we wish that more activities of this type would be scheduled on a regular basis for the incarcerated patients. Nevertheless, we feel that there are two plausible rival hypotheses to account for the significant findings associated with this study's data analysis.

The technical report of this investigation does not indicate whether the judges rated the Monday tapes and pictures prior to rating the Friday tapes and pictures. If they did, then it seems to us that instrumentation becomes a definite alternative explanation for the significant findings.

In general, *instrumentation* is the term used to describe situations wherein changes in the measuring instrument between the pretest and post-test make it look as if an inert intervening treatment has an effect. In this particular study, the Bales measuring

---

[1] But even a longitudinal strategy has its problems. To overcome the defects inherent in the cross-sectional and longitudinal approaches, a more complex model has been devised that minimizes these defects but which requires that some groups be followed longitudinally while others be looked at cross-sectionally. For more infomation, see K. Schaie. "A General Model for the Study of Developmental Problems." *Psychological Bulletin,* 1965, *64,* 92–107.

[2] F. Boas, *Changes in the Bodily Form of Descendants of Immigrants.* Immigration Commission Document No. 206, Washington, D. C., U.S. Government Printing Office, 1910.

[3] W. W. Gruelich, "Growth of Children of the Same Race Under Different Environmental Conditions." *Science,* 1958, *123,* pp. 515–516.

instrument was used for rating both the Monday and Friday material, and obviously it did not change. But the ability of the raters to use it certainly may have. We submit that the two sets of judges may have rated the Friday tapes and pictures differently from the Monday material simply because they were better able to use the Interaction Matrix after having some experience with it. Hence, unless the judges were well trained in the use of the rating scale or unless the order of the materials was counter-balanced, we consider the instrumentation to be a potential contaminating factor in this study.

The second rival hypothesis is the Rosenthal effect. The staff and patients probably expected the camp-out to facilitate social interaction. And this expectancy could very well have distorted the judges' perceptions when they listened to the Friday tapes and looked at the second set of pictures. It is not at all unlikely that they selectively heard and saw things that confirmed their expectations, while not noticing occurrences that ran contrary to their hopes. Even the researchers agree with this possible problem, for they comment that "It's quite possible that both staff and patients were biased in their expectations and perceptions" (Tuttle *et al.,* p. 78.) In light of the researchers' aware-ness of the potential rating bias, we wonder why the ratings were not done by people who did not go on the camping trip—with the Monday or Friday source of data being concealed from these raters.

57. Dirty Words

Both the design and analysis of this study are appropriate to answer the question of whether college students show more emotionality in response to socially taboo words, as well as whether they take longer to identify those words. Unfortunately, in our opinion, the researcher's interpretation of the latter finding as a phenomenon of the perceptual system does not seem justified.

Since it would take longer to recognize unfamiliar words, the researcher did consider the plausible rival hypothesis of unfamiliarity of college students with the critical words and rejected it, no doubt correctly, on the basis that the college students he knew were quite familiar with such words. However, he failed to consider the possibility that, although the students stated when asked that they responded equally promptly to all words, the delays for the critical words were a result of a slight (or possibly strong) reluctance to blurt out these words in a laboratory setting. As the study was conducted considerably before the women's liberation movement began, we feel safe in suggesting that the temper of the times could be used to support the rival explanation. We suspect that these results would not appear if the study were conducted today.

58. Feeling Good and Helping

In this study, the request to participate in the social psychology experiment was supposedly unconnected with the distribution of certificates for a free hamburger. Recall that the researchers considered these events to be "apparently unrelated," primarily (we suspect) because the person giving out the certificates was not the one who distributed the request for help. In our opinion, many of the Whopper subjects may have seen the connection between these two events, and we contend that they may have purposely failed to send in the post card because they realized that an attempt was being made to manipulate their behavior.

Being university professors, we walk between campus buildings a lot—more times than we care to count. But in all the time we've gone back and forth across our campuses, we have *never* run into anyone who was passing out certificates for free merchandise. Furthermore, we have *never* been approached by anyone who requested our participation in an experiment; such requests are typically posted in written form on bulletin boards inside buildings, particularly the psychology building.

We suspect that many of the 47 Whopper subjects in the experiment on helping behavior were just like us and had never been bothered as they traversed their campus grounds. But look what happened to them on this particular day. First they got the certificate for the free hamburger. This event by itself was probably enough for many of the 47 to begin wondering what was going on. And then, 50 seconds later, they were stopped and asked to participate in a study—an experiment in *Social Psychology*, no less! If most of these subjects didn't put two and two together, either they were asleep and on their way to a 7 A.M. class, or else students on that particular campus have trouble adding.

It has been our observation that people don't like to have their behavior manipulated. Upon learning that someone is trying to manipulate them, many people typically react by behaving in the opposite way from what is expected. Hence, we suggest that only a small number of Whopper certificate recipients sent in their post cards because they saw the connection between the two interruptions of their walk across campus and realized that the free certificate was being given in an attempt to influence their decision about the post card.

Maybe the certificate was, in fact, enough to evoke the hypothesized good feeling that the researchers were trying to develop. And maybe the 47 recipients of the certificate, or at least many of them, would have been more inclined, as a consequence of their unexpected good fortune, to be more helpful and have better dispositions the rest of the day. With a different plan for measuring this effect, the relationship might have been documented. But as it was, the cause-and-effect relationship was not supported empirically, and we are left with the sad possibility that many of the good feeling subjects, upon seeing through the study, spent the rest of the day in an angry mood, with residual hostility against social psychologists remaining long after the study was completed.

59. Head Start

We know how much weight Donald Campbell and Albert Erlebacher (two psychologists at Northwestern University) would give to the Westinghouse/Ohio University report—very little. They made their position quite clear in a paper criticizing both the methodology and the statistical procedures used in studies of Head Start programs. Since the statistical discussion is quite technical, we will concentrate only on the methodology.

Campbell and Erlebacher's chief criticism was of the effect of matching on the results. Since it would be more difficult to find matches for the most disadvantaged children, it is likely that the studies ended up matching those at the upper end of distribution in the Head Start classroom with those at the lower end of the control classroom. Thus, both samples being compared were extreme relative to their respective populations. Any time the samples are chosen as a consequence of being extreme, we can expect to find the statistical artifact of regression toward the mean. That is to say, the mean of a group chosen because it is extreme will tend to be less extreme (closer to the population mean) when measured a second time.

The amount of regression is a function of the correlation between the two measures, with lower correlations resulting in greater regression. This is a consequence of the chance component of the scores at the first measurement, in that high scorers were "lucky" the first time measured and will be less so the second time. Similarly, low scorers were "unlucky" the first time and will also be less so on second measurement. Thus, in the absence of any differential treatment of the two groups, we would expect the lower-class group mean to decrease and the middle-class group mean to increase as a function of the less-than-perfect correlation due to error of measurement. If we now add a constant to each child's score (both maturation and testing would have this effect) in order that all changes will be in the positive direction, the results will show greater gains for the middle-class control group than for the Head Start group—in other words, exactly the findings reported in the Westinghouse/Ohio University evaluation.

The irony of these findings is heightened when we consider the effects of matching on post-test scores. Campbell and Erlebacher used this procedure on data from a computer simulation and concluded that "of children scoring the same at time two, the Head Start children have gained .495 points while the Control children have lost .152" (p. 193.) This will make sense when you realize that the pretest mean of the Head Start group will have been *lower* initially, while that of the control group will have been higher.[1] Thus, in the absence of adding the constant, the control group would appear to have lost ground from the pretest to the post-test.

Although there were criticisms of Campbell and Erlebacher's criticism, we chose to side with them. We assume that you will do the same.

60. Hand Calculators

We were wrong. The three different results were not caused by carelessness in entering the correlational data. We never would have guessed the true cause of the outcome discrepancy, and we felt (and still feel) somewhat startled at learning what it was.

Our colleague, who considers himself to be meticulously careful, reports that he was sure that something crazy was going on with his calculator and that *he* was not the problem. So he called Texas Instruments, the people who manufactured and service calculators like the one he was using. After he told them about his three different answers for the same data set, Texas Instruments suggested that our colleague charge up his calculator with the electricity adapter and try entering the data again. Our colleague plugged his calculator in, waited a while, entered his data a fourth time, and—lo and behold—the answer in the calculator display window was exactly the same as the first of the three answers that had been obtained before.

According to the Texas Instruments owner's manual, the batteries in our colleague's

---

[1] Since regression is a statistical phenomenon, it also occurs when the post-test is used to create the extreme groups.

hand calculator typically provide two to three hours of continuous operation before they need to be recharged. The owner's manual also says that the batteries should be recharged when the display window goes blank. But what the manual *doesn't* say is that the calculator loses its accuracy just before the batteries completely wear down. To us, this is a very disconcerting situation. How many researchers, we wonder, are getting inaccurate results without knowing it because they are using their calculators with weak, almost-worn-down batteries? And how many times might we or someone else presume that discrepant results have been caused by a student or colleague's being sloppy and careless in the use of the calculator, when in fact a different, nonhuman cause is responsible for the observed results?

61. Bumper Stickers

Although the study seems to confirm the original claims of police harassment, we would like to offer a few alternative explanations. First, a selection bias could have occurred, in that the fifteen students who agreed to put themselves in legal jeopardy were more likely to be politically oriented and sympathetic to the Black Panther cause. This in turn (as the original study points out) could have influenced their normal driving habits. In other words, they may have driven more recklessly than normal in order to attract police attention, which would then confirm the research hypothesis. Second, the author reports that the students became "nervous" and "edgy" during the study; perhaps this nervousness influenced driving habits, and perhaps the police tend to pay more attention to drivers with these characteristics. Third, it seems possible that a police officer stopping someone who appears tense, but who does not try to talk his or her way out of the citation, would be more likely to give the citation as well as to search the vehicle. Thus, although we are certainly not condoning police harassment, nor recommending that you run out and buy a Black Panther sticker, we believe that the jury is still out on this study.

62. Debriefing

In this study on instructional objectives, a statistically significant difference was found to exist between the two comparison groups in terms of their average scores on the 12-item post-test. We suspect that there *was* a real difference between the two conditions being compared. However, we are somewhat unwilling to accept the researchers' interpretation of the observed difference. Whereas they concluded that the treatment (the list of instructional objectives) given to the experimentul group had a beneficial effect, we would like to suggest that the two-point differential on the quiz may have been produced in part (or totally) by a negative effect associated with the control group.

As you will recall, the nine members of the control group showed up for class one day and were immediately asked to go to a nearby room. The instructor went with them, and for about ten minutes they discussed an examination that had been taken a few days earlier. Then they were asked to return to the regular classroom, with the added request that they not tell anyone in the other half of the class what they had been doing. And upon being reunited with the other ten students, members of the control group (and the other 10 as well) began to hear a lecture on a new topic, two-way analysis of variance.

Although the 19 subjects were supposedly naive to the fact that an experiment was being conducted, we contend that all of the students probably figured out what was going on. These were master's level students who had most likely participated in countless research investigations prior to this one. And since the content of their course that summer dealt with statistics and research, they were probably even further sensitized to the possibility of an experiment when they arrived for class that day and were split into two groups. If they had been asked to explain the basis for the group division, we strongly suspect that most of all of the 19 students would have correctly guessed, "At random."

Thus, our first point is that college students often figure out that they are serving as subjects in an experiment, even if the researcher carefully avoids telling them. Our second point, somewhat related to the first, has to do with perceived group membership. We are fairly confident that the ten students who remained in the regular classroom to examine the list of instructional objectives realized that they had received a potentially helpful treatment—if not right away, during the ten minute session when they were by themselves, then most likely during the actual lecture when it became evident that the instructor's comments were providing answers to the items on the instructional objectives list. And we're also fairly confident that most of these experimental subjects thought ahead to the possibility of an end-of-class quiz covering the lecture material.

But what went through the minds of the nine students in the control group? Our guess is that they incorrectly assumed that *they* were the experimental group. (Recall that they, too, had an activity during the time they were in the nearby room; moreover, the instructor went with them and could have been perceived as administering their treatment.) This would have been all right (even desirable) except for the fact that their treatment may have given them a false set, thereby causing them to get less out of the lecture than they normally would.

During the control group's ten-minute presession, they discussed a previously administered course quiz. Because of the nature of this presumed treatment, we suspect that these subjects looked ahead to the end of the class session and guessed that they would be examined on the content covered by the previous quiz. They probably thought that the experiment had something to do with retention and review. And during the lecture on two-way analysis of variance, these subjects may have been paying less attention to what the instructor was saying than they normally would and more attention to a mental review of their recent discussion with the instructor and an attempted recall of the actual test items that they had seen on the previous quiz.

In an attempt to make our point in a different way, let us suppose that the available subject pool had been randomly split into three subgroups rather than two. Further suppose that two of these groups were treated in precisely the same way as the two groups were in the actual experiment. How would the quiz scores have turned out, we wonder, if the third subgroup had simply been contacted and told to report to class ten minutes after the regular starting time? If our theory is right about the possible negative set created by the ten-minute discussion of the previous course examination, then we would find that the subjects engaged in this preclass activity would score lower on the 12-item quiz than the group of subjects who simply came to class ten minutes late. Moreover, the group getting the instructional objectives might not perform any better than the group that came late, thereby showing that the list of objectives did not really have any beneficial impact at all.

However, there may have been a far easier way to find out whether the rival hypothesis that we are talking about was actually operating. In a word, the subjects could have been debriefed. This technique, used now by some researchers but not nearly as many as should, simply involves talking to some or all of the subjects following the collection of the post-test data. The subjects are asked whether they knew that an experiment was in progress, whether they had any idea what the researcher's hypothesis was, whether they knew which group (experimental or control) they were in, and whether they gave honest answers to the questions on the post-test. Based on their responses to these queries, the researcher can usually identify more confidently the true reason for the groups' earning dissimilar scores on the post-test.

In the actual experiment on instructional objectives, it would have taken no longer than three or four minutes to debrief the 19 subjects with a short written questionnaire following the collection of the quiz papers. We seriously think that the researchers would have been in a better position to argue about the beneficial effects of their instructional objectives had they done this.

63. Teenagers and Drugs

There are some obvious problems with this study. For one thing, the selection of participants was done by one of the authors (a physician). Perhaps he inadvertently chose those with a higher probability of a positive response to the Ritalin therapy. A second problem involves the use (or nonuse) of statistical tests. For the most part, results were reported as "positive improvement," judged, apparently, by the authors of the study. A third problem concerns the continuation on Ritalin of those who showed improvement. It seems possible to us that some adolescents may take longer to respond to the therapy—perhaps another few weeks would have led to improvement in those for whom the drug had been ineffective, perhaps not. The adolescents were also continuing to get attention from nurses and physicians during this stage of the study. The extra attention from these authority figures might also serve as a rival hypothesis to the treatment.

Finally, without going into the details (see Problem 81), this study has all the shortcomings usually associated with a one-group pretest–post-test design (for example, the adolescents might have improved in the absence of treatment). Thus, we can hardly support the conclusions drawn in this study.

64. Being Partial: Not Always a Bad Thing

We think that years played, as a variable, should have been held constant or partialled out. At the time this sports editorial appeared, some of the 32 pitchers listed in the chart had played only eight years in the major leagues; others had been pitching in the big leagues for twice as long, and one had been in majors for 20 years! Clearly, the more years a pitcher accumulates in the major leagues, the larger the expected differential between career wins and career losses. When experience is taken into consideration (by dividing the won/lost differential by the number of years in the major leagues, thereby providing an index of average yearly won/lost differential), the ordering of the list changes substantially. Bob Gibson, with 15 years' experience, drops to fourth place. The pitcher originally in fifth place takes over the top position. And the pitcher originally in the twenty-second spot ends up in the thirty-first position.

We are not sure that a simple difference between games won and games lost is the best way to assess who is the best pitcher. Surely, the hitting ability of the pitcher's teammates helps him to win games, as does the fielding ability of the other eight individuals on the team. The concept of earned-run average is also another important variable. But one thing we know for sure: the chart presented in the newspaper should have taken into consideration how many years each pitcher had spent in the big leagues.

65. Childless by Choice

As you have no doubt realized, there are a few problems with this study. For one thing, the groups differed drastically on the proportion of married women (none in the tubal ligation group, 11 of 18 in the nonpermanent contraception group). Second, since according to the authors, "the psychiatrist is often called on to be a decision-maker in the case of a young woman seeking sterilization," it seems likely to us that such women would feel compelled to overstate wildly their hostility towards children, in much the same way as couples seeking a divorce must exaggerate their feelings in states with highly restrictive divorce laws. Had they responded otherwise, it is possible that the psychiatrist would have denied them the operation. In other words, we consider the interview to have been a highly reactive measurement occasion. A third problem concerns the lack of statistical analyses other than the comparison of proportions (no tests were reported).

Although studies of this issue are difficult to do well, we believe the researchers could have done better.

66. The Price of Beer

In this study, each of the 60 subjects was required to judge the quality of each brand of beer. However, the technical report of this study states that the subjects, on each of the 24 visits from the researcher, "were free to choose whichever brand they wished" (Mc Donnell, p. 331.) You may be thinking that each subject could have selected the *same* brand throughout the experiment—probably Brand "M," the high-priced brand. Were this the case, then the evaluation of the other two brands (which were never tasted) would constitute *anticipated* perception of quality, and the results would have to be interpreted differently from the way they were. However, the researcher reports that each brand was selected at least 25 percent of the time, and we presume that all subjects had some exposure to each brand. Hence, we do not have, as yet, a plausible rival hypothesis.

But what about the order in which the subjects selected their beer during the 24 visits from the researcher? Even if each subject had selected each brand an equal number of times, you may be thinking that a majority of the subjects drank one brand during the first eight visits while saving a different brand for the last eight visits. Had this been the case, type of beer would seem to be confounded with weeks of the experiment. However, since all three brands were actually the same, this was not a problem. If the subjects evaluated the brand consumed first differently from the brand consumed at the end, only one explanation could be offered—the price difference. Hence, order effects do not constitute a plausible rival hypothesis in this study.

A third possible explanation for the perceived differences among the three brands is related to possible differences among preferences for letters. As we indicated elsewhere (see Problem 6), people will sometimes choose one item over another simply because of the letters used to label the two items. In the beer experiment, however, we suspect that the influence of the price information had a much greater impact than the influence of the letters. Hence, we conclude that the labels of the bottles constitute an implausible rival hypothesis for the observed results.

Now, if we eliminate label effects, order effects, and exposure effects, is there anything left for us to consider as a plausible rival hypothesis? In our judgment, there certainly is! The subjects in this study were, by their own admission, beer-drinking college students. We do not know how much beer these subjects would normally consume during the two-month duration of the experiment, but we suspect that it was *more* than the 24 bottles supplied by the researcher. In other words, we suspect that many of the 60 subjects—and maybe most or all of them—were also drinking their own beer during the eight weeks of the study. And if these college students were similar to the ones we know, they probably drank a variety of brands during this time period. If some of this beer was expensive and good-tasting while some was inexpensive and not so good, then we contend that subjects could very well have been thinking about their own high-, middle-, and low-priced beers as they filled out the researcher's questionnaire. To rule out this rival hypothesis, which seems very plausible to us, the researcher should have made sure that only the researcher's beer would be consumed during the eight weeks of the experiment.

67. A "T" Party

Both the measures and the design used in this study appear appropriate to answer the researcher's questions. However, we do have two major criticisms—assignment of participants to groups and the number of analyses run on the data. Assuming that type of treatment was assigned randomly to the days of the week, the assignment to treatment groups during the February and March sessions is a good solution; however, the use of a control group that chose to wait a few months for the treatment seems suspect. Despite the similarities between the groups on the various pretest measures, it still appears plausible to us that the same variables that led to the choice of different sessions could still have resulted in a selection bias. For example, perhaps greater concern about their children or enthusiasm for such a program led some parents to choose the early sessions. These and other unmeasured (perhaps even unmeasurable) variables could only have been prevented from causing systematic group differences by true random assignment.

Because of the large number of analyses run, we believe that the *experiment-wise error rate*—the probability of at least one difference appearing by chance alone would be high. It was fortunate that so many significant analyses were reported in support of the researcher's conclusions in that discounting the few (unidentifiable) chance results still leaves a fair amount of convincing evidence. We are willing to accept the treatment group differences but not the differences between the treatment groups and control groups.

68. Assessing Personality Through Handwriting Samples

Without meaning to impugn the professional integrity of Dr. James Bruno or other graphologists, we simply cannot accept the implied conclusions of the investigation conducted by *Parade* magazine. As we see it, the very plausible rival hypothesis connected with this study is that Dr. Bruno knew or simply guessed that the anonymous handwriting sample given to him was from President Carter. Based on the knowledge or assumption that this "government employee" was actually the President, Dr. Bruno could very likely have written his seven-paragraph personality analysis on the basis of public information about Jimmy Carter.

Dr. Bruno is a very famous graphologist, and he has conducted handwriting analyses for corporations, lawyers, universities, and "think-tanks." Consequently, we would be very surprised if he (and other well-known graphologists) had not become familiar with Jimmy Carter's handwriting during and after the 1976 election. Being a graphologist, Dr. Bruno was probably frequently asked to compare Carter's handwriting with that of other candidates and past presidents. And hence he very well may have recognized it during the study conducted by *Parade* magazine.

But suppose Dr. Bruno did *not* recognize the handwriting sample as Carter's. For the sake of argument, let's imagine that he had never seen any of Carter's handwriting prior to the little research study. Even if this were the case, we contend that Dr. Bruno quite possibly *guessed* that the handwriting sample came from Carter. To substantiate this claim, we selected 127 college students and asked them who had seen the previous week's issue of *Parade*, the issue that contained the report of the handwriting study. An 8½-by-11-inch sheet of paper was distributed to the 72 who indicated that they had not. This sheet had a handwriting sample at the top of the page (the same sample as that given to Dr. Bruno), plus these instructions presented in the middle of the page:

> Your task is to identify the person who has "authored" the above handwriting sample. The only hints we will give you are (1) the content of the handwriting sample and (2) the knowledge that the individual is a government employee. Without discussing this matter with anyone else or looking at their response, please write your guess on the blank line presented at the bottom of this page.

Among our group of 72 naive subjects, 36 (exactly 50 percent) correctly guessed the name of President Carter. We submit that many of these individuals could have written relatively accurate personality assessments on the "anonymous" author of the handwriting sample, even without any training as graphologists. The defense rests!

69. Yo! Ho Ho! and a Bottle of Rum

The reported success rate of over 80 percent does not tell us very much, even when it is compared with the previous, much lower rate. It is possible that different criteria for success were used in arriving at the two figures. It is also possible that the change to a volunteer Navy has placed the commanding officers under pressure to achieve high success rates. Both of these possibilities would be considered problems of instrumentation; that is, the ratings may have changed as a result of changes in the measuring process and not as a result of actual changes in the phenomenon being measured.

In their discussion section, the researchers point out other flaws in the study; thus, we will conclude by allowing the researchers to criticize their own study. For example, they state, "Without control groups one cannot be sure the changes noted in association with the treatment were caused by the therapy" (Edwards and Bucky, p. 184). We are also informed that "there is some evidence that levels of anxiety, depression, and hostility. . . decrease rapidly with the cessation of drinking no matter what the therapy" (p.184).

We agree. The use of the one-group, pretest–post-test design simply does not allow for meaningful assessment of treatment effects.

70. Teaching Machines Versus Textbooks

In our opinion, there is a problem connected with the way in which the subjects received their learning material (the 19 frames). The subjects using the teaching machine were presented with this material *individually,* either one at a time (because there was only one teaching machine) or all at once but in separate learning carrels (if there were several teaching machines available). On the other hand, the subjects using the printed booklets studied *in a group.* Actually, there were two groups for the subjects using the text, each containing about 15 people.

It is our contention that in many situations people do not behave the same way in a group as they do when they are alone. As college professors, we consistently observe a reluctance on the part of students to be the first one to turn in an examination paper. Our students, during learning and testing, are sensitive to what other learners are doing, and we suspect that this peer sensitivity could have been operating among the subjects of the experiment who studied the 19 frames in a group setting. Isn't it possible that some of these subjects were distracted by what their colleagues were doing? Or that they studied more diligently because this seemed like the thing to do.

We don't know, of course, whether there actually was an effect created by studying the 19 frames individually or in a group, nor do we know the direction of the effect if it did, in fact, exist. But if this effect were present, then the results may well be misleading. Possibly, the teaching machine is better than the text for *all* students, regardless of the student's interest; or maybe the text is better. Because individual/group study was confounded with the machine/text presentation of material, it is very difficult to interpret clearly the results of this study.

71. Intelligence and Strangeness

In this study, selective sampling is clearly a problem. The "attraction" literature in social psychology[1] tells us that it is likely that teachers selected students who were already better adjusted socially, were from upper-middle-class homes, and were well liked by all (including the teacher). It should not surprise us to find these characteristics continuing into adulthood. For example, the sample showed a relatively low divorce rate, which we know to be correlated with a low rate of parental divorce; perhaps children from broken homes were not chosen by the teachers and thus were underrepresented in the final sample. Also, the overrepresentation of upper-middle-class children could have accounted for the large number of professional degrees, higher income, and so on.

As we see it, it is unlikely that every bright child had an equal probability of being selected into Terman's sample. If this were the case, then this sampling bias serves as an alternative explanation for the conclusion that gifted children are supernormal. The jury is still out on this question, but truth is sometimes stranger than fiction.

72. Dormitory Hours

The results of this study make it look as if the presence of residence hall hours has no effect on the academic performance of first-quarter college women. We feel, however, that the researchers may have committed a logical flaw in their conduct of this investigation. To be more specific, while the adjusted first-quarter GPAs for the hours and no-hours groups give the impression that the women required to observe hours would have earned about the same grades under the no-hours condition, we think that they very well might have done much worse if given the opportunity to come in at night whenever they pleased.

Were the two groups really equal to begin with? And did the statistical adjustment based on predicted GPAs remove any initial difference that may have existed? In our opinion, the answer may be a firm no. Let us now try to explain.

There are probably several reasons why the 371 sets of parents chose not to allow their daughters to ignore the dorm hours. However, we suspect that many of them were fearful that their daughters would "goof off" and not spend enough time studying and sleeping if permitted to stay out as long as they wished. During high school, these daughters may have shown their parents—when given the opportunity—that they could *not* deal with freedom in a fully mature way. On the other hand, we are sure that many of the parents in the other group gave their daughters permission to disregard the dorm hours because the girls had proven themselves in high school.

But the predicted college GPAs for these two groups were very similar! And if the above reasoning were correct, wouldn't we expect the hours group to have a lower predicted GPA than the no-hours group? Not necessarily. We think it is possible that the two groups performed about the same in their high school coursework and on the

---

[1] For example, see E. Berscherd and E. Wallster . "Physical Attractiveness." In L. Berkowitz, ed., *Advances in Experimental Social Psychology*, (New York: Academic Press, 1974), vol. 7, pp. 158–215.

college entrance exam because the "goof-off" group, being under the watchful eye of their parents at that time in their lives, simply didn't "goof off" very much. We certainly know several people who achieve quite nicely when operating in a supervised setting, but take the supervisor away and watch out!

In this research study, the similarity of the predicted GPAs for the two groups meant that the comparison of the hours and no-hours groups virtually involved the obtained GPAs. In other words, the researchers are asking us to believe that an appropriate control group for the hours group is the no-hours group—or stated differently, that the hours group would have earned about the same grades as the no-hours group if it had been able to ignore the dorm hours. We simply cannot accept this argument, for we feel that the hours group would have performed less well than it did (or than the no-hours group did) had the girls been able to come in at night whenever they wanted.

The statistical adjustment technique used by the researchers can work nicely if the initial differences that exist between the comparison groups are, in fact, noticed and used. But in the study on dorm hours, the inclination not to study (which we believe was present among the two groups to different degrees) was not reflected in the two sets of predicted GPAs. And as a consequence, the data collected and reported in this study are not giving us a valid notion of how the hours group would have performed during their first college term without having to adhere to the hours regulation.

Just to clarify the point, consider this hypothetical study. Suppose a researcher had two intact groups of available subjects but does not know that one is a group of people with very high IQs while the other is a group with average IQs. Further suppose that both groups are exposed to a course dealing with a new foreign language that no subject has ever heard of before the experiment. The experimental group (made up of all the average IQ people) gets to attend the class discussions *and* meet with the instructor for individual tutoring sessions. The control group (made up of all the high-IQ people) gets to go to class but does not receive the individual tutoring. On a post-test, the two groups perform about equally well. And since both groups earned about the same low score on the pretest, the researcher concludes that the two groups were equivalent to begin with and that the tutoring didn't have any beneficial effect.

Obviously, such an inference would be a mistake. The fact the average-IQ group did as well on the post-test as the high-IQ group indicates that the tutoring most likely *did* help out substantially. And the similarity of the pretest scores does not indicate initial equivalence. Unless the two groups were first exposed to some of the new course material and allowed to demonstrate their differential ability to learn, the difference between the groups in IQ would not be expected to show up on the pretest. Likewise with the dormitory hours study. We feel that the similarity in college grades does not show that the hours regulation was ineffective, and the near-identical predicted GPAs for the two groups do not mean that the two groups were initially equivalent.

73. Alcoholics in Control

Although the authors of this study considered three alternative explanations for their findings, we believe that there were at least two others that should have been considered. First, it seems very likely that there was a selection bias in that the control group consisted of women with jobs as well as women active in community affairs—all of whom were volunteers. Both groups would very likely believe themselves to be in control of their lives and thus score higher on internality. The difference in this study could reflect the high internality of the control group as much as anything else. Second, it seems to us that the six-month period over which the alcoholic group was tested (as contrasted with the presumably shorter period over which the control group was tested) could have led to differences if the residents of the halfway house discussed the scales with each other during course of the study. The control group presumably did not have as much opportunity for such discussion. All in all, however, we consider the selection bias the more serious problem—serious enough to make us hesitant about accepting conclusions that go against a number of other studies.

74. Disabled Counselors

It seems possible that the disabled counselors were selected more often than the able-bodied counselor because of the handsomeness variable rather than the disability variable. The researchers certainly tried to control for handsomeness by pairing each of the three counselors with each of the three disability conditions (wheelchair, crutches, nothing). However, we still think that the counselors, and not their disability, may have been the cause of the observed differences in subject preference. Let us explain why.

The three counselors who were used in the various photographs of this study did not, in reality, have any physical disability. Hence, they were acting in two of their three photographs, when they were paired with the wheelchair and the crutches. Perhaps when they were in these two situations, the counselors tried harder to appear empathetic toward the client who was also in the picture. If this happened, then the counselors' attempts to appear more empathetic may have resulted in facial expressions that were more desirable from the standpoint of a prospective client.

Or, maybe the three counselors in the study felt silly when pretending to be physically disabled. If so, possibly their facial expressions seemed more jovial in the wheelchair and crutches photographs. And in that case, the results of the experiment would potentially indicate that clients prefer happy counselors rather than counselors who appear to be more serious-minded.

Our main point concerning the rival hypothesis can be summed up as follows. We believe that the three treatments (levels of disability) may have had an influence on the facial expressions of the counselors in the photographs. The experimental subjects were led to believe that they should be concentrating, in part, on the variable of handsomeness. Hence, the disabled counselors may have been selected more often for the 20 hypothetical problems because when in the "disabled" photographs, they looked different from the way they appeared in the "able-bodied" photograph. That is, maybe the three counselors appeared more (or less) handsome when paired with a wheelchair or crutches. If so, the counterbalancing technique of having nine photographs, with each counselor paired with each level of disability, would *not* solve the problem.

To rule out this rival hypothesis, the researchers could have taken the nine photographs and cut out the portion that showed each counselor's face (and possibly his arms if gestures were being used to make a point). Then, using an independent set of subjects, the three pictures of each counselor's face could be given to one-third of these new subjects, with the task being to rank the three pictures in terms of empathy, jovialness, handsomeness, or some such characteristic. If the faces from the wheelchair and crutches photographs were selected, in this new study, about an equal number of times in the first, second, and third positions, then our suggested rival hypothesis would be proven not to apply. But as the original study stands, there *is* an alternative explanation for why the disabled counselors were selected more frequently.

As added support for our theory, consider what happened at the end of the original experiment. The 48 subjects were interviewed individually, to see if they suspected any experimental deception. (Recall that subjects were told the experiment dealt with handsomeness when it really dealt with levels of disability.) In one of these debriefing interviews, the subject stated that he had been influenced by the "smile" of the counselor. Isn't it possible that other subjects were also influenced by this sort of stimulus but chose not to say so? Or that they were influenced in the same way in an unconscious manner? And isn't it also possible, as we have previously argued, that there were more or bigger smiles in the wheelchair and crutches photographs?

75. The Principle of Least Interest

The following question should have crossed your mind: is there a relationship between anxiety level and age, education, religion, or other such demographic variables? Fortunately, it also crossed the minds of the researchers, who found no such relationship. It should also have crossed their minds that (aside from ever-present third variables) the direction of causality between primary group ties and low anxiety was as likely to be in one direction as in another. It seems plausible that those who are less anxious in stress situations are those who are more likely to form stronger ties with their primary groups.

Although these researchers were very careful to label their findings as "merely suggestive," we believe that they fell into a subtle, but very common, trap. After recognizing the limitations of the study in the methods section, they forgot those limitations when they reached the discussion section. As in many studies, the interpretation of the findings gives an impression of strength, whereas we believe that the conclusions ought to be expressed more tentatively. The researchers failed to heed their own warning.

76. Popcorn

Maybe Orville Redenbacher's corn *is* better than other brands. However, we have used it at home and still have trouble with leftover unpopped kernels or burned corn stuck to the bottom of our pan. Since we are somewhat skeptical of the unbiased attitude and scientific aloofness of people who conduct "experiments" for magazine advertisements and television commercials, we do have a few rival hypotheses in mind that might explain the different amounts of corn in the two poppers.

The experimental equipment involved two popcorn poppers, 4 ounces of Redenbacher's popping corn, and 4 ounces of some other ordinary brand of popping corn. We will presume that the two poppers were identical (possibly brand new) and that there really were 4 ounces of each brand. Even though these features of the experiment were constant across the two comparison groups, we wonder whether the cards were purposefully stacked against the ordinary brand.

For one thing, we wonder about the age of the popping corn. Isn't it possible that the kernels from the ordinary brand were old, stale, and too tired to pop the way they would have earlier in their lives? Second, what about the size of the kernels? Maybe a large group of Redenbacher's kernels were culled to produce 4 ounces of small kernels, while 4 ounces of large kernels from the ordinary brand might have been used. Maybe small kernels will produce a greater volume of popped corn than will the same amount (in ounces) of large kernels.

Third, we wonder about the heat in the two poppers. Sometimes poppers have temperature controls, and if the two in the picture did, maybe the ordinary brand of corn was popped at too low or too high a temperature. Fourth, what about the type of cooking oil used in the two poppers? We are not told that it was the same, nor that the kernels from the two brands were put into the cooking oil at the same time.

Fifth, what about the time at which the two batches of popcorn were started and the time of the picture? Isn't it possible that Orville started cooking his corn earlier than he did the ordinary brand, that the picture was taken just as his batched finished, and that the other batch continued to pop and produced an equal amount after the camera's shutter had clicked? And finally, perhaps the two brands were weighed at different times. Possibly popping corn weighs less after being popped than before. This would mean that 4 ounces of popped Redenbacher corn would constitute a bigger pile than 4 ounces of unpopped corn from the ordinary brand, which was then popped.

As we stated earlier, maybe Orville Redenbacher's Gourmet Popping Corn is the best popcorn on the market. And maybe its superior quality is the true explanation of why the two poppers in the picture have different amounts of popcorn in them. But then again, it is also possible that one or more of the rival hypotheses mentioned above constitute the only reasons for the observed difference. We leave it up to you to determine how plausible each of our alternative explanations really is. But as you do this, please remember, *caveat emptor* ("let the buyer beware").

77. Cigarette Smoking and Physical Fitness

Did a high level of cigarette smoking cause subjects to perform less well on the stressful physical tests? Possibly so. However, we wonder whether the cause-and-effect relationship, at least in part, might be in the *opposite* direction—from the fitness tests to the smoking frequency! Obviously, how a subject performed on the fitness tests could not affect, retrospectively, the amount of smoking that took place prior to the day of the experiment. But we do feel as if performance on the tests could potentially influence the way in which the subjects responded to the question about their smoking behaviors. In short, we question the validity of the self-report data on frequency of smoking.

As you will recall, the last of the five tests for all 88 subjects was the 1-mile run. On this test, performance varied tremendously. The standard deviation was 86.01 seconds, meaning that the range between the fastest and slowest runners was about seven minutes. (The mean time for all subjects was eight minutes 48 seconds.) Thus, among the total group there were some pretty slow runners. In fact, we wonder whether the slow ones actually kept on running for the entire 1-mile run; it is quite likely that some had to stop and walk so as to catch their breath.

Well, following the 1-mile run, the subjects were asked to indicate how much they smoked. For those who did poorly on the 1-mile run, we contend that the question about smoking could have suggested to them a reason why they did poorly and encouraged them to exaggerate how many cigarettes they had been smoking per day. This unconscious distortion of their true smoking behavior could have given these poor runners a reason for why they did not do better. For the subjects who did well in the mile run, we think that just the opposite could have happened. With these individuals, the fact that they ran fast may have influenced them, consciously or unconsciously, to underestimate the amount of smoking they did.

If the subjects had been asked about their smoking behavior just *before* the five tests, we are positive that this type of problem would not have occured. Obviously, the performance on the mile run could not affect the self-report data on smoking if the self-report data came first. However, a different type of problem might have been created. By asking subjects to indicate their smoking frequency just before they performed, we might cause some persons to perform poorly simply because they are under the *impression* that heavy smokers do not do well in physical activities. This impression could be incorrect—in fact, it was the hypothesis being tested in this study—but it could still operate to affect performance. Not many people perform well when they do not think they should! Clearly, the best solution to the problem of when to collect the smoking data would be to obtain this information from the subjects at a time that was not near the actual physical testing—and preferably in such a manner that would not cause any subject to see the possible connection between the smoking information and the fitness tests.

But what if the smoking data *had* been collected in an appropriate manner? Given the same set of results as the researcher obtained, would this prove a cause-and-effect relationship between smoking and physical fitness? The answer is no. Possibly, a third variable—unmeasured in the study—is the true reason why people who smoke a lot perform poorly on fitness tests. In other words, perhaps smoking and poor fitness are both consequences brought about by some other causal agent. Maybe nervousness is such a third variable, with some individuals smoking a lot and running slowly because they are in a chronic state of nervousness. Or possibly the third underlying variable is the physique—maybe people with anemic-looking bodies smoke a lot to compensate for their appearance and run slowly because they simply don't have well-developed muscles. And there are, of course, many other such underlying third variables that we could posit as the true reason why some people run more slowly than others and smoke more.

78. To B-Mod or Not To B-Mod

The description of this study should have raised at least some of the following questions in your mind: What is the effect of the staff's being aware of the parents' group assignments? Does having two therapists present at the treatment group sessions, but not at the placebo group sessions, really result in equal status attention? What about the reliability of both the coding scheme and the expectancy questionnaire? What is the effect of the small number of families used? What is the correct unit of analysis? Why were some of the statistical tests one-tailed and some two-tailed? Why were results reported for only one of the 29 observational categories?

With no statement to the contrary, the participant assignment procedure makes it quite possible for the treatment staff to have inadvertently been generally more helpful and concerned about the treatment group than about the placebo group. Our second question appears to answer itself—status attention is badly confounded with group assignment. As for reliability, although the authors did report a mean observer agreement of 82 percent (the range was 63 to 92 percent), no reliability was reported for the expectancy questionnaire. In combination with the small sample size, this raises serious questions about the authors' acceptance and interpretation of their finding of no difference in expectancy level of the two groups. A graph of the expectancy data was presented in the original article, and it appeared that the treatment group had consistently higher expectations of success. It seems to us that the small number of families resulted in little statistical power. Accepting the hypothesis of no difference under these circumstances is fraught with danger. Furthermore, the correct unit of analysis in this study is undoubtedly the group of three families, and not the separate families. This would yield four, rather than twelve, subjects for the study.

Since no theoretical case is made for the reporting of a one-tailed test of significance in a situation where the two-tailed test would not have been significant, we are unable to give you an explanation. Although we strongly recommend the use of two-tailed tests for most situations, we would have been more sympathetic had the authors consistently used one-tailed tests. Finally, if only one of the 29 observational categories was "clinically relevant," (no explanation given), we wonder why the authors bothered to code the other 28 categories. Even if they only analyzed the data on that one category because the other categories were clearly not going to yield significant results, the effect on the error rate is the same as if they had computed all 29 tests. The probability of at least one chance difference being found in analyzing the observational categories is still very high.

We would like to commend the authors for having given two plausible explanations for their finding that the placebo parents believed their children had improved despite reporting no improvement in symptom behavior. At the same time, however, we believe that they overlooked at least one other equally plausible explanation, namely, that learning that other parents had similar (or worse) problems may have made these parents less distressed about their children's symptom behaviors.

Although we cannot recommend this study to our friends, we think it does point out the difficulties of doing clinical research, particularly in a field setting.

79. Student Resignations at West Point

The rival hypothesis connected with this study was not initially suggested by us. Instead, it came directly from the researchers themselves and was discussed at the end of the formal report of the investigation. It has to do with the time interval during which the data were recorded and a possible effect that the informative booklet might have before this time period.

As you recall, the booklet was sent to 246 experimental subjects about a month before the start of the summer training program. The 11 members of this group who did not show up on July 1 were not counted as experimental resignations, and yet the booklet very well may have caused these individuals to resign early. The booklet's descriptions of the mundane and stressful activities may have led these 11 people (or at least some of them) to see that the military experience was not for them, so they didn't go. But since the data on resignations from the experimental group were collected only *after* the program began, it looks as if the booklet prevented more resignations than may have been the case, simply because the 11 no-shows were disregarded. (Recall that the size of the two comparison groups was 234—the number of experiment group cadets who actually began the program.) As the researchers put it,

> One could argue that those who did not report after accepting their appointments still had some doubts, and the booklet convinced them not to come. The "doubters" were still in the control group on July 1 but subsequently resigned, thus creating the significant difference reported. (Ilgen and Seely, p. 454).

Although the researchers considered this alternative explanation for their results, they argued that the booklet most likely did not cause very many of the 11 experimental no-shows. Data from previous investigations and a somewhat complex analysis of their own data were used as a basis for the researchers' conclusions about the booklet's probable lack of effect on early resignations in the experimental group. And thus the major conclusion of the study was that the booklet worked. Our major point is that the researchers were sensitive to a possible rival hypothesis, and you, as a critical thinker, should have seen this alternative explanation as well.

80. Miss America

If you have concluded that the pretest–post-test difference (1.6 percent versus 16.3 percent) was attributable to changes in the interviewers or scoring criteria, you could be right. However, we don't think that these explanations constitute plausible rival hypothesis. Most likely, all interviews were very structured and conducted in a similar fashion at both the pretest and post-test time periods. We seriously doubt that any hints were given during the post-test interview or that the criterion for successfully answering the question changed from pre to post.[1]

Another thought you may have had is that the *same* group of 15,000 individuals was interviewed during the pretest and then again during the post-test. The promotional material does not rule out this interpretation, for it states that "in February and March 1975 a second wave of over 15,000 interviews was conducted." It doesn't say that the post-test interviewees were different from the pretest interviewees. If they were the same, then clearly the pre-post percentage change could be attributable to the stimulus of the first interview rather than to the intervening outdoor advertisements. However, we again feel that this is an improbable competing explanation. We strongly suspect that the people interviewed during the pretest were not included in the post-test sample.

So much for implausible rival hypotheses. Now let us consider two plausible explanations. First, the promotional material gives the impression that the impact of the other media stopped at the time of the pretest and that only outdoor advertising was in effect during the pretest–post-test time period. (In another section of the promotional material, IOA states: "Through a 2-month posting, Outdoor had done what all of the

---

[1] A change in the measuring device between pre and post is called *instrumentation*.

other media, combined, had failed to do.") However, Miss Ame[...]
television and radio concurrently with the outdoor advertising[...]
ued to appear in newspapers and magazines during this t[...]
Therefore, we cannot single out billboard advertising as *the r*[...]
increased awareness of her name. Possibly, this increased awar[...]
a cumulative effect of the other media.

Our second suggestion, however, is the one that we believe to be the most plausible
rival hypothesis of all. That is simply that the unusual nature of the Miss America
poster caused it to become a topic of conversation in the 44 metropolitan markets. We
live in one of these metropolitan areas, and soon after the Miss America posters went
up we read about the project in our local newspapers, heard about the project on our
local radio stations, and saw the poster on a segment of the local television news report.
Above and beyond the fact that Miss America's name was appearing, in a normal way,
in all these media during the two-month test period (our first plausible rival hypothesis), her name appeared in these other media *because of* the unique nature of IOA's
poster and research study. Had these media failed to cover this story, we strongly
suspect that less than 16.3 percent of the post-tested sample would have correctly
known Miss America's name.

Suppose you are in the position of trying to sell a new brand of canned baked beans.
You could, of course, begin to advertise your product through outdoor advertising. If
you did, IOA's promotional materials would lead you to believe that after two months
of posting there would be a tenfold increase in the percentage of the consuming public
who were familiar with your particular brand of baked beans. We feel this might be
true—if you could get radio, television, and the newspapers to help out by also
promoting your product.

81. Groups for Parents

Is the Groups for Parents approach really as effective as its authors claim? As a
consequence of the researchers' use of a one-group pretest–post-test design, it is almost
impossible to answer this question.

First, we must consider the rival hypothesis of experimental mortality (this refers to
those participants who dropped out of the study before its completion). This raises the
possibility that those who were not finding the approach helpful were more likely to
drop out than those for whom the approach was succeeding. This would also account
for the high rate of client satisfaction reported in the study.

Second, instrumentation could account for the increases in both reinforcement rates
and compliance rates; that is, since in both cases the parents were the measuring
instruments, it is likely that they were better able to identify both types of behaviors
even when the rate was unchanging. We must also consider the rival hypothesis of
history; other events outside the study may have been taking place during the eight-
week experimental period which affected the dependent variables. It is also possible
for the problems to have eased up on their own during this time, thus giving rise to the
rival hypothesis of maturation.

Other rival hypotheses to be considered include both testing (perhaps the pretest
influenced the parents' responses to the post-test) and statistical regression. The latter
is a statistical artifact caused by a less-than-perfect correlation between the pretest and

e post-test. This results in the pretest mean of a group selected for its extremity being less extreme than the post-test mean. For example, the children of basketball players would be tall, but on average would not be as tall as their parents. Similarly, the children of those below the mean on height would still be short, but not as short as their parents. Thus, in this study parents were referred as a consequence of having extreme problems—we would not expect their problems to be as extreme on second measurement.

Needless to say, although the program may well be effective (no data to the contrary are reported), we would not enroll on the basis of the data presented in this study.

82. Unequal Egalitarianism?

Before the passage, in 1972, of Title IX of the Educational Amendments, females constituted a tiny fraction of the college and university faculty population. At any given rank, the percentage of women was very small, especially at the upper ranks (associate and full professor). Today, males continue to outnumber females as full-time faculty members, but there has been a concerted effort since 1972 on the part of many institutions to hire more females and to promote them more fairly.

However, as the percentage of female faculty increases due to new appointments, the relative average yearly salary for females has tended to go down. This is because there were, prior to 1972, a small group of females (at all ranks) possessing varying amounts of experience. The average yearly salary was previously based on this group; but as more and more females were hired or promoted, the average number of years' experience for any group dropped. Consequently, the gap between men's and women's salaries, in spite of inflation and a new policy of equal pay for both sexes, has tended to increase.

To make our argument clear, consider this hypothetical example. Suppose College X has seven faculty members employed at the assistant professor rank. Five of the seven are males, with their annual salaries and previous experience as follows: $12,000 (no experience), $13,000 (1 year's experience), $14,000 (2 years' experience), $15,000 (3 years' experience), $16,000 (4 years' experience). The two female assistant professors earn $12,000 (no experience) and $14,000 (2 years' experience). Further assume that at the end of the year the most experienced male faculty member resigns to take a job elsewhere, everyone else is given a 10 percent raise, and the vacancy is filled by a brand new female professor (no experience) who is hired at $12,960—$960 more than the previous year's starting salary to keep up with 8 percent inflation. Given these facts, the average salary for men increases 10 percent from the first year to the next year, while for women the average salary increases only 6.6 percent.

Does the discrepancy between the 10 percent and 6.6 percent figures presented in the previous paragraph indicate that males are treated more favorably than women? We do not think so. And the data in our fictitious example could have been constructed so as to apply to professors at any single rank, or to professors in general. Our point is simply this: if the NCES average salaries for the two-year duration of their study were based upon everyone who was working in either year (that is, not restricted to those working both years), and if the percentage of women at any one rank (or overall) increased due to new hiring and /or promotion, then the NCES statistics would make it look as if men were being treated more favorably when in fact both sexes may have received identical raises, with women being given a preference in hiring when other things are held constant.

For those who question the logic of our suggested rival hypothesis, consider a United Press International newspaper story printed two weeks after the article we have been discussing. This second article also dealt with men's and women's salaries. The Department of Labor indicated that the difference between yearly salaries for men and women (in all occupations) has been increasing, with the discrepancy being $3433 in 1974. The government report claimed that two major factors have contributed to the widening gap. With respect to the second explanation, readers were told:

> The dynamic rise in womens' labor force participation has resulted in a larger proportion of women who are in or near the entry level. Many women who started work were forced to take low-paying beginner jobs, while most men had more years of employment experience.[1]

Before concluding, it is important for us to add a final comment. We have argued that the NCES statistics showing a 0.6 percent differential between men's and women's salary increases *could* have been attributable entirely to variables other than sex discrimination. Since the original article, "Unequal Pay," did not indicate whether experience was taken into account, this variable is a legitimate rival hypothesis for the cause implied in the article, discrimination. However, even if experience and other pertinent variables *were* to be taken into consideration, we suspect that there would still be a differential (though not as large as the NCES figure of 0.6 percent) between men's and women's salaries. Discrimination against females has become a less frequent occurrence during the past few years, but it has not been eliminated.

83. Adopting the Sick Role

In observing friends and relatives who have two or more children, we have noticed that parents do, in fact, seem to be less concerned about minor physical problems in their second (and third) children than was the case with their first. Seeing that the first-borns survived their runny noses and mild fevers can do wonders for making parents a bit more realistic and a bit less nervous when it comes to raising the next child who comes along. Since we ourselves are parents, we can state that we have noticed this change in parental behavior on a first-hand basis—for our first-borns saw the friendly physician far more than their siblings.

Thus, we do not disagree with the idea that first-borns receive a different type of parenting when it comes to medical problems. But we find it somewhat hard to believe that this difference would show up on the three-item questionnaire years later when the children had become adults and students in college. Instead, we contend that other known differences between first-borns and their siblings could be the true cause of the significant difference between the two means. For example, intelligence may be the explanation.

First-born children have been shown to score significantly higher than younger siblings on traditional tests of intelligence. Regardless of whether the primary reason

[1] "Men's Wages Average $3433 Above Women's." *Knoxville News-Sentinel, November 29,* 1976, p. 9.

for this intellectual differential is hereditary or environmental, the fact remains that first-borns show up on tests as being smarter. Other research has shown that people who are superior intellectually are not anemic or physical rejects as many people think; rather, they are equal to or better than their less bright counterparts in terms of physical attributes.

One could argue that the smart thing to do upon noticing a physical abnormality—even a small one—is to contact a physician. (Certainly the medical profession would endorse this point of view!) Hence, the differential tendency to seek medical assistance may be caused by first-borns' being intellectually superior, and it may actually be unrelated, in a causal sense, to the differential parenting that these individuals received.

To make our point in a different way, suppose that we could somehow get our hands on a group of brand-new first-born and later-born children, and further suppose that we could arrange things such that the two groups received equal parental concern for the physical symptoms of disease and injury and also equal exposure to doctors and nurses. Were we able to make certain that the two groups of children were raised in this egalitarian fashion, would it guarantee that the two groups would perform equally on the three-item questionnaire administered 20 years later? Of course it would not. And the reason is that the two groups might not be the same with respect to one or more variables besides parenting.

Following this same pattern of logic, the discovery that two groups differ on some effect variable and also differ on some *potentially* causal variable does not firmly establish a cause-and-effect relationship—unless there are no other possible causal variables that distinguish the two groups. But in the particular study under consideration, we do not feel as if parenting is the only variable that differentiates first-borns from later-born children and that could potentially cause the two groups to score differently on the questionnaire. We offer intelligence as one such variable. But we are confident that there are many other alternative variables that could be suggested as well.

84.   School Adjustment Problems

One question that arises concerns the possible bias introduced by dropping families in order to match the two groups on the demographic variables. Fortunately, the researchers did look for differences between the 56 small families dropped and the 133 small families remaining in the study, and they found that while those remaining had significantly higher maladjustment scores, they did not differ on any of the other criterion measures.

The possibility also arises that although the two groups were matched on six demographic variables, other demographic differences might still exist. Differences in religous beliefs may be correlated with family size, as well as with different emphases on the importance of a strict upbringing or the importance of learning. It is also the case that family size is correlated with the length of time the family has been in existence; thus, larger families would tend to have older parents. A related problem involves the birth order of the children; the study might actually be comparing the youngest children from large families with the oldest children from small families, in which case we would not be surprised to find differences in the types of problems encountered.

85. Typed Papers and Grades

It seems to us that typed papers received better grades than handwritten papers because of differences between students, as a group, who typed their papers and students, as a group, who did not type their papers. Stated differently, we suspect that other variables, besides the presumed causal variable of typing, were not held constant across the two comparison groups. As a consequence, we believe that a case can be made for any of these other variables being the true reason for why the two groups differ in the grades they receive.

Let us consider two of the ways in which the typing and nontyping groups could have differed. First, think of motivation. Isn't it likely that the student who goes to the trouble to type a paper is more highly motivated than the student who does not go this extra mile? And isn't it likely that this higher motivation has led to a more extensive reading (and rereading) of assigned material, an examination of materials not assigned, a discussion of the paper topic with peers and/or parents, and other activities that put the student in a better position to write a high-quality paper? Second, what about the variable of financial well-being? Aren't students who own typewriters more likely to come from well-to-do families? If so, their parents probably have more than the average number of books around the house; they probably have been exposed to more places and cultural events through family trips; and they probably have been encouraged by their parents to adopt a value system that encourages high grades. We are confident that the typing students would probably differ from the nontyping students in several other ways, but lack of space precludes a complete listing of all such variables. Suffice it to say that it is highly unlikely that the two groups were the same except for the variable of having typed or not typed their papers.

Not too long ago, a pair of researchers conducted a tightly controlled experiment dealing with the neatness of essay examinations and grades.[1] In this study, all variables *were* held constant except the one of interest—paper neatness. This worthy goal was accomplished by constructing four versions of the same essay response; in other words, the four versions were identical in content, wording, spelling, length, and so on. The only difference was in appearance: one version was beautifully handwritten, one version was copied with average handwriting neatness, one version was handwritten in a nearly illegible manner, and one version was typed. When the papers were graded by 420 prospective high school teachers, it turned out that there was no significant difference between the typed and very neatly handwritten versions of the essay. (And believe it or not, the mean grade given to the typed paper was slightly *lower* than the mean grade given to the essay copied in neat handwriting!)

Loneliness

Yes—we *do* feel that there are some plausible rival hypotheses. With respect to the Boston Irishmen, we think that they may be no more lonely than their brothers in the homeland. Their higher coronary death rate may be attributable to any of several variables, other than loneliness, that distinguish Boston from Ireland—for example,

[1] J. C. Marshall and J. M. Powers, "Writing Neatness, Composition Errors, and Essay Grades," *Journal of Educational Measurement*, 1969, 6, pp. 97–101.

worse drivers, more competition from women who are entering the job market, an extremely high cost of living, air pollution, and so on.

Nevada's higher death rate from heart disease than neighboring Utah *may* be attributable to the more "freewheeling, single-oriented atmosphere" as compared with the tradition of close family ties associated with the Mormons. But then again, it may not. For one thing, the majority of people who gamble in Reno and Las Vegas are vacationers from other states. Furthermore, the large number of divorces granted in Nevada do not involve just Nevada residents; we suspect that many people from Utah travel to Nevada to take advantage of a shorter waiting period for their divorces. Finally, we must point out that the amount of alcohol consumed per person is probably quite different in Nevada from what it is in Utah. Isn't it possible that drinking, rather than loneliness, is the true cause of heart disease differential?

Roseta, Pennsylvania has only one-third as many heart attacks as the surrounding towns. And since Roseta is less culturally diversified, Dr. Lynch points to this variable as the causal agent. But we wonder whether the ages of the people living in Roseta match those in the neighboring communities. There is a tendency to live one's entire life in a culturally homogeneous community, with young adults staying rather than moving away. Consequently, the average age in Roseta could be far below that in the surrounding towns. Or possibly the type of work engaged in by residents of Roseta is less strenuous. Or possibly Roseta has a larger number of physicians and a better health awareness program.

So far, we have discussed separate rival hypotheses for each of the three samples. Let us now suggest one hypothesis that may be common to all three—diet. In general, single people simply do not eat well-balanced meals as frequently as do married couples. (Have you ever tried cooking a roast for one?) Therefore, their mediocre or poor diets—probably with high cholesterol content—may be the true cause of single persons experiencing higher rates of heart attacks and disease.

For the above reasons, we cannot place ultimate faith in Dr. Lynch's theory. As we see it, there are some very plausible rival hypotheses associated with the Boston, Nevada, and Roseta "evidence." But beyond this conclusion, we question the assumption that divorced and single people are lonelier than those who are married. Please don't get us wrong; we are not knocking marriage (for we both consider ourselves to be quite happily married). But we do know several people who are just as happy even though they have never been married or have tried it out and found that it did not work. We concur with the notion that loneliness is brought about by social isolation, at least for most people like us. But we do not accept the assumption that single and divorced people are socially isolated and that they are therefore in a state of loneliness.

87. Sesame Street

Since we find that watching sporting events in color is well worth the price, we are glad to have spent the extra money on a color television set. This, in fact, does lead us to wonder whether there is a correspondingly greater effect from watching Sesame Street in color. Since data showed that nearly twice as many advantaged children, who were also more likely to own color television sets, watched Sesume Street as disadvantaged children, it seems likely that they as a group would benefit more than the disadvantaged children for whom the show was presumably intended.

Furthermore, it seems to us that encouragement to view was confounded with the effects of the show. This is rendered all the more plausible by data from Philadelphia that showed that the nonencouraged children watched as much as those children selected for encouragement. Nonexperimental encouragement was most likely coming from their advantaged parents. Other data from Durham, North Carolina, showed that the effects of encouragement disappeared rapidly when the visits stopped, thus increasing the plausibility of encouragement as a rival causal agent to the content of the show itself.

Finally, the differences between advantaged and disadvantaged in this study seem equally as attributable to differences in geographic locations as to differences in social class. Thus, we do not believe that the study adequately assessed the effects of watching Sesame Street in the absence of encouragement.[1]

88. Financial Woes of Colleges and Universities

To assess adequately the validity of the claims made by educational administrators that their institutions (especially private colleges) are in a near-crisis state, we feel that it would be necessary to have statistics regarding each institution's income (from tuition, alumni gifts, grants, and investments) and its financial obligations (salaries, taxes, and mortgages). If the typical institution has less money coming in than it has to pay out, then it *is* in financial trouble. And we believe that many colleges are now experiencing this sort of difficulty and consequently having to dip into normally untouched endowment funds to make the financial sheet balance.

Does an increase in the number of institutions indicate that no financial difficulties are being experienced? Absolutely not. Some of the new schools may be responding to a legitimate need for their services in a new geographical or specialty area. And they may do well. But other new institutions may fall flat on their faces because they did not heed the warning signs currently in evidence. Simply stated, the relationship between the number of institutions and their financial strength is not of a cause-and-effect nature.

For those of you who don't think that colleges and universities are having financial difficulty, we simply suggest that you go and talk with three people: the student who has just been told that tuition is going up, the faculty member whose teaching position no longer exists, and the university president. And show any of these people that little editorial!

---

[1] A complete discussion of the Sesame Street evaluation, along with a reanalysis of the data, can be found in T. Cook, H. Appleton, R. Conner, A. Shaffer, G. Tamkin, and S. Weber. *Sesame Street Revisited* (New York: Russel Sage Foundation, 1975).

89. Moral Development Across the Life Span

You should have noticed that we failed to give the authors' interpretation of the data we presented. We told you exactly what the authors told us; namely, that there were age differences. There was no attempt to relate these differences to some underlying construct other than "life experiences." We have an equally serious concern about their analytic approach. It seems redundant to use both a method for contrasting means from *qualitatively* different groups (Scheffé's) and a method that assumes the age groups are on a continuum that can be scaled at intervals (trend analysis).

Although age appears to be scaled at intervals, thus making trend analysis more appropriate, there is a subtle difference between age and age groups that would lead us to choose Scheffé's (or some similar) method in this case. When we examine the mean ages for each of the six groups as reported by the authors (given in years and months: 12,0; 16,4; 27,5; 37,10; 58,4; and 79,10), we find that these means are not equally distant from one another. Were we to plot on graph paper the relationship between mean age and age group, we would also find a curvilinear relationship. Thus, we would prefer to treat the groups as qualitatively, rather than quantitatively, different.[1]

A more common problem, which this study shares with many others, is that of sampling. Although we were not so told, the sampling appeared to be on the basis of easy access to the participants. We were told that certain individuals were excluded from the oldest age group. Thus, it seems to us that the sampling in this study adds to the previously mentioned age-cohort confusion. In short, had the authors interpreted their data, we would have been reluctant to accept their interpretation.

90. A Hypothetical Basketball Game

Although we do not gamble very much money on professional (or nonprofessional) sports, it is conceivable that someone might tempt us into wagering a few dollars on the outcome of the rookie versus Portland basketball game, presuming that such a game could actually be arranged. Even though we are somewhat unsophisticated about basketball strategy and play making, it would not take us very long at all to decide which team to bet on. We would definitely want to back the Portland Trailblazers, despite the 20-point differential in cumulative scoring averages between the two groups of five players. As we see it, there are a couple of alternate explanations for why the cumulative scoring average for the five rookies is higher than the cumulative average of Portland's starters, besides the possible explanation of superior ability among the rookies.

Our first rival hypothesis has to do with the number of minutes played per game in the past by each of the ten participants of our hypothetical basketball contest. Since Portland's striking success through the first half of the 1977–78 season was due, at least in part, to a strong "bench" (second-string players), the average number of minutes

---

[1] It is possible to use trend analysis with unequally spaced groups, but the researchers gave no indication that they had done so.

played per game by the starting five Trailblazers was probably much smaller than would have been the case if the reserves were of mediocre or low calibre. In contrast, the average number of minutes played per game by some of the rookies was probably very high, as in the case of Bernard King, who was playing for New Jersey (the worst team in the NBA, with an obviously weak bench).

Obviously, a player can not score when sitting on the bench. And we strongly suspect that Portland's starting five spent much more time on the bench than did the five rookies. For this reason, the scoring averages of the two sets of players are not comparable. What would happen, we wonder, if a sports statistician computed the average number of points scored *per minute played* (rather than per game) for each of the five rookies and veterans? Wouldn't these new averages give us a better idea of how the hypothetical game would turn out?

But let us suppose, just for the sake of argument, that the rookies were playing the same amount of time in each game as the Portland starters. Could we then have confidence that the rookies would win the hypothetical game by 20 points? Our answer is again a firm no, and our reasoning here has to do with our second rival hypothesis, opportunity to shoot and score. In case you don't already see our point, let us quickly explain.

In order to have a high scoring average, a basketball player not only needs to be off the bench and in the game but also needs to be given the ball. Since some of the five rookies mentioned—especially King and Davis—are the highest-scoring players on their respective teams, we suspect that their regular teammates recognize their scoring potential and consequently pass them the ball at almost every opportunity. But think about what happens when King and Davis and the other three rookie stars are brought together to form a team. When King has the ball and is trying to work in toward the hoop to score two points for his team, Davis and the other three rookies are unable to score. Conversely, the per-game scoring averages of the Trailblazers' starting line-up comes from situations in which they are playing with one another. In short, even a recomputation of the scoring averages to reflect point production per minute played would not give us an accurate picture of how the rookies would score when playing together. We definitely feel that even these adjusted scoring averages would exaggerate how many points the rookies would score as a team.

Besides our two main alternate explanations, you may have thought of other reasons why the rookies would not, in all likelihood, beat Portland's first five by 20 points. For one thing, the rookie team does not have a tall (by NBA standards) center to get rebounds under the defensive hoop and inside shots under the offensive hoop. And it would literally take years for the rookie team to become totally familiar with one another's moves on the court, in order to be able to anticipate where each other would be in the next second or two. Portland's starting five probably has this familiarity with each other's strengths, weaknesses, and tendencies.

We will conclude by asking you to think about that oft-repeated saying that goes something like this: "The whole is often *not* equal to the sum of its parts." We think that this saying has relevance to that final sentence of the newspaper article. And for anyone who disagrees, we simply ask you to check the record book to see how the College All-Star football game in Chicago—which pitted the best graduating college seniors against the top pro team from the previous year—almost always turned out. After a quick glance at the resulting scores, we think you, too, would want to put your money on Portland's starting five.

91. Do Snowstorms Increase Absenteeism?

Although this is the best use of a snowstorm in a study that we have seen, we believe that the researcher overlooked a few points. For one thing, it is clear that he views the attitudes as causing the behavior. Considerable support exists among some social psychologists for the opposite conclusion; namely, that behavior causes attitudes. For example, perhaps the participants in this study noticed that co-workers in their group consistently made more efforts to attend when "under the weather" than did workers in other groups. After such social pressure led them to attend under similar circumstances, they have perceived themselves as liking their jobs more. After all, why else would they try so hard to get to work?

This leads us to a related rival hypothesis; that is, differing social demands within the different groups may have caused both the attitudes and the behaviors. To the extent that different groups establish their own norms for attitudes and behaviors, the two would not be causally linked except through the third variable of social setting. The plausibility of this rival explanation seems to be increased by the anonymous nature of the initial data collection. It is possible that many of those whose attitudes were surveyed the previous year either no longer worked in the same group or no longer worked for the company, and that the demands of the setting rather than individual attitudes were responsible for the relationship.

So, while we commend the researcher for his creativity, we do not advise him to wait until the next snowstorm before considering the issues in this discussion.

92. Acting Like an "A" Student

We find it hard to believe that the phrase "as if you were an 'A' student" (given only to the experimental subjects) could bring about the observed difference between the two groups. Instead, we feel as if there may have been a methodological problem associated with the study. To be more direct, we wonder whether the 15-minute lecture was really as dull for the experimental group as it was for the control group.

Recall that the two sets of instructions were *read to* the 39 subjects. (The instructions were not printed and *read by* the subjects.) This means that the subjects had to be divided into two separate rooms for at least the preliminary part of the study, and we strongly suspect that the subjects remained separated when given the lecture. If so, then the dull lecture read to the experimental group may not have been precisely as dull as the same lecture presented to the control group.

If we are right in assuming that the groups were separated for the lecture, then we wonder who read the lecture. It might have been two different people, perhaps the researcher and his assistant or possibly two of the researcher's assistants. If two different individuals were doing the reading, then we contend that reader differences, and not variations in the instructions, could have brought about the significant difference observed on the test. We know (and we're sure you do, too) several people who can pick up a truly exciting document and make it excruciatingly dull through their poor reading technique, while there are others who simply have beautiful voices and intonation and are therefore interesting to listen to regardless of the material being read.

Suppose, however, that it was not two people doing the reading but rather just one individual, who presented the lecture to one of the groups and then later to the other group. Here again, we would have to ask, who was the reader? In our eyes, there are three possibilities: the researcher himself, a research assistant who was aware of the experimental hypothesis and knowledgeable about which group had received the potentially motivating instructions, or someone who was "blind" to the study's purposes and each group's prelecture treatment. If the reader was either of the first two individuals, then we think that there may have been an unconscious tendency to read the lecture in a more interesting manner to the group that had been predicted to do better.

Bringing everyone together for the lecture may have been undesirable since the listeners would probably find out from one another about the different prelecture instructions. Such knowledge, if it existed, might completely undermine the study. Therefore, it may have been preferable to keep the experimental and control groups separated. Once again assuming that this was, in fact, the way the investigation was conducted, we suggest that the use of a video- or audiotape machine to present the lecture would have ensured that the level of dullness was exactly the same for both groups. Granted, the results of such a study might not generalize as easily to typical class situations in which lectures are presented in person by the professor. However, use of the audio- or videotape would completely eliminate the rival hypothesis that we suggest may have been associated with the actual experiment. And in our opinion, elimination of rival hypotheses always takes precedence over generalization.

93. Wrong Number

Although this study is an excellent example of a creative approach to field research and has good generalizability, we believe that an obvious alternative was ignored. Since blacks were selected on the basis of last names but whites were not, it seems likely that the black sample had a significantly larger number of people in it named Williams (the name of the caller). Thus, if there were actually equal rates of helping in the two populations, the oversampling in one group of people named Williams who were more likely to help other people named Williams, regardless of race, would confound the findings of the present study. This alternative would also account for the researcher's report of greater helping on the part of the blacks in the study.

94. Are Reading Problems Inherited?

We might use the familial/nonfamilial distinction in our research, but then again we might not. The method of creating the subgroups does not seem to define the construct very well. It immediately raised in our minds at least one question: why weren't the control children also checked for relatives with reading problems? Perhaps an equivalent proportion of the control group would have been classified as familial. In other words, the LD/control differences might well represent random differences between groups that don't really differ on the dimension used to distinguish them. Thus, instability is a plausible threat to the conclusions drawn in this study.

We agree that further study is needed.

95. Ethics of Random Assignment

As we pointed out in the description of this study, matching, as opposed to a random precedure, was used to generate the control group. What problems are created by this approach? Although there is no question that the groups are similar to one another on the matching variables, there is no guarantee that they are comparable on other equally important variables. It is equally clear that the groups differ on the most important variable—namely, having ended up in the hospital. Finally, although t-tests were used for many tests of significance, this study is essentially correlational (that is, it asks what differences are correlated with group membership); thus, the question of causality should spring to mind. While it is quite plausible, it is not at all clear that undernourishment is the cause of later developmental problems (to be fair, the authors did cite some animal work in support of this causal link; however, we did not tell you that in the problem). It is possible that some other variables outside the study caused both undernourishment and the later associated problems.

While we have given you some things to think about in considering this study, we hesitate to recommend undernourishing your children. At best, it qualifies as abuse and neglect and will get you arrested in a number of states.

96. Japanese Women and Business Profits

The Nomura study found that the high-profit companies employed more women than the low-profit companies did, and that women in Japan are paid 40 percent less than men. The not-too-subtle argument seems to be that the high-profit companies wanted more women around because these women could be paid less; if the new law mandated equal salaries, the value of having women on the payroll would no longer be as great. We disagree with this possible interpretation of the facts.

In our judgment, the high-profit companies may have been doing better in terms of net earnings because they employed more women and because women work harder than men. Our male readers may not like to hear this, but recent research has shown that women take shorter coffee breaks, are absent less frequently, and accomplish more within a specific amount of time. Given our hypothetical situation, you—as chairman of the board—should opt for the hiring of more women than men (if you could get away with such a policy!).

97. Stop Signs

We would not feel the least bit safer! For one thing, it is possible that drivers responded only to the change from one form of stop sign to another. Had the change been from standard signs to those written on the ground, the same effect might have been found.

The rival hypothesis of history must also enter into consideration. For example, a series of bad accidents between the pre- and postobservations might have led to a temporary change in driving behavior that was unrelated to the experimental manipulation. Other aspects of history might include such things as the weather or a national holiday. A further rival hypothesis was indicated by the researcher in stating that a larger proportion of the postobservations were made in the morning. Perhaps Nigerian drivers are more considerate through greater use of turn signals at that time than in the afternoon on their way home.

From the narrative description given by the researchers of the traffic situation in Nigeria, even a better controlled study and a lot of good luck charms would leave us leery of driving in that country.

98. A Student-Designed Graduate-Level Course in Business

Although we are advocates of giving students a say in their course content and structure (at least in upper-division graduate seminars), we do see a couple of rival hypotheses that interfere with a clear interpretation of this study's results. Granted, the difference between the way the experimental and control subjects responded to the 22-item evaluation instrument *may* have been brought about by the manipulated variable of participative management. However, differential ratings may have been associated (either partially or totally) with other variables that distinguished the experimental and control classes.

Our first concern has to do with possible student differences. Recall that the two experimental classes were offered during the daytime session of the winter quarter, while the two control classes met at night during the spring term. We suspect that student ability remains fairly constant across adjacent terms in the same academic year at Pittsburgh or any other educational institution. However, we are not so confident that daytime students are the same as those who attend school at night. At our schools, students who attend during the day tend to be younger, more energetic, and unlikely to be working full-time. Conversely, students who attend our night classes tend to be older, less energetic, and more likely to be fully employed. As we see it, the lower ratings associated with the two control classes in the spring may have been caused by the students' being a more critical lot (due to their work experience out in the "real world") who were being instructed when they were fatigued and ready for a dull television show or bed.

Our second concern has to do with potential instructor differences. Only one instructer was used in this study for all four sections of the business course, and in a sense this instructor was serving as his own control. Nevertheless, we submit that he may have been less effective with the two control classes during the spring quarter than with the experimental classes during the winter. Just as it's more difficult to be a student in a night course than a student in a day course, we assure you (based on first-hand experience) that it's also more difficult to teach night courses. The instructor also gets tired at the end of a full workday, and a night class can easily become a somewhat painful experience. This is expecially true if the night class meets once a week for three hours, as is usually the case.[1]

Besides potential instructor differences created by the day/night variable, we wonder whether the experimental and control groups received differential treatment from the instructor. If the researcher and the instructor were the same person, then it seems clear to us that this person's preferences in terms of research results may have caused him (possibly unconsciously) to be a better teacher when dealing with the experimental classes. He may have been more friendly to the students, more punctual in starting and ending class, more available to students out of class, and so on. But what if the researcher and the instructor were different people, with the latter kept naive about the former's research hypotheses? Were this the case, we simply doubt that it took the instructor very long to figure out what the researcher was hoping to show.

99. The Effects of Television

We have two major concerns about this study. First, the reduction from the 260 couples who were randomly assigned to the 183 couples remaining in the study, in conjunction with the different number of couples in each experimental group, led us to conclude that it was more difficult to keep people in some of the groups than in others. If this is true, the resulting bias due to differential mortality might be a rival hypothesis for this study. Given that the initial group similarities were based on the 260 couples, it is possible that husbands were more likely to stay in some groups than in others.

A second problem with this study involves the use of the wives as observers. Aside from the ethical objections to such a procedure, we believe that there are methodological flaws as well. We assume that keeping the wife from watching television with her husband was partly an attempt to keep her from being affected by the content of the shows and partly an attempt to keep her from knowing to which group her husband was assigned. It appears inconceivable that the researchers were successful in the latter of these attempts. For example, it seems plausible to us that a woman whose husband was watching only violent shows for a week (as opposed to a less extreme mixture) would realize the purpose of the study and inadvertently report more "hurtful" behaviors. We would expect a comparable result for women with husbands in the prosocial group.

---

[1] The technical report did not indicate how many times per week the four classes were meeting. If the daytime classes met three times a week for one hour per session and the night classes met once a week for three hours, then we obviously have another rival hypotheses.

100. Exercise, Heart Attacks, and Buses

We believe that there are two additional rival hypotheses worthy of consideration. The first one is related to differential tension associated with the two jobs. The conductors probably experienced very little tension as they went up and down the bus collecting fares from the passengers; the worst thing that they probably had to deal with in their jobs was a passenger who attempted to ride free by sneaking around from one seat to another. Normally, however, we suspect that the conductors actually enjoyed their interaction with other people while on the job.

But on the other hand, each driver had the safety of everyone on the bus as his responsibility. And as anyone who lives in or visits a city knows, driving in rush-hour traffic is anything from restful. Having to dodge pedestrians, being cut off by other vehicles, watching for signal changes—these activities can bring about temporary outbursts of anger and chronic nervousness. Imagine how it would affect your heart to be in the driver's seat of a bus for eight hours each working day!

Granted, the people who took the job as drivers were probably better able to cope with the traffic events that normally make a person's frustration level increase and fingernail length decrease. But despite this possible difference between the bus drivers and more typical drivers, we feel that the increased rates of heart disease and coronary death among the bus drivers very well might be causally related to the nature of their job duties. If people like us had been behind the wheel of those double-decker buses, maybe the rate of heart problems would have been five or ten times higher than that among the conductors.

The second rival hypothesis that we have in mind is age. Suppose the employees assigned to the driver jobs were older and those assigned to the conductor jobs were younger. (Isn't this quite plausible if the person making the assignments felt that the conductor jobs required lots of mobility, or if seniority was a basis for job assignment?) If the drivers were older, then we would expect more heart attacks among this group for reasons completely unrelated to job function.

Which rival hypothesis is the right one: Dr. Morris' explanation (which deals with initial weight and fitness), our first suggestion (which deals with the nature of the job activities), or our second suggestion (which deals with age)? We are not sure. Possibly they all are correct, and all three identified variables were operating jointly to produce the health differential among the two groups. Or maybe none of them is correct; maybe the original explanation—exercise—is the true reason. In general, whenever more than one variable is identified as a possible and plausible cause of some event, we're left in a quandary as we attempt to make valid interpretations of the data. With Dr. Morris' study, there are at least four such variables. Hence, we really do not know whether Dr. Morris was right in 1953, right in 1956, partially right both times, or not right at all.

APPENDIX A

Bibliography

Problems

Sources

1 The Common Denominator." *Knoxville News-Sentinel,* August 6, 1976.

2 Johnson, E., Smith, S., and Myers, T. I. "Vigilance Throughout Seven Days of Sensory Deprivation." *Proceedings, 76th Annual American Psychological Association Convention,* 1968, pp. 627–628.

3 Cannon, W. B. and Washburn, H. L. "An Explanation of Hunger." *American Journal of Psychology,* 1912, *29,* pp. 441–452.

4 Woodside, A. G. "A Shopping List Experiment of Beer Brand Images." *Journal of Applied Psychology,* 1976, *56,* pp. 512–513.

5 Cerbus, G. and Travis, R. J. "Seasonal Variation in Personality of College Students as Measured by the MMPI." *Psychological Reports,* 1973, *33,* pp. 665–666.

6 "Coke-Pepsi Slugfest." *Time,* July 26, 1976, pp. 64–65.

7 Wexley, K. N. and Thornton, C. L. "Effect of Verbal Feedback of Test Results upon Learning." *Journal of Educational Research,* 1972, *66,* pp. 119–121.

8 Counts, H. "Your Lawn and Garden." *Knoxville News-Sentinel,* August 10, 1975.

9 Schaefer, C. E. "Imaginary Companions and Creative Adolescents." *Developmental Psychology,* 1969, *1,* pp. 747–749.

10 Williams, R. L. "Response Strength as a Function of Pre- and Post-reward Delay and Physical Confinement." *Journal of Experimental Psychology,* 1967, *74,* pp. 420–424.

11 Gleason, E. M. "Stability of Dogmatism and Relationship of Dogmatism to Performance in Two Air Force Officer Schools." Doctoral dissertation, University of Tennessee, 1973.

12 Marlowe, D. "Psychological Needs and Cooperation: Competition In a Two-Person Game." *Psychological Reports,* 1963, *13,* p. 364.

13 Haase, R. F. and Ivey, A. E. "Influence of Client Pretesting on Counseling Outcome." *Journal of Consulting and Clinical Psychology,* 1970, *34,* p.128.

14 Bouchard, T. J. "A Comparison of Two Group Brainstorming Procedures." *Journal of Applied Psychology,* 1972, *56,* pp. 418–421.

15 Garlington, W. D. and Dericco, D. A. "The Effect of Modeling on Drinking Rate." *Journal of Applied Behavior Analysis,* 1977, *10,* pp. 207–211.

16 Quereshi, M. Y. "Teaching of Undergraduate Psychological Statistics With and Without a Textbook." Paper presented at the 85th Annual American Psychological Association Convention (San Francisco), August, 1977.

17 Fredericson, E. "Distributed Versus Massed Practice in a Traumatic Situation. *Journal of Abnormal and Social Psychology,* 1950, *45,* pp. 259–266. [The rival

hypotheses associated with this study are also discussed in Underwood, B. J. *Psychological Research.* New York: Appleton-Century-Crofts, 1957, pp. 143–144.]

18 Roberts, A. H., Kewman, D. G., and McDonald, H. "Voluntary Control of Skin Temperature: Unilateral Changes Using Hypnosis and Feedback," *Journal of Abnormal Psychology,* 1973, *82,* pp. 163–168.

19 Dawley, H. H. and Aurich, L. W. "Case Study: Elimination of Smoking Behavior Through Aversive Smoking and Other Procedures." *Psychological Reports,* 1975, *37,* pp. 799–802.

20 Morse, J. A. and Tillman, M. H. "Effects on Achievement of Possession of Behavioral Objectives and Training Concerning Their Use." Paper presented at the American Educational Research Convention (New Orleans), 1972.

21 Catt, V. and Benson. P. L. "Effect of Verbal Modeling on Contributions to Charity." *Journal of Applied Psychology,* 1977, *62,* pp. 81–85.

22 Crocker, L. M. and Brodie, B. J. "Development of a Scale to Assess Student Nurses' Views of the Professional Nursing Role." *Journal of Applied Psychology,* 1974, *59,* pp. 233–235.

23 Langley, E. M. and Gehrman, J. L. "Impact of Practicum-Field Experience on Perceptions of Counselor Characteristics." *Journal of the Student Personnel Association for Teacher Education,* 1971, *9,* pp. 76–80.

24 Tinbergen, N. "Social Releasers and the Experimental Method Required for Their Study." *Wilson Bulletin,* 1948, *60,* pp. 6–52. (Reported in *The Study of Instinct.* New York: Oxford University Press, 1951.)

25 Voevodsky, J. "Evaluation of a Decelerating Warning Light for Reducing Rear-end Automobile Collisions." *Journal of Applied Psychology,* 1974, *59,* pp. 270–273.

26 Shindell, S. *Statistics, Science, and Sense.* Pittsburgh: University of Pittsburgh Press, 1964, pp. 44–45.

27 Fairweather, G. W. and Simon, R. "A Further Follow-up of Psychotherapeutic Programs." *Journal of Consulting Psychology,* 1963, *27,* p. 186.

28 "Weaker Sex." *Parade,* September 11, 1977, p. 10.

29 "Dynamiting Language." *Time,* August 16, 1976, p. 56.

30 Schein, W. E., Maurer, E. H., and Novak, J. F. "Impact of Flexible Working Hours on Productivity." *Journal of Applied Psychology,* 1977, *62,* pp. 463–465.

31 "The Different Distance Ball." An advertisement placed in Delta Airline's *Sky* magazine, April, 1977.

32 "Bread: You Can't Judge a Loaf by its Color." *Consumer Reports,* May, 1976, pp. 256–260.

33 Freeman, S., Walker, M. R., Borden, R., and Latane, B. "Diffusion of Responsibility and Restaurant Tipping: Cheaper by the Bunch." *Personality and Social Psychology Bulletin,* 1975, *1,* pp. 584–587.

34 Beatty, W. W. and Beatty. P. A. "Hormonal Detriments of Sex Differences in Avoidance Behavior and Reactivity to Electric Shock in the Rat. *Journal of Comparative and Physiological Psychology,* 1970, *73,* pp. 446–455; Beatty, W. W. "How Blind is Blind?" *Psychological Bulletin,* 1972, *78,* pp. 70–71.

35 Maw, W. H. and Maw, E. W. "Differences Between High- and Low-Curiosity Children in Their Recognition of Verbal Absurdities." *Journal of Educational Psychology,* 1972, *63,* pp. 558–562.

36 Roose, K. D. and Anderson, C. J. *A Rating of Graduate Programs.* Washington, D. C.: American Council on Education, 1970; Cox, W. M. and Catt, V. "Productivity Ratings of Graduate Programs Based on Publication in the Journals of the American Psychological Association." *American Psychologist,* 1977, *32,* pp. 793–813.

37 "It Pays to Stick to 55." Scripps-Howard Newspapers, May, 1977. (*Knoxville News-Sentinel,* May 17, 1977, p. 10.)

38 Golightly, C., Huffman, D. M., and Byrne, D. "Liking and Loaning." *Journal of Applied Psychology,* 1972, *56,* pp. 521–523.

39 Ivancevich, J. M. and Lyon, H. L. "The Shortened Workweek: A Field Experiment." *Journal of Applied Psychology,* 1977, *62,* pp. 34–37.

40 Peretti, P. O. and Lucas, C. "Newspaper Advertising Influences on Consumers' Behavior by Socioeconomic Status of Consumers." *Psychological Reports,* 1975, *37,* pp. 693–694.

41 "Dentists Beware." *Parade,* July 31, 1977, p.11.

42 Fiske, D. W. and Goodman, G. "The Posttherapy Period." *Journal of Abnormal Psychology,* 1965, *70,* pp. 169–179.

43 Schuh, A. J. and Crivelli, M. A. "Animadversion Error in Student Evaluations of Faculty Teaching Effectiveness." *Journal of Applied Psychology,* 1973, *58,* pp. 259–260.

44 "Barcardi Rum Tops Vodka and Gin in the Ultimate Martini Test." *Cosmopolitan,* June, 1976, p. 103.

45 Rosenthal, T. L. and Zemmerman, B. J. "Modeling by Exemplification and Instruction in Training Conservation." *Developmental Psychology,* 1972, *6,* pp. 392–401.

46 Wolfson, W. "Profile Drawings and Procrastination." *Perceptual and Motor Skills,* 1963, *17,* p. 570.

47 Jeannerte, P. R. and Webb, W. B. "Strength of Grip on Arousal From Full Night's Sleep." *Perceptual and Motor Skills,* 1963, *17,* pp. 759–761.

48 Rogers, P. "Two Year Old's Use of Objects in Peer Interaction," Doctoral dissertation, George Peabody College for Teachers, 1976.

49 Mazer, G. E., Severson, J. L., Axman, A. L., and Ludington, K. A. "The Effects of Teaching Background on School Counselor Practices." *Journal for the Student Personnel Association for Teacher Education,* 1965, *4,* pp. 81–84.

50 Baker, W. J. and Theologus, G. C. "Effects of Caffeine on Visual Monitoring." *Journal of Applied Psychology,* 1972, *56,* pp. 422–427.

51 Kelsey, H. W. *Improve Your Bridge.* New York: Hart Publishing Company, 1971.

52 Belmont, L. and Birch, H. G. "Re-individualizing the Repression Hypothesis." *Journal of Abnormal and Social Psychology,* 1951, *46,* pp. 226–235. [This study and one of the alleged rival hypotheses is also discussed in Underwood, B. J. *Psychological Research.* New York: Appleton-Century-Crofts, 1957, p. 149.]

53 Tidball, M. E. "Perspective on Academic Women and Affirmative Action." *Educational Record,* 1973, *54,* pp. 130–135.

54 Kirkman, D. "Food Additives and Child Ailment Link Challenged." *Scripps-Howard Newspapers,* June, 1977. (*Knoxville News-Sentinel,* June 12, 1977, p. C-8.)

55 Doppelt, J. and Wallace, W. "Standardization of the WAIS for Older Persons." *Journal of Abnormal and Social Psychology,* 1955, *51,* pp. 312–330.

56 Tuttle, L. P., Terry, D., and Shinedling, M. M. "Note on Increase of Social Interaction of Mental Patients During a Camp Trip." *Psychological Reports,* 1975, *36,* pp. 77–78.

57 McGinnies, E. "Emotionality and Perceptual Defense." *Psychological Review,* 1949, *56,* pp. 244–256.

58 Schellenberg, J. A. and Blevins, G. A. "Feeling Good and Helping: How Quickly Does the Smile of Dame Fortune Fade." *Psychological Reports,* 1973, *33,* pp. 72–74.

59 Cicirelli, V. G. "Project Head Start, a National Evaluation: Summary of a Study." In D. G. Hays (ed.), *Britannica Review of American Education.* Volume 1. Chicago: Encyclopedia Britannica, 1969; Campbell, D. T. and Erlebacher, A. E. "How Regression Artifacts in Quasi-Experimental Evaluations Can Mistakenly Make Compensatory Education Look Harmful." In J. Helmuth (ed.), *Compensatory Education: A National Debate.* Volume 3. New York: Brunner/Mazel, 1970.

60 Layne. B. H., Assistant Professor, Georgia State University (Atlanta). Personal communication, June 17, 1977.

61 Heussenstamm, F. K. "Bumper Stickers and Cops." *Transaction,* 1977, *8,* pp. 32–33.

62 Huck, S. W. and Long, J. D. "The Effect of Behavioral Objectives on Student Achievement." *Journal of Experimental Education,* 1973, *42,* pp. 40–41.

63 Lerer, R. J. and Lerer, M. P. "Response of Adolescents with Minimal Brain Dysfunction to Methylphenidate." *Journal of Learning Disabilities,* 1977, *10,* pp. 223–228.

64 Siler, T. "Best of the Best." *Knoxville News-Sentinel,* April 18, 1975, p. 18.

65 Kaltreider, N. B. and Margolis, A. G. "Childless by Choice: A Clinical Study," *American Journal of Psychiatry,* 1977, *134,* pp. 179–182.

66 McDonnell, J. D. "Effect of Pricing on Perception of Product Quality." *Journal of Applied Psychology,* 1968, *52,* pp. 331–334.

67 Tavormina, J. "Relative Effectiveness of Behavioral and Reflective Group Counseling with Parents of Mentally Retarded Children." *Journal of Consulting and Clinical Psychology,* 1975, *43,* pp. 22–31.

68 "Handwriting Analysis." *Parade,* October 9, 1977, p.6.

69 Edwards, D. and Bucky, S. F. "Personality and Attitudinal Change for Alcoholics Treated at the Navy's Alcohol Rehabilitation Center. "*Journal of Community Psychology,* 1977, *5,* pp. 180–185.

70 Cahoon, D. A., Peterson, L. P., and Watson, C. G. "Relative Effectiveness of Programmed Text and Teaching Machine as a Function of Measured Interests." *Journal of Applied Psychology,* 1968, *52,* pp. 454–456.

71 Terman, L. M. and Oden, M. H. *The Gifted Child Grows Up.* Stanford, Calif.: Stanford University Press, 1947.

72 Sims, O. S. and Suddick, D. E. "The Effect of Residence Hall Closing Hours on Grade Averages of Freshmen Women." *Journal of the National Association for Women Deans and Counselors,* 1972, *35,* pp. 178–179.

73 Obitz, F. W. and Swanson, M. K. "Control Orientation in Women Alcoholics." *Journal of Studies on Alcohol,* 1976, *37,* pp. 694–697.

74 Brabham, R. E. and Thoreson, R. W. "Relationship of Client Preferences and Counselor's Physical Disability." *Journal of Counseling Psychology,* 1973, *20,* pp. 10–15.

75 Hauser, S. and Hobart, C. "Premarital Pregnancy and Anxiety." *The Journal of Social Psychology,* 1964, *63,* pp. 255–263.

76 "My Orville Redenbacher's Gourmet Popping Corn Will Blow Your Top Off." *McCall's,* August 17, 1976, p. 150.

77 David, K. H. "Age, Cigarette Smoking, and Tests of Physical Fitness." *Journal of Applied Psychology,* 1968, *52,* pp. 296–298.

78 Walter, H. I. and Gilmore, S. K. "Placebo Versus Social Learning Effects in Parent Training Procedures Designed to Alter the Behavior of Aggressive Boys." *Behavior Therapy,* 1973, *4,* pp. 361–377.

79 Ilgen, D. R. and Seely, W. "Realistic Expectations as an Aid in Reducing Voluntary Resignations." *Journal of Applied Psychology, 1974, 59,* pp. 452–455.

80 *The First Medium.* Institute of Outdoor Advertising, 1975. (Also, a special Miss America promotional brochure put out by the Institute of Outdoor Advertising.)

81 Sadler, O. W., Seyden, T., Howe, B., and Kaminsky, T. "An Evaluation of 'Groups for Parents': A Standardized Format Encompassing Both Behavior Modification and Humanistic Methods." *Journal of Community Psychology,* 1976, *4,* pp. 157–163.

82 "Unequal Pay." *Parade,* November 14, 1976, p. 28.

83 Franklin, B. J. "Birth Order and Tendency to 'Adopt the Sick Role'." *Psychological Reports,* 1973, *33,* pp. 437–438.

84   Searcy-Miller, M. L. and Cowen, E. L. "School Adjustment Problems of Children from Small Versus Large Families." *Journal of Community Psychology,* 1977, *5,* pp. 319–324.

85   "Students Who Type Usually Receive Better Grades." *Time,* August 30, 1976, p.1; *Typing and Improved Academic Performance.* A promotional brochure put out by Smith-Corona, July, 1976.

86   "Loneliness Can Kill You." *Time,* September 5, 1977, p. 45.

87   Ball, S. and Bogatz, G. A. *The First Year of Sesame Street: An Evaluation.* Princeton, N. J.: Educational Testing Service, October, 1970; Bogatz, G. A. and Ball, S. *The Second Year of Sesame Street: A Continuing Evaluation.* Vols. 1 and 2. Princeton, N. J.: Educational Testing Service. November, 1971.

88   "Financial Woes of Colleges and Universities." Scripps-Howard Newspapers, June, 1977. (*Knoxville News-Sentinel,* June, 22, 1977, editorial page.)

89   Bielby, D. D. V. and Papalia, D. E. "Moral Development and Perceptual Role-Taking Egocentrism: Their Development and Interrelationship Across the Life Span." *International Journal of Aging and Human Development,* 1975, *6,* pp. 293–308.

90   "Sports Notebook." *The Christian Science Monitor,* January 6, 1978, p.23.

91   Smith, F. J. "Work Attitudes as Predictors of Attendance on a Specific Day." *Journal of Applied Psychology,* 1977, *62,* pp. 16–19.

92   Cullen, J. B. "Social Identity and Motivation." *Psychological Reports,* 1973, *33,* p.338.

93   Gaertuer, S. and Bickman, L. "A Nonreactive Indicator Measure of Racial Discrimination: The Wrong Number Technique." In L. Bickman and T. Henchy (eds.), *Field Research in Social Psychology.* New York: McGraw-Hill, 1972, 162–169.

94   Rugel, R. P. and Mitchell, A. "Characteristics of Familial and Nonfamilial Disabled Readers." *Journal of Learning Disabilities,* 1977, *10,* pp. 308–313.

95   Chase, H. P. and Martin, H. P. "Undernutrition and Child Development." *The New England Journal of Medicine,* 1970, *282,* pp. 933–939.

96   Shearer, L. "Intelligence Report: Women and Profit." *Parade,* October 16, 1977, p.19.

97   Ugwuegbu, D. C. E. "The Stop Sign is For the Other Guy: A Naturalistic Observation of Driving Behavior of Nigerians." *Journal of Applied Psychology,* 1977, *62,* pp. 574–577.

98   Kilmann, R. H. "Participative Management in the College Classroom." *Journal of Applied Psychology,* 1974, *59,* pp. 337–338.

99   Loye, D., Gorney, R., and Steele, G. "Effects of Television: An Experimental Field Study." *Journal of Communication,* 1977, *27,* pp. 206–216.

100   Gilmore, C. P. "Taking Exercise to Heart." *The New York Times Magazine,* March 27, 1977, pp. 38–42, 81–83.

APPENDIX B

20 Categories of Rival Hypotheses

20 Categories of Rival Hypotheses (And a Classification of the 100 Problems)

(1) Correlation Causality	(2) Cross-Sectional/ Longitudinal	(3) Experimenter Effect	(4) History	(5) Instability
3, 9, 37, 75, 77, 83, 91, 95, 100	22, 55, 89	7, 16, 21, 28, 78, 98	5, 19, 23, 30, 39, 41, 66, 69, 80, 81, 97	8, 31, 63, 65, 94
(6) Instrumentation	(7) Matching	(8) Maturation	(9) Mortality	(10) Observer/Rater Effect
56, 60, 69, 80, 81	35, 84, 95	47, 48, 81	2, 16, 22, 27, 42, 79, 81, 99	34, 40, 56, 99
(11) Order Effect	(12) Regression	(13) Sampling Bias	(14) Selection	(15) Statistical, Other Than Instability and Regression
21, 31, 44, 66, 97	11, 35, 59, 81	18, 44, 51, 61, 63, 66, 71, 89, 93	22, 29, 30, 49, 53, 65, 67, 72, 73, 85, 98	20, 53, 64, 67, 72, 78, 89
(16) Subject Effect	(17) Testing	(18) Treatment Confound	(19) Valid Data/ Self-Report	(20) Different Interpretation of Data
25, 26, 30, 31, 38, 58, 61, 62, 65, 68	5, 13, 23, 80, 81	1, 6, 7, 12, 14, 15, 16, 17, 18, 25, 28, 32, 37, 45, 52, 66, 70, 73, 74, 78, 87, 92, 98	9, 19, 25, 36, 48, 57, 65, 77	8, 18, 88, 96

(1) Correlation and Causality

If a group of people or objects is measured with respect to two variables, and if neither of the variables is experimentally manipulated, then the simple finding of a direct or indirect relationship between the two variables—through some sort of correlation coefficient (r_{pb} or 0) or statistical test (t or X^2)—cannot serve as legitimate evidence for the claim that one variable has a causal influence on the other. Quite possibly, both of the variables are causally linked to some unmeasured third variable.

(2) Cross-Sectional/Longitudinal

Researchers are often interested in identifying developmental trends in people or animals—that is, physiological or psychological changes that are simply a product of aging. One popular strategy involves measuring, at one point in time, subjects who differ widely in age, and then comparing the age subgroups on the variable(s) of interest to infer the developmental trend. The other simple strategy involves measuring a single group of subjects repeatedly as they age, with developmental inferences drawn from an observation of how the group's performance varies with time. Unfortunately, neither of these strategies is able to assess validly the developmental process. In the cross-sectional approach, subgroup differences may have been brought about by differential lengths of exposure to improving (or worsening) environmental or nutritional conditions, not by age differences. In the longitudinal approach, changes over time might well be tied to nonmaturational events that are unique to that one group's life span.

(3) Experimenter Effect

If there are two or more conditions (levels) of a manipulated treatment variable, and if the treatments are administered to the subjects by someone familiar with the researcher's hypotheses and hoped-for results, then it is possible that the comparison groups will be treated differently along dimensions other than that associated with the formal independent variable. In nonexperimental descriptive studies wherein comparisons are made between the way two or more status groups (such as males and females) react to the same stimulus, the same sort of bias can exist if the stimulus is being presented to the subjects by a person who has a preference (possibly unconscious) that the groups show up as dissimilar.

(4) History

When a group of subjects is measured before and after exposure to some sort of treatment (or nonexperimental activity or event), a pretest—post-test change or lack of change in the data collected may be attributable to something other than the treatment and that took place outside the confines of the experiment between the pre- and post-test measurements. Clearly, history can make a treatment look as if it made a difference when in fact the treatment was inert. Or, worse yet, a truly beneficial (or detrimental) treatment may end up looking as if it was detrimental (or beneficial) if its effect is confounded with a negative (or positive) historical event.

(5) Instability

Instability refers to the fact that sample statistics almost never turn out to be the same as the corresponding population parameters, even though the sample is chosen so that its estimates of the population values are unbiased. If two treatments having either the same effect or no effect were applied to groups of randomly formed subjects, we would expect the sample means (or other statistics) to differ. When expected differences are neglected by a failure to set up levels of significance and statistical tests, the researcher ends up drawing conclusions that are almost certain to constitute Type I errors whenever H_o is true and Type III errors about half the time when H_o is false by a small amount.

(6) Instrumentation

Sometimes a measuring instrument's ability to yield accurate data changes in a systematic manner over time, as when the norms of a standardized test gradually (or sometimes quickly) become obsolete. It is as if the springs of a scale had become stretched. If such an instrument is being used to measure a single group of people so as to provide pretest and post-test data, the change in the measuring instrument may make it appear as if the treatment had more or less of an impact than was really the case. The problem of instrumentation might also arise in post-test—only designs if all the members of one group are measured before any members of other groups and the instrument is affected by use (such as a scale). Another likely situation in which this rival hypothesis becomes confounded with treatment effects occurs when observers or raters are required to use a complex recording form, when there are different people doing the recording at pre and post (or for each group in a multigroup study), or when practice effects or boredom leads to a change (over time) in the recorder's ability to use the instrument in the proper manner.

(7) Matching

In comparing two or more treatments against one another (and possibly against a control condition), researchers often use the technique of matching to decide which subjects will be exposed to the treatment conditions, or which from among a large pool that received the treatment will be measured and/or have their data analyzed. Sometimes the researcher uses this technique because it is impossible to assign subjects randomly to the various comparison conditions; at other times the researcher is probably under the impression that matching works as well as or better than randomization. Regardless of the reasons for its use, the technique of matching does not ensure that the comparison groups are equivalent. While it does rule out the possibility that the treatment variable will be confounded with group differences on the variable(s) used to do the matching, there still remains the possibility that one or more of the nearly infinite number of variables *not* used in the matching process is more related to the obtained group differences than the treatment variable. And as we explain carefully in the solution to problem 35, matching can also bring forth the phenomenon of regression towards the mean.

(8) Maturation

Many characteristics of humans, animals, and plants change over time as a natural consequence of internal events associated with the aging process. If pretest and post-test data are collected on a single group of experimental subjects, a pre-post change may be attributable to the intervening treatment that was administered by the researcher. However, in many such studies it is impossible to rule out the possiblity that maturation has caused a beneficial (or detrimental or inert) treatment to look as if it had an impact different from what was actually the case.

(9) Mortality

If subjects drop out of a one-group pretest—post-test design, or if there are differential rates of (and reasons for) attrition in multigroup designs, conclusions regarding treatment effects may be misleading. As is the case with other rival hypotheses, mortality may cause a truly beneficial treatment to look worthless or detrimental, a truly detrimental treatment to look worthless or beneficial, or an inert treatment to look as if it has had a good or bad impact.

(10) Observer/Rater Effect

In some research studies, people observe the subjects and record their reactions to the treatments that have been administered. In other studies, people rate audiotapes, videotapes, or photographs of the subjects or some written documents (like essay tests) or other tangible items produced by the subjects while under the possible influence of the treatments. In either situation, the conclusions of the study could be misleading if the observers or the raters were aware of the purpose of the research investigation, if they knew which subjects had received each treatment, and if this information (maybe just good guesses on their part) served to bias the data they recorded.

(11) Order Effect

When two or more levels of a treatment factor are being compared in a design in which all subjects are exposed to and measured under each and every treatment condition, it is important to vary the order in which the treatments are presented. This can be done by counterbalancing or by randomly arranging the order in which each subject receives the treatments. If neither of these protection measures is taken, then any observed differences between the treatment conditions may actually be the results of a learning (practice) or fatigue effect, not true treatment differences. Or, the treatments may actually differ in their effectiveness but turn out looking alike (or different in the wrong way) because of the compensating influence of treatment and order effects.

(12) Regression

If a group of individuals is preselected to receive a treatment because of its initial high or low standing on some measured variable, and if the pretest has a correlation lower than $+1.00$ with the instrument used to collect post-test data, the group mean on the post-test will be less extreme (as compared to the average score that would have been earned by all people in the larger pool from which the subjects were drawn, had they been given the post-test) than is the group's pretest mean (as compared to the "grand" mean based on all pretest scores collected). Consequently, a remedial group may improve between pre and post and thus make an inert treatment look as if it was effective. Worse yet, if the regression phenomenon is strong enough, it could potentially cause a truly detrimental treatment to look good.

(13) Sampling Bias

Sometimes researchers use a single group of subjects within the context of a longitudinal descriptive investigation or a repeated measures experiment. And sometimes these subjects are sampled in such a way as to make them *unrepresentative* of the total group from which they were drawn, in the sense that there is a built-in bias toward favoring one of the treatment conditions or behaving longitudinally in accord with the researcher's hypotheses. Another type of sampling bias exists when the components of a treatment condition are nonrandomly drawn from the population of available components, with conclusions stated as if they apply to the population. Here again (as with sampling bias with subjects), it is not an issue of external validity that we are concerned with, but rather a purposeful or unconscious sampling that causes the results and conclusions to be unrealistic.

(14) Selection

When two or more groups receive different treatments (with one group possible serving as a control), a failure to assign subjects randomly to the comparison conditions means that true treatment effects are confounded with group differences in initial status and/or the likelihood of changing in the future (for reasons unrelated to the treatments). Neither matching nor the analysis of covariance has the ability to compensate completely for these potential group differences along dimensions other than the manipulated independent variable. When the independent variable is not truly manipulated by the researcher but is rather of such a nature that subjects put themselves into preferred treatment conditions, this rival hypothesis becomes exceedingly plausible.

(15) Statistical, Other Than Instability and Regression

At times, researchers analyze their data by procedures that are statistically or logically incorrect. Sometimes, the result is simply a Type I error probability that exceeds the nominal level of significance reported by the researcher. On other occasions, the error in analysis may mean that the conclusions drawn are totally unjustified on the basis of the data collected—with entirely different conclusions being likely had those data been analyzed in a logically correct manner.

(16) Subject Effect

The subjects who receive a particular treatment may figure out, even if not directly told, what treatment they have been given, what the other group(s) in the study received (if there are other groups), and what the research hypotheses are. This information may cause the groups to perform differently on the criterion variable(s) simply because of the way the subjects *expect* their treatments to affect their behavior, attitudes, or knowledge. As a consequence, treatments with no true relative effects may show up as different. Or, truly different treatments may show up as equivalent (or different, but ordered incorrectly) if the subjects' expectations are not congruent with the true treatment effects. Finally, it should be noted that the procedures of a study may be such that the subjects think they know which treatment they got, when in reality they are recipients of an entirely different treatment. (A subject effect, as defined here, is analogous to but slightly different from the well-known Hawthorne effect.)

(17) Testing

When a group is tested twice, the individuals usually earn higher scores (if the measuring instrument has right and wrong answers) or more "normal" scores (if the measuring instrument is dealing with personality characteristics) on the second testing. This phenomenon has been shown to exist even though the examinees are given no feedback between testings, even if no opportunity exists to study or experience historical events or to change, and even when the second test is a parallel form of the first one.

(18) Treatment Confound

Many of the rival hypotheses listed previously deal with activities, changes, or phenomena that are confounded with the treatment and therefore have the potential to distort a study's results. These categories do not, however, allow for a complete accounting of the things that are sometimes confounded with the treatment (such as instructor differences in a study comparing two methods of teaching something). Treatment confound has been defined to accommodate these numerous and varied other types of confounding.

(19) Valid Data/Self-Report

Sometimes the validity of a study's data is questionable. For one reason or another, the subjects may consciously perform at something other than their maximum level. When the data are of a self-report nature, subjects may be consciously or unconsciously motivated to withhold their honest thoughts. Or the data collected sometimes constitute quantitative information on the wrong dependent variable. Obviously, any of these data-based problems may cause the true treatment effects to be hidden from view.

(20) Different Interpretation of Data

In a sense, whenever a plausible rival hypothesis exists, we have a different interpretation of the data and summary statistics. Therefore, different interpretation of data could be said to apply whenever one of the previous 19 errors applies. However, this category has been defined because we sometimes come across research conclusions that are subject to different interpretations even though none of the preceding rival hypotheses is applicable. For example, the flea study reported at the beginning of the Foreword belongs in this final category. So does the implied claim (made in Problem 96) that the top businesses in Japan are financially successful because they have a higher proportion of females on their payroll and because women are paid lower salaries than men. In our opinion, there is a different way to interpret these data relating to the same factors of financial success and numbers of employed women.

Index